Origami Pop-ups
To Amaze and Amuse

Jeremy Shafer

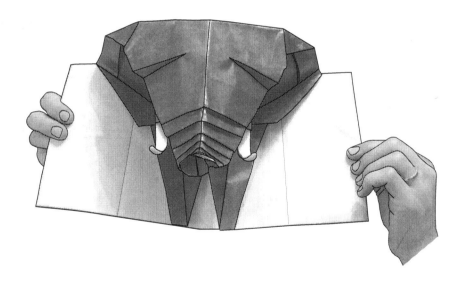

ORIGAMI POP-UPS
TO AMAZE AND AMUSE

Copyright © 2013 by Jeremy Shafer
All rights reserved.

No part of this publication may be copied or reproduced by any
means without written permission of the author.

ISBN-13: 978-1494299026

ISBN-10: 149429902X

Back cover photo: Banyan Tree Park, Lahaina, Hawaii (Photographer: Alicia Shafer)

Introduction

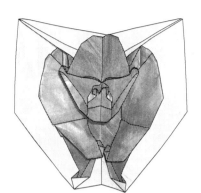

Gorilla Pop-up Card
(page 94)

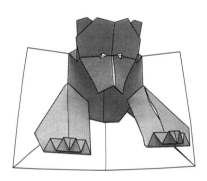

Grizzly Bear Pop-up Card
(page 100)

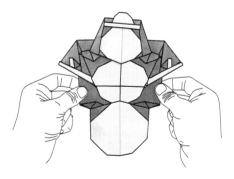

Snowman Pop-up Card
(page 140)

Dear Aspiring Origamist,

A major risk of becoming a serious origamist is that your home will become inundated with origami. While that might be okay and even desirable for diehard origamists, their families are likely to suffer. They will resent how these invasive species of folded creatures are multiplying uncontrollably and taking up vital common spaces. Utterances of, "Clear the dining room table!" and "Clean your room!" will grow in frequency and intensity, and, in extreme cases, even the bathroom will fall victim to the scourge of folded objects!

The good news is that there is help available for you or your loved one. If you've purchased this book, then you've taken what might seem like a small step for man, woman, boy or girl, but is in fact a giant step for managing to get the origami infestation under control. You see, a big part of the problem is that origami models tend to be three-dimensional, which means that when folded in great numbers they can take up enormous space. And, if you try to squish them together in a small box, they will inevitably get ruined, which will often cause the origamist to explode into a fit of rage, and rightfully so!

With pop-up cards and models that lie flat, on the other hand, you can stack hundreds of them together and still fit them in an orderly row on your bookshelf, perhaps even next to this book, or better yet, stuck in between its pages! On a bookshelf, they will not only look orderly, but they might even look academic, especially if sandwiched between math or science textbooks. Besides, origami actually does connect to math and science in a number of ways, but that is beyond the scope of this book. The focus of this book is to teach one-piece origami pop-up cards and flattenable models that will hopefully amaze and amuse your friends.

Even if you aren't yet wading through origami piled head-high, folding origami that lies flat is clearly the solution for any origamist with limited space, and let's face it, space is always limited, unless we're talking about outer space, but, that would extend far far beyond the scope of this book!

Returning back to earth, on a more personal note, as an entertainer, having origami that squishes flat has been a lifesaver. The most

Rearing Pegasus Pop-up Card
(page 119)

Barbershop Quartet
(page 146)

E.T. Pop-up Card (page 108)

Number Three Pop-up Card
(page 160)

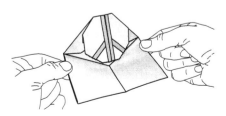

Peace Sign Pop-up Card
(page 213)

challenging part of doing a gig, for me, is the logistics of getting to the gig, because I use so many props – unicycles, juggling clubs, juggling balls, Hoberman Spheres, and, of course, my box of origami which contains a few dozen of my origami show pieces. As you can imagine, I don't have the space or time to carefully house each model in its own box as many origami artists do when they exhibit. Instead, my routine is to cram them all into my one box, a practice which has required me to focus on designing models that can be easily crammed together without getting damaged, and, the fruit of that pursuit is this book!

This book is comprised of models that lie flat but when opened become three dimensional. The advantage of this is not only that they store flat, but also, when opened they become 3-D and recognizable. So, when demonstrating the models, for the audience there is the element of suspense at not knowing what the model is going to be, the element of surprise when it's opened and they recognize what it is, and finally, we hope, the element of amazement, especially if we have explained to them beforehand that all of the models are from one sheet of paper without using tape, glue or cutting.

But there is also a fourth element, humor, which helps transform an ordinary origami show-and-tell session into what can be called a performance. I've found that using humor is especially important when performing for kids because that's what keeps them engaged and entertained and also because, unlike adults, they usually can't grasp or appreciate that the models are folded from one uncut sheet of paper. Following in the footsteps of my most recent book, Origami Ooh La La, I've once again added "Perform It" boxes in which I offer silly comic routines for performing the models in front of kids. Some of the routines might also work on adults, especially if they are sufficiently tipsy, but for sober adult audiences, I've found it's best to stress the amazingness of origami and not try to be too silly. However, even with a group of sober adults, I get good giggles when I put silly origami hats on them, and they especially love watching me be silly with the kids.

Many of the models in this book have served me well in my career as an entertainer, but I know entertaining is not for everyone and that there are many other reasons people fold origami, such as to engage their fidgety fingers, or to relax, or simply to have fun. Some like it because origami challenges and stimulates their mind, others because creating intricate figures out of a simple piece of paper gives them a thrill. I imagine many people will find these models to be useful as gifts or as greeting cards. Whatever your reason, I hope this book will help nurture your passion for origami and satisfy your folding needs without taking up boxes and boxes of space!

Increasingly,
        Jeremy Shafer

P.S. If you find your origami cravings insatiable, there are many self-help resources available on the Internet, in particular, my YouTube Channel: **www.youtube.com/jeremyshaferorigami** which is home to over 200 videos showing how to fold my most recent designs (see video index, pages 240-255) And, as you probably know, there are thousands of other origami videos and diagrams on the Internet to help you along with your addiction!

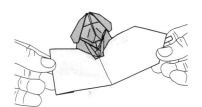

Puppy Pop-up Card
(page 80)

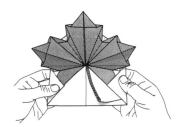

Maple Leaf Pop-up Card
(page 229)

Magical Transforming Octahedron
(page 241)

Heart Pop-up Card
(page 193)

$ Cobra Pop-up Card
(page 92)

$1 Dollar Cobra Pop-up Card (page 92) **in action**

CONTENTS

Introduction 1
Contents 4
Notation 10
Tips for Following Diagrams 10
Basics 11
More Basics – Traditional Flapping Bird 15

Birds Bugs and Bats ... 17

And Head 18

Grasshopper Head 19

Dragonfly 20

Swan 22

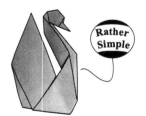

Angelfish Swan Pop-up Card 23

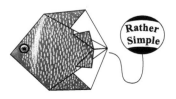

Pajarita 25

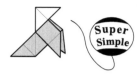

Pajarita Pop-up Card 25

Star Bird Pop-up Card ... 27

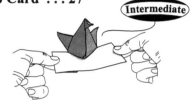

Crane Pop-up Card ... 31

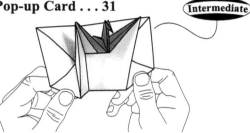

Kissing Love Birds Pop-up Card 33

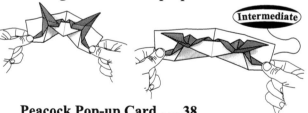

Peacock Pop-up Card ... 38

Bat Pop-up Card. ... 42

4 *Origami Pop-ups*

Bat . . . 46 — Rather Complex

Flapping Bat . . . 49 — Intermediate

Flapping Butterfly Pop-up Card . . . 56 — Intermediate

Flapping Dragonfly Pop-up Card . . . 61 — Rather Complex

LAND ANIMALS . . . 68

Panda Bear Pop-up Card . . . 69 — Super Simple

Simple Bunny Pop-up Card . . . 70 — Rather Simple

Bouncing Bunny Pop-up Card . . . 72 — Intermediate

A Bunch of Bunny Variations . . . 75

Magic Bunny . . . 76 — Rather Simple

Puppy Pop-up Card . . . 80 — Intermediate

Surprise Guest for Dinner Pop-up Card . . . 84 — Intermediate

Hello Kitty!

Elephant Pop-up Card . . . 87 — Intermediate

$1 Dollar Cobra Pop-up Card . . . 92 — Intermediate

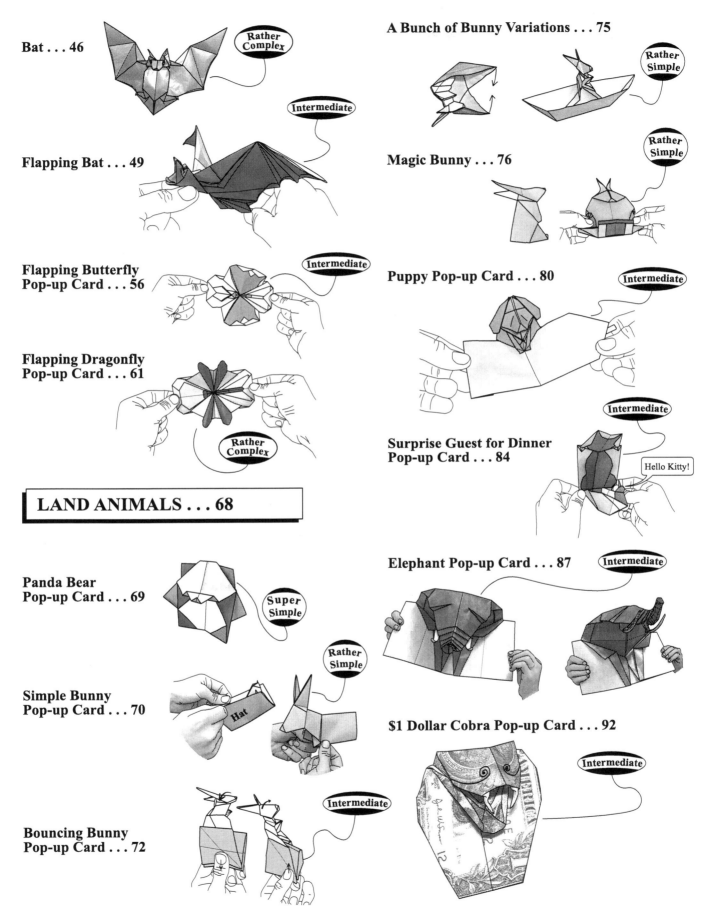

Contents **5**

Gorilla Pop-up Card . . . 94

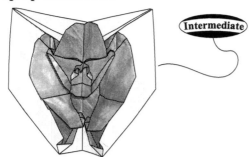

Grizzly Bear Pop-up Card . . . 100

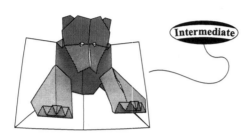

FANTASY ANIMALS . . . 105

Pippy Cyclops Pop-up Card . . . 106

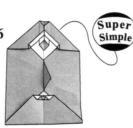

E.T. Pop-up Card 108

Flapping Dragon Pop-up Card . . . 114

Rearing Pegasus Pop-up Card . . . 119

POP-UP PEOPLE . . . 124

Baby on a Bed . . . 125

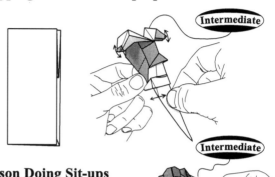

Flapping Jester Head Pop-up Card 127

Person Doing Sit-ups Pop-up Card . . . 131

Pop-up Housewife . . . 134

Pop-up Househusband 138

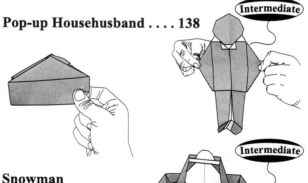

Snowman Pop-up Card . . . 141

6 *Origami Pop-ups*

Barbershop Quartet 146

Hug Me! Envelope 148

Number Pop-up Cards . . . 152

Last One Standing . . . 153

Number One Pop-up Card . . . 154

Number Two Pop-up Card . . . 157

Number Three Pop-up Card . . . 160

Number Four Pop-up Card . . . 163

Number Five Pop-up Card . . . 165

Number Six Pop-up Card . . . 168

Number Seven Pop-up Card . . . 171

Number Seven Pop-up Card Take Two! . . . 173

Number Eight Pop-out Card . . . 174

Number Nine Pop-up Card . . . 176

Zero Pop-up Card . . . 179

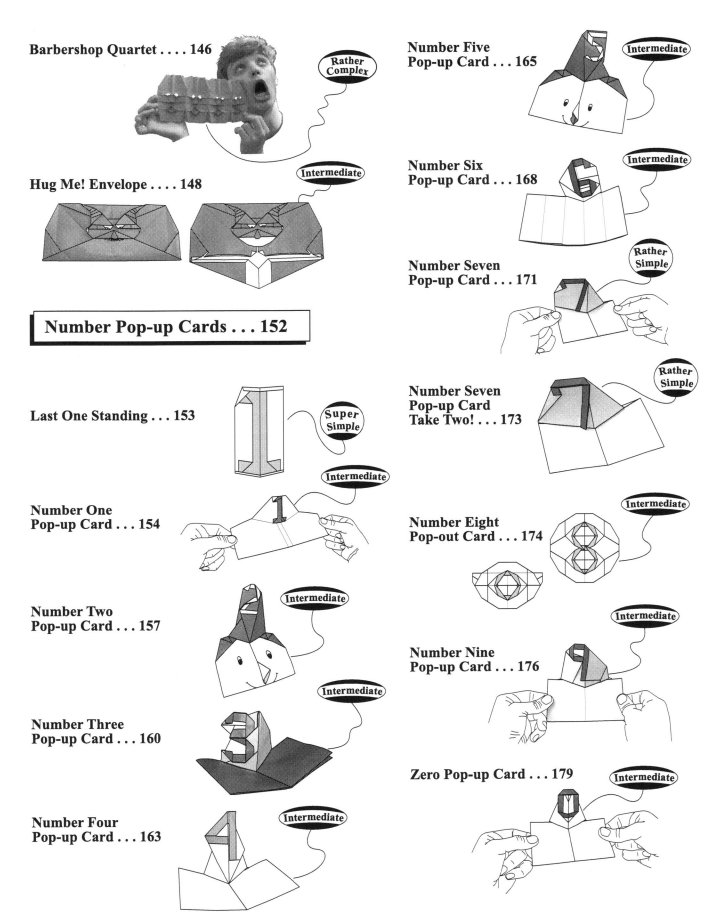

Contents 7

THINGS ... 181

Anything Pop-up Card ... 182

Pop Star ... 184

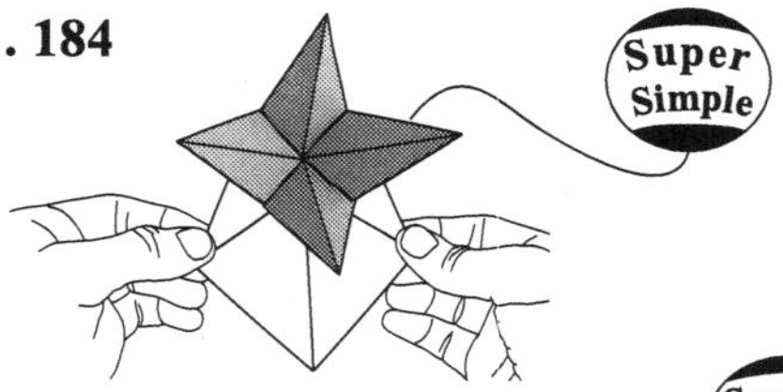

Alien Predator Pop-up Card ... 185

Pop Star Christmas Tree ... 186

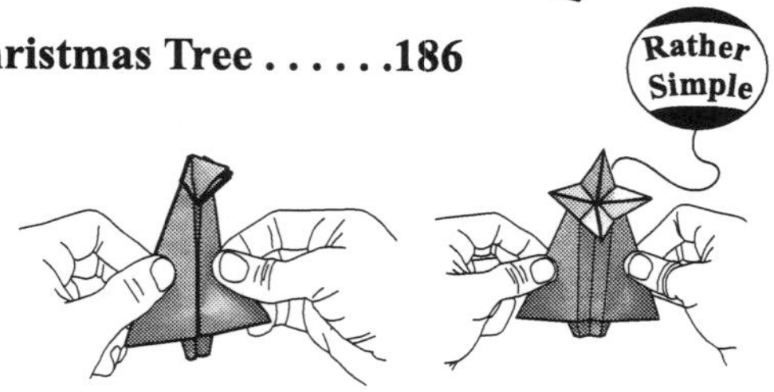

Star Pop-up Card ... 188

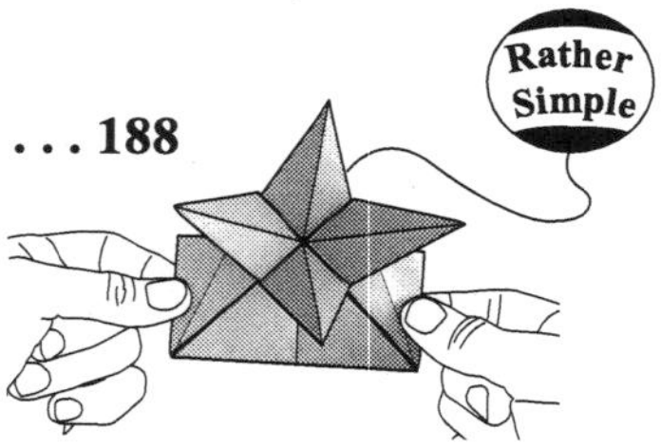

Winter Tree Pop-Up Card ... 190

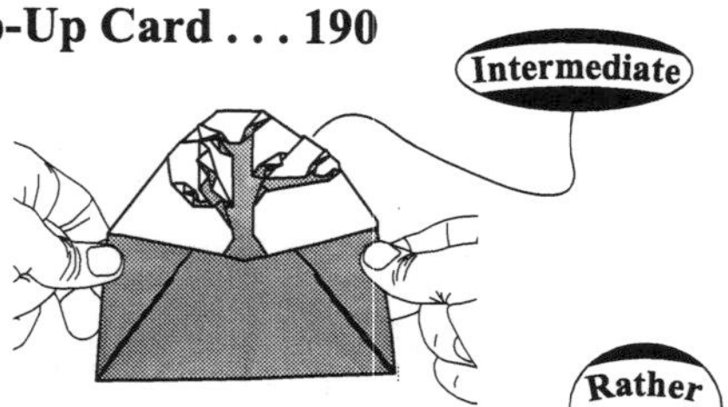

Heart Pop-up Card ... 193

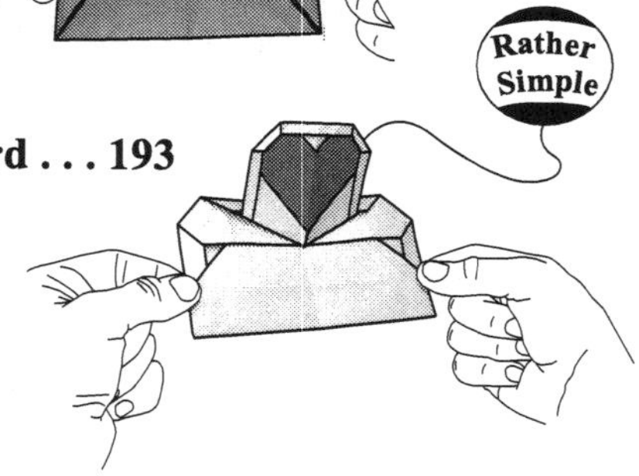

Sacred Heart ... 195

Speaking One's Heart ... 197

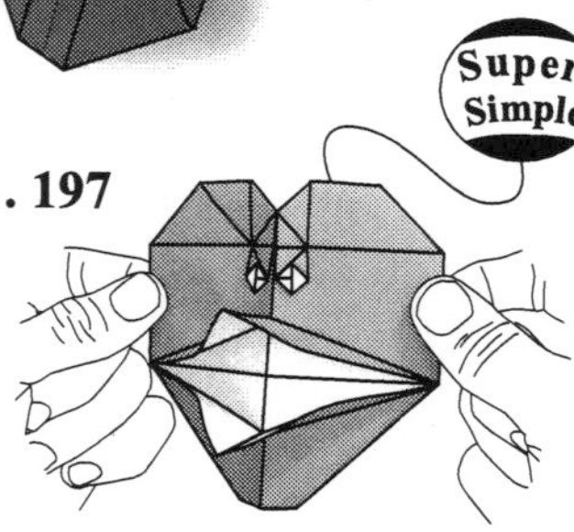

Harlequin Heart ... 198

Book of Love ... 200

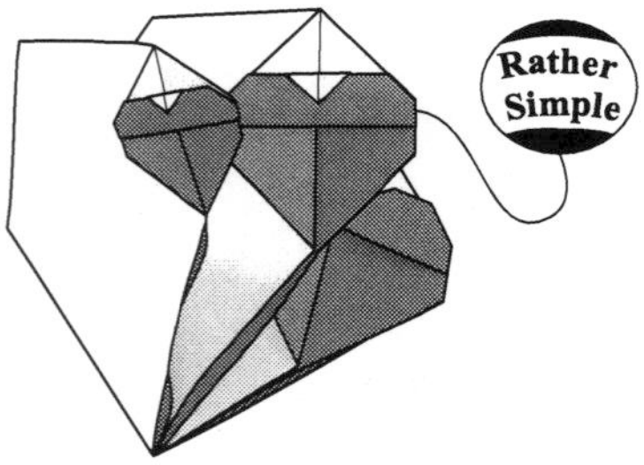

Flip Book of Love ... 202

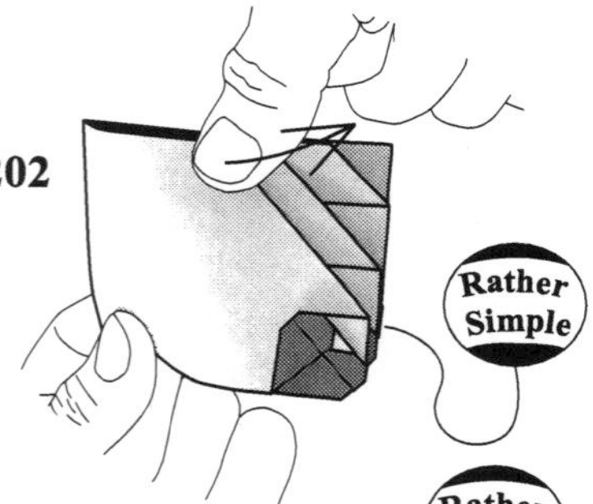

Book of Love with Foldouts ... 202

TV Heart ... 203

8 *Origami Pop-ups*

Lovey-Dovey Heart Card.... 205

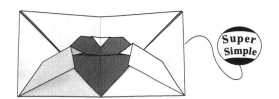
Super Simple

Star Greeting Card.... 206

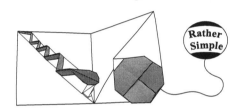
Rather Simple

Miracle of Life Greeting Card.... 207

Rather Simple

Go Fish Greeting Card.... 208

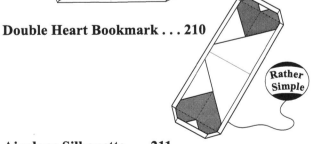
Rather Simple

Double Heart Bookmark... 210

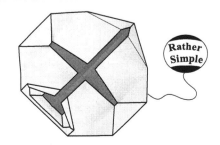
Rather Simple

Airplane Silhouette... 211

Rather Simple

Peace Sign Pop-up Card... 213

Intermediate

Pop-up Cubicle... 217

Intermediate

Cherry Blossom Pop-up Card... 220

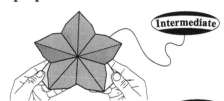
Intermediate

Clematis Pop-up Card.... 224

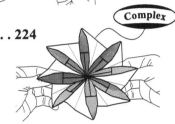
Complex

Maple Leaf Pop-up Card.... 229

Rather Complex

Stress Reliever.... 236

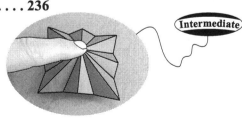
Intermediate

JeremyShaferOrigami YouTube Tutorials Contents 240

Pop-ups, Flashers, Stars, Hearts, Flowers, Extreme Action, Scary Origami, Dollar Origami, Popular Culture, Astonish and Amuse, Miscellaneous.

Contents **9**

NOTATION

Line Styles

Valley Fold	– – – – – –
Mountain Fold	–·–·–·–·–
Crease	———
Covered up edges or folds or where the paper ends up	··············

Arrows and Symbols

- Fold from here to there
- Valley-fold and unfold
- Fold behind
- Fold behind and unfold
- Unfold
- Push in or Apply force
- Pleat-sink
- Open between these two layers
- Turn the model over
- Slide out paper from underneath
- Repeat once
- Repeat three times
- Rotate the model (180°)
- Exploded view—the next drawing will be larger
- Imploded view—the next drawing will be smaller
- Eyeball—the next drawing is from the point of view of this eyeball
- Focus on this spot
- Inflate or blow

Anatomy of the Origami Diagram

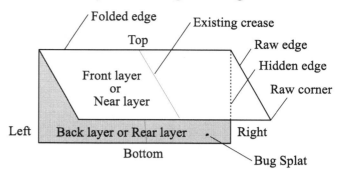

Labels: Folded edge, Existing crease, Top, Raw edge, Hidden edge, Front layer or Near layer, Raw corner, Left, Back layer or Rear layer, Right, Bottom, Bug Splat

Tips for Following Diagrams

Make folds as precise as possible. Following the arrows, carefully line up each fold making sure it's exactly where it's supposed to be. Most of the steps in this book have clear guidelines to follow such as, "Valley-fold edge-to-crease," or, "Valley-fold on the black dots." In these cases, any error made will get magnified; if the beginning folds of a model are off, then the end folds will be REALLY off! However, some steps will require that you use your judgement as to the placement of the folds. In these cases exact placement is not important, but, for best results, you should still try to make it look as much like what's shown in the diagram as possible.

Look ahead to the next step. If, for instance, you're on step 4 of a model, your goal is to make the model look like the diagram in step 5. So before doing step 4, you should look at the diagram in step 5 to see what you're aiming for.

Orient the paper. Make sure the paper is oriented exactly as it is shown in the diagram.

Fold on a flat surface. Most folders, including myself, fold on a flat surface simply because it's easier.

Make sharp folds (unless otherwise stated). Fingernails are a good tool.

Don't get in over your head. All the models in the Contents are labeled Super Simple, Rather Simple, Intermediate, Rather Complex, and Complex.

If you are a beginning folder, it's a good idea to start with the super simple models. You're welcome to start out with the complex diagrams, but if you get stuck, before you tear up the paper out of frustration, please come back and attempt something easier.

Choosing Paper

Almost any paper that doesn't break when folded is good for origami. But, since most of the models in this book are bi-color, it's best to use paper that is a different color on each side. I recommend using standard "origami paper" which comes in an assortment of colors and is white on the back side. It's sold at most arts and craft stores and online.

For my show pieces I like to paint the paper with acrylic paint. This makes the model stronger, more colorful and also makes it waterproof. Another technique to make the paper stronger is to laminate it. A cheap (but time consuming) method of laminating paper is to completely cover one side with clear packing tape.

Basics

This is a pictorial glossary showing how to do the basic folds which appear throughout origami diagrams. All origami maneuvers can be broken down into mountain folds and valley folds. Mountain folds, indicated by dot-dot-dash lines, are convex like a mountain ridge. Valley folds, indicated by dash-dash lines, are concave, like a valley.

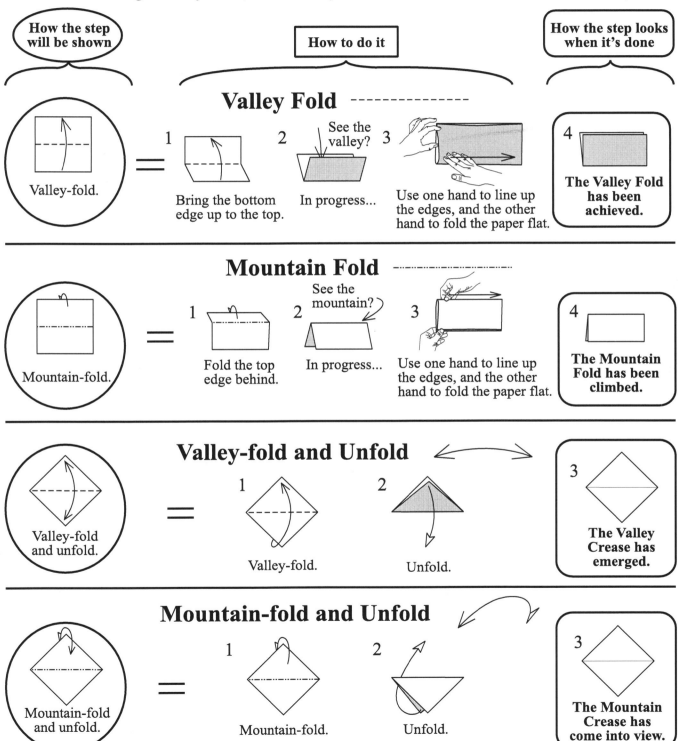

Basics 11

Kite Base

Fold a Kite Base.

=

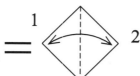
1. Begin with white side up. Valley-fold and unfold in half.

2. Valley-fold.

3. **The Kite Base has taken off.**

To get ready for the next fold, valley-fold the Kite Base in half and rotate 90° counter-clockwise.

Inside Reverse Fold

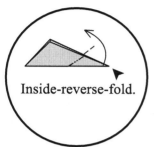
Inside-reverse-fold.

=

1. Valley-fold and unfold.

2. Reach in and lift the point up through the middle as shown.

3. Continue lifting.

4. Now flatten it along the existing creases.

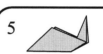
5. **The Inside Reverse Fold has risen.**

Outside Reverse Fold

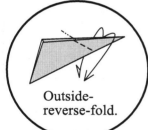
Outside-reverse-fold.

=

1. Valley-fold and unfold.

2. Unfold the kite from behind.

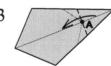
3. Valley-fold, so that the fold line goes through point **A**.

4. Mountain-fold the bottom half behind.

5. Rotate the small flap counterclockwise in a hinge action, so that the folds end up on the existing creases.

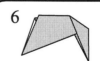
6. **The Outside Reverse Fold has fallen into place.**

Squash Fold

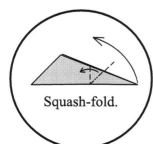
Squash-fold.

=

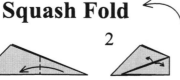
1. Valley-fold.   2. Puff out the pocket.   3. Lift the flap and squash it flat.

4. **The Squash Fold has been committed.**

12 *Origami Pop-ups*

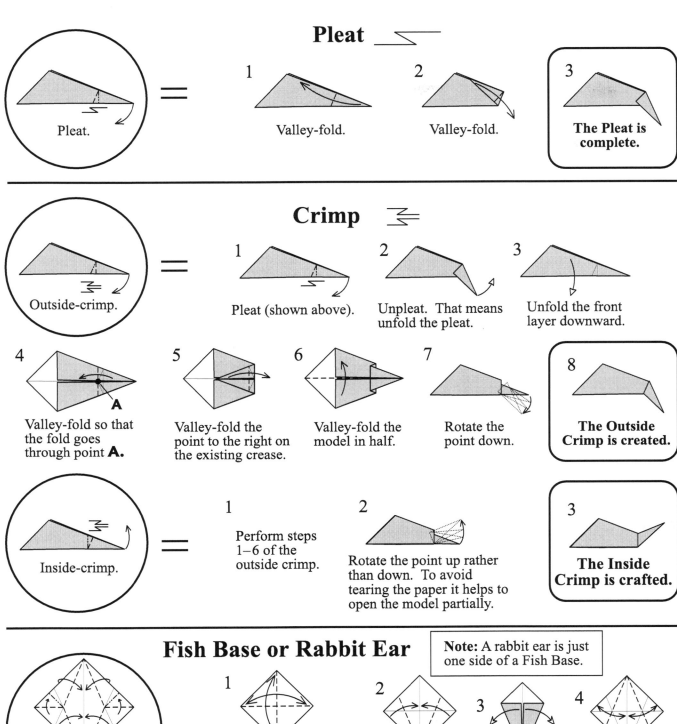
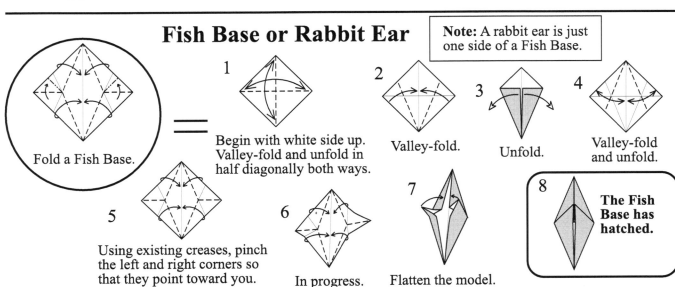

Basics 13

Waterbomb Base

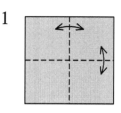

This symbol means, "Turn over."

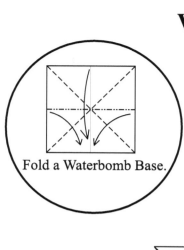

Fold a Waterbomb Base.

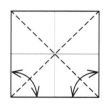

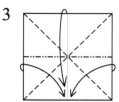

1 Begin colored side up. Valley-fold and unfold in half both ways. **Turn over.**

2 Valley-fold and unfold diagonally in half both ways.

3 Bring the midpoints of the three upper sides down to the midpoint of the lower side.

4 In progress.

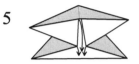

5 Even more progressive!

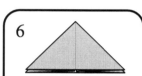

6 The Waterbomb Base has exploded into existence.

Sink

Note: The sink arrowhead is also used when a point gets reverse-folded into the model.

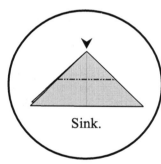

Sink.

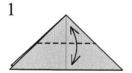

1 Begin with a Waterbomb Base (see above). Valley-fold and unfold.

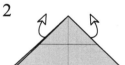

2 Completely unfold.

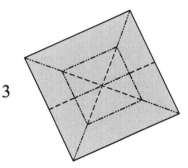

3 Starting with the mountains, make the indicated folds.

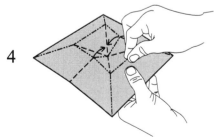

4 Mountain-pinching in progress. Return the paper to the configuration of step 1, but with the central portion pushed in.

5 The Sink is sunk.

14 *Origami Pop-ups*

More Basics... Traditional Flapping Bird

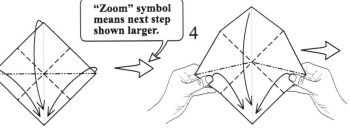

Now that you have learned some basics, it's time to learn a few more, but this time while folding the traditional Flapping Bird, which in my opinion is one of the most amazing origami models of all time. It requires making several basic folds such as Petal Fold and Square Base, which is why I've included it here in the Basics section.

1

Colored side up. Valley-fold and unfold diagonally both ways. **Turn over.**

2

Valley-fold and unfold in half both ways.

3

"Zoom" symbol means next step shown larger.

Bring the three corners down to the lower corner folding on existing creases. The following two steps show this fold in progress.

4

Step 3 slightly in progress. Continue bringing the three corners downward.

5

Step 3 further in progress. Flatten completely.

6 Square Base

The Square Base is complete. Valley-fold the left and right front flaps to middle crease.

7

Valley-fold the top down.

8

Unfold the two flaps but leave the top folded down.

9 Petal Fold

Now it's time to do a Petal Fold. Lift the front flap slightly.

10

Keep lifting.

11

Here we have a boat. Collapse the sides of the boat to the middle line.

12

The Petal Fold is complete. **Turn over.**

PERFORM IT!

Hold up the finished Flapping Bird and ask the audience, **"What is this?"** [Audience says, "A bird."] Make the wings flap and say, **"It's a flapping bird! Everyone flap your wings like a bird!"** [Audience flaps their arms.] Exclaim, **"Stop! That was close! You guys almost flew away!"**

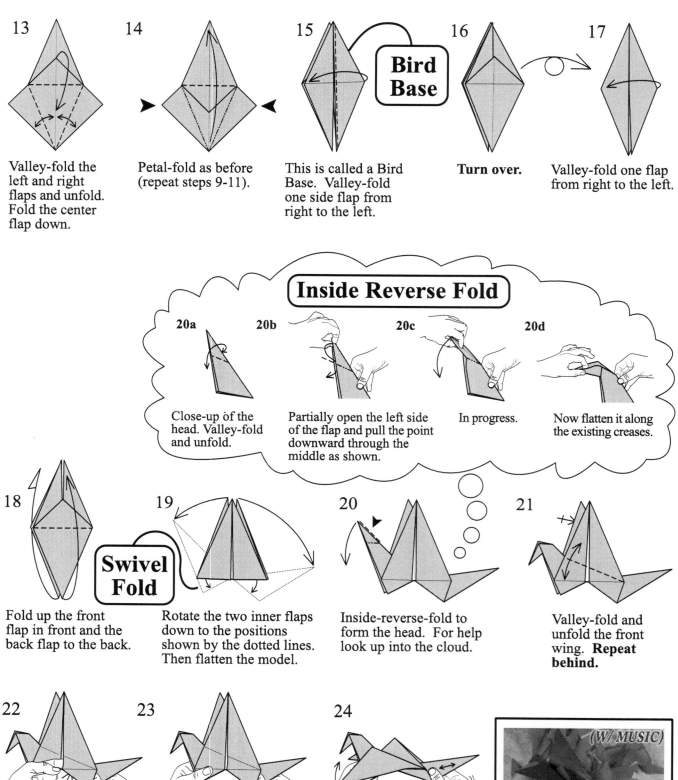

13 Valley-fold the left and right flaps and unfold. Fold the center flap down.

14 Petal-fold as before (repeat steps 9-11).

15 This is called a Bird Base. Valley-fold one side flap from right to the left.

16 Turn over.

17 Valley-fold one flap from right to the left.

Inside Reverse Fold

20a Close-up of the head. Valley-fold and unfold.

20b Partially open the left side of the flap and pull the point downward through the middle as shown.

20c In progress.

20d Now flatten it along the existing creases.

18 Fold up the front flap in front and the back flap to the back.

19 (Swivel Fold) Rotate the two inner flaps down to the positions shown by the dotted lines. Then flatten the model.

20 Inside-reverse-fold to form the head. For help look up into the cloud.

21 Valley-fold and unfold the front wing. **Repeat behind.**

22 Holding exactly as shown, put your finger in the pocket and then take it out. **Repeat behind.**

23 To make the wings flap, hold firmly as shown, and pull your right hand straight down and then to the right.

24 **The Bird has been flapped.** Push the tail back in and the wings will go back up. Pull the tail out and push it in, flapping to your heart's content!

Video tutorial on youtube.com! **Search:** shafer flapping birds fast

16   *Origami Pop-ups*

Bugs, Birds and Bats

This book is organized by topic into chapters. While most of the models are actual pop-up cards, for the sake of variety (and to fill 257 pages!) some regular models are interspersed throughout, but they all share the characteristics of being able to be stored flat (without getting ruined!) and being able to be opened into three dimensions, so they are "pop-ups" in the broader sense. **Note:** Some of the regular models require some unfolding in order to lie flat.

This chapter focuses on the three B's – Birds Bugs and Bats. Hey, what is the similarity between winged creatures and origami? For both, the sky is the limit! May you soar through this chapter and beyond! On with the folds!

Ant Head

By Jeremy Shafer ©2005

This recently discovered specimen is heading up the new field of ant-omology. It might not bring you fame and fortune, but it will certainly make a nice trophy for your biology teacher to pin up on the wall!

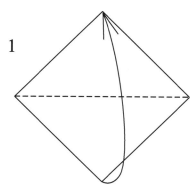

1. White side up, valley-fold in half diagonally.

2. Valley-fold in half and unfold.

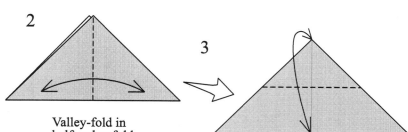

3. Valley-fold top-to-bottom and unfold (both layers).

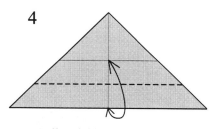

4. Valley-fold edge-to-crease and unfold.

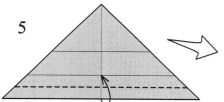

5. Valley-fold edge-to-crease and unfold.

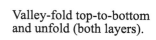

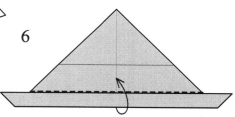

6. Valley-fold on the edge.

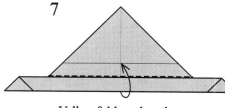

7. Valley-fold on the edge.

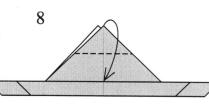

8. Valley-fold one flap point-to-point.

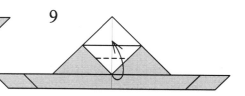

9. Valley-fold the flap to just beyond the folded edge.

18 *Origami Pop-ups*

10

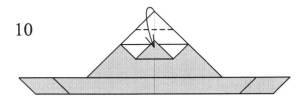

Valley-fold the flap to just beyond the folded edge.

11

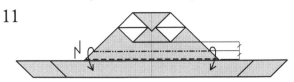

Pleat (all layers).

12

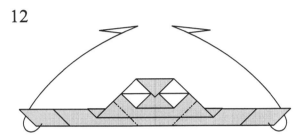

Mountain-fold to taste forming the two antennae.

13   14

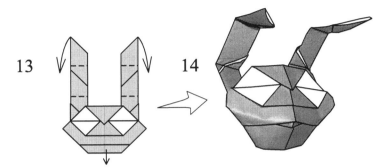

Make two valley folds on each antenna so that they extend in front of the face. Pull the lower mouth downward and shape to taste.

The ant head is done. Disclaimer: No ants were dismembered in the designing of this model.

PERFORM IT!

Say to the audience, "I would like you to meet my ant, Hedda." Hold up the model and say, "As you can see, she's the Hedda the ant colony."

Grasshopper Head

(Rather Simple)   By Jeremy Shafer ©2005

If fried grasshoppers are more to your taste, then this is the model for you!

12

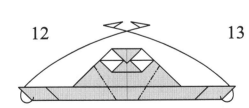

Begin by folding steps 1-10 of the Ant Head. Mountain-fold the two ends, crossing them behind so that they overlap.

13

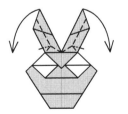

Narrow the antennae with rabbit ears. What's a rabbit ear? See page 13!

14

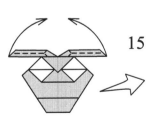

Narrow the antennae even more with rabbit ears or just squish them thin. Shape to taste.

15

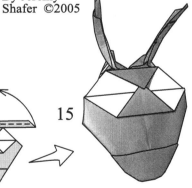

The Grasshopper Head is finished. Now it just needs to find some *body* to attach itself to!

PERFORM IT!

Hold up the model and say, "This is a grasshopper head. You see, it has two blades of grass and it can hop." Make it hop on one antenna.

Ant Head 19

Dragonfly

By Jeremy Shafer ©2009 **Rather Simple**

This dragonfly lost its legs in battle, but it really doesn't care, because it's a "Dragonfly," not a "Dragonwalk."

1

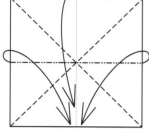

Begin by folding a Waterbomb Base (see page 14).

2

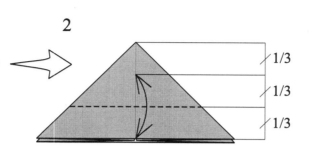

Valley-fold horizontally and unfold, estimating thirds.

3

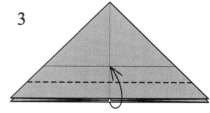

Valley-fold to the crease (all layers).

4 5 6

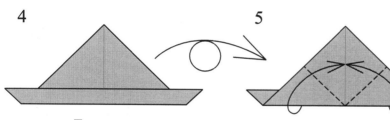

Turn over. Valley-fold edge-to-crease.

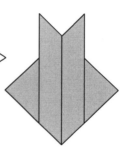

Turn over top to bottom.

7

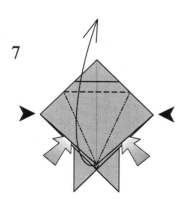

Petal-fold. What's a petal fold? See page 15, steps 6-12.

8

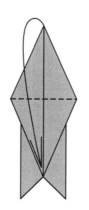

Valley-fold the flap back down.

9

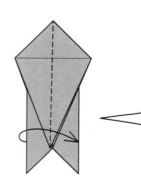

Valley-fold in half.

20 *Origami Pop-ups*

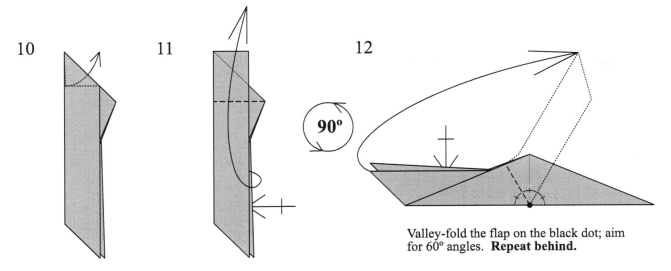

10 Pull out the interior flap.

11 Valley-fold the front flap. **Repeat behind.** Rotate 90° counterclockwise.

12 Valley-fold the flap on the black dot; aim for 60° angles. **Repeat behind.**

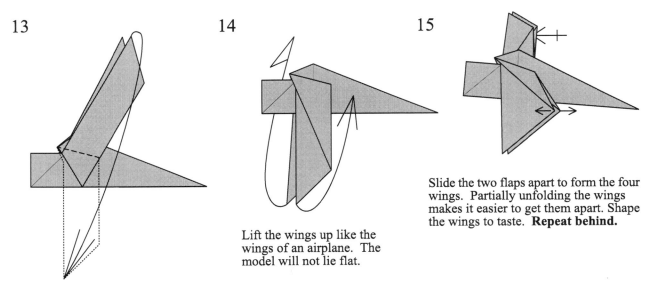

13 Valley-fold. **Repeat behind.**

14 Lift the wings up like the wings of an airplane. The model will not lie flat.

15 Slide the two flaps apart to form the four wings. Partially unfolding the wings makes it easier to get them apart. Shape the wings to taste. **Repeat behind.**

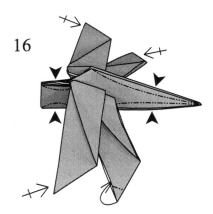

16 Reverse-fold the tips of the four wings, and squeeze the head and the tail, shaping them to taste.

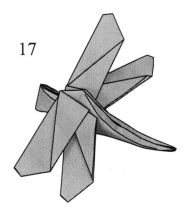

17 **The completed Dragonfly.**

PERFORM IT!

Hold up the finished model and ask, **"What is this?"** [Audience says, "A dragonfly."] Say, **"Yes, and it can even fly. Do you want to see?"** [Audience says, "Yes!"] **"Ready, set, everyone say, 'Fly!'"** [Audience says, "Fly!"] Throw the model into the audience and say to whoever picks it up, **"Wow, look it even landed gracefully at your feet! Now can you make it fly back?"**

Dragonfly

Swan

While there can never be too many swans a swimming, seven on this page is plenty!

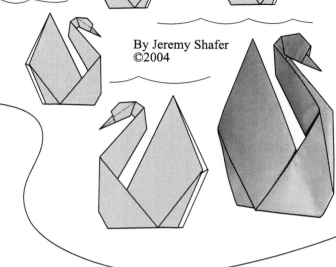

By Jeremy Shafer
©2004

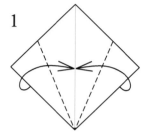

1. White side up, valley-fold edge-to-crease.

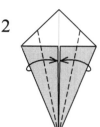

2. Valley-fold edge-to-edge.

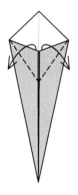

3. Valley-fold. This is a judgement fold; just try to make it look like the next step.

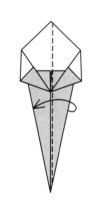

4. Valley-fold in half.

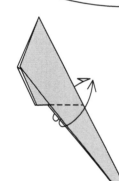

5. Outside-reverse-fold on the interior edge. What's an outside reverse fold? See page 12.

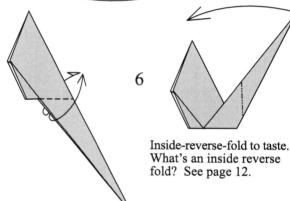

6. Inside-reverse-fold to taste. What's an inside reverse fold? See page 12.

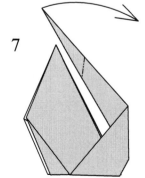

7. Inside-reverse-fold to taste.

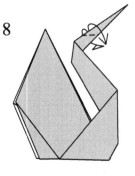

8. Outside-reverse-fold to taste.

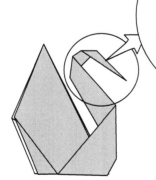

9. Pull out paper from inside the head to make the head wider.

22 *Origami Pop-ups*

10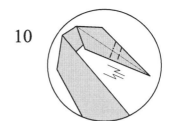

Crimp to form the beak.
What's a crimp? See page 13.

11

One Swan is ready for a swim on top of a table. Fold six more to complete the hepta-gaggle.

12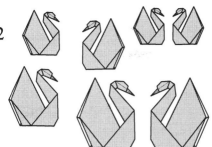

Seven Swans a Swimming!
Now you just need to fold
Six geese a laying,
Five golden rings,
Four calling birds,
Three french hens,
Two turtle doves
And a partridge in a pear tree!

Oops! Don't forgot the
twelve drummers drumming,
Eleven ladies dancing,
Ten lords a leaping,
Nine pipers piping, and the
Eight maids a milking!

Thoughts Behind the Folds

I was commissioned to design this model and fold 50 of them by a local Macy's as part of a juggling gig I did at the store to promote their Swarovski jewelry and figurines.

Angelfish Swan Pop-up Card

Rather Simple

13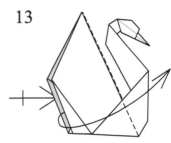

For this variation I recommend re-folding the model but switching colors, so that the swan comes out white and the angelfish comes out colored. Valley-fold the front flap to the right and **repeat behind**.

14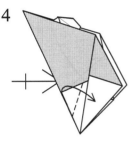

Valley-fold the flap to taste. **Repeat behind.**

15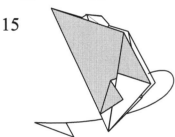

The Angelfish Swan Pop-up Card is complete, but you can only see half of the fish. In order see the whole angel fish simply open the card from behind and embellish to taste.

16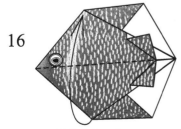

The Angel Fish has been spotted.
Close the fish to turn it back into a swan

17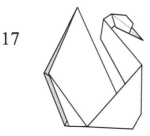

The Angelfish has swanned.

PERFORM IT!

Hold up the closed model (step 15) and say, **"This here is half a fish. Would you like to see the whole fish"** [Audience says, "Yes!"] Show the angelfish (step 16) and exclaim, **"There it is! And, it's name is 'Swan.'' Do you know why?"** [Audience says, "Why?"] Show the swan and say, **"Because it really IS a swan! And what do swans eat?** [Audience says, "Fish?"] Show the angelfish again and say **"That's right, fish! And what do people say to fish?"** [Audience says, "What?"] **"They say, 'GO, fish!'"** Yell at the model, **"GO!!! fish!"** Put the model back in the box and say, **"Ok, it went."**

Swan

Traditional Pajarita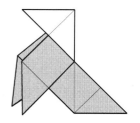

The Pajarita, which in Spanish means "Little Bird," is a much-loved traditional model of Spain, but what is it doing in this book? It's a warm-up for the next model, "The Pajarita Pop-up Card." Besides, I think you'll find my method of folding it new and interesting.

1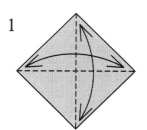

Colored side up, valley-fold and unfold diagonally in half in both directions.

2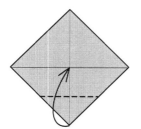

Valley-fold one corner to the center.

3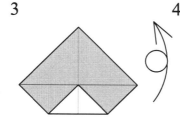

Turn over bottom to top.

4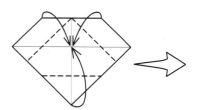

Valley-fold three corners to the center.

5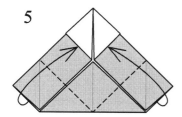

Valley-fold edge-to-edge.

6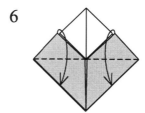

Valley-fold the two flaps edge-to-edge.

7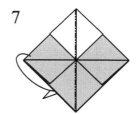

Mountain-fold in half.

8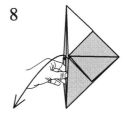

Pull out the middle layers.

9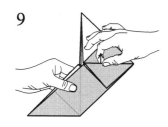

Slide the horizontal edge slightly upward.

10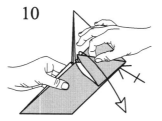

Pull the flap downward releasing the trapped layers. **Repeat steps 9 and 10 behind.**

11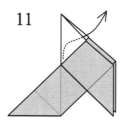

Pull out the interior flap.

12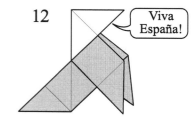

The Pajarita is completita.

PERFORM IT!

Hold up the model and say, "**This is the Pajarita, the little bird that is a huge symbol of patriotism in Spain.** Its full name is Papiratis Pajariticus, and, like most bird species, it prefers wetter climates, like, for instance, the low flatlands of Spain. Do you know why?" [Audience says, "Why?"] "Because..." Sing, "**...THE RAIN IN SPAIN FALLS MAINLY ON THE PLAIN!**" (from musical, *My Fair Lady*)

Pajarita Pop-up Card

 By Jeremy Shafer
©2003

This modelo es fantastico for niños y niñas, amigos y amigas, señores y señoritas y especialmente aficionados de pajaritas!

1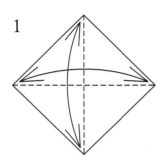
White side up, valley-fold in half diagonally in both directions and unfold.

2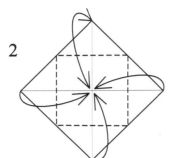
Fold all four corners to the center. Unfold the top corner.

3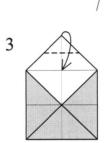
Valley-fold to the intersection of creases.

4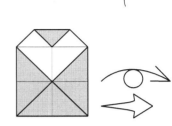
Turn over.

5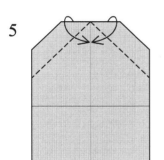
Valley-fold edge-to-crease.

6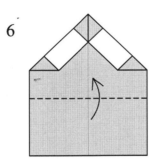
Valley-fold on the existing crease.

7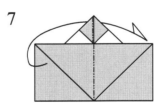
Mountain-fold the model in half.

8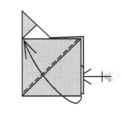
Valley-fold the front flap. **Repeat behind.**

9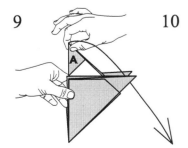
Holding as shown, pull out flap **A**; reverse and flatten it.

10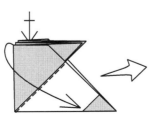
Valley-fold the front flap downward. **Repeat behind.**

11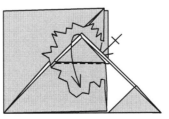
Cut-away view. Valley-fold the triangular flap downward. **Repeat behind.**

12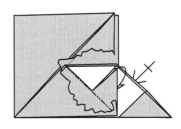
Mountain-fold the interior flap downward. **Repeat behind.**

Pajarita Pop-up Card **25**

13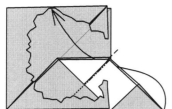

Reverse-fold the flap on the folded edges.

14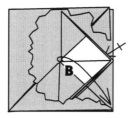

Carefully unfold flap **B** downward releasing the trapped layers. **Repeat behind.**

15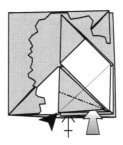

Reverse-fold. **Repeat behind.**

16

Pull out the interior flap; reverse and flatten it.

17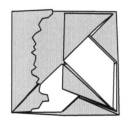

The Pajarita Pop-up is ready to make its grand appearance. Restore the torn paper that you hopefully did not really tear!

18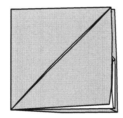

Open the card.

19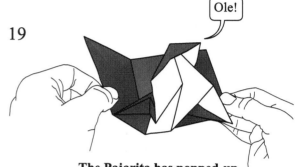

The Pajarita has popped-up from its siesta and is now en camino a la fiesta! Open the card wider and the pajarita will spread its wings as if soaring through the beautiful sky singing mariachi... "Canta, no llores, porque cantando se alegran, Cielito Lindo, los corazones!" (Translation: "Sing, don't cry, because singing, my pretty sky, warms people's hearts!")

PERFORM IT!

Hold up the closed card and say, **"Inside here is a super model! Ready, set, everyone say, 'Pop-up!'"** [Audience says, "Pop-up."] Say, **"It's a bird! It's a Plane! It's..."** Open the card. **"...just a bird. But not just any bird! It's... Super Pajarita! Do you want to see it fly?"** [Audience says, "Ya!"] Throw the model straight up in the air as high as you can and try to catch it. Ask, **"Did you see it perform all those amazing spinning tricks in the air. No wonder why the Pajarita is the pride of Spain! Everyone say, '¡Olé!'"** [Audience says, "¡Olé!"]

Star Bird Pop-up Card

By Jeremy Shafer ©2008

What exactly is a Star Bird? Previously, it was a Milton Bradley Space Ship toy popular in the 1980's. But since that fad is dead, a new definition must be found, and what better time than now!... So, I hereby declare *Star Bird* to be defined as any bird that can transform into a star. And, so far, I know of only one – the bird in this origami pop-up card! And now you too can get in on this trendy new trend and own your very own Star Bird today!

1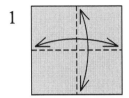
Colored side up, valley-fold and unfold.

2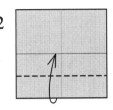
Valley-fold edge-to-crease.

3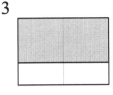
Turn over left-to-right.

4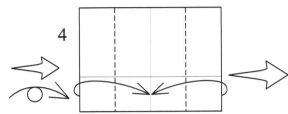
Valley-fold edge-to-crease.

5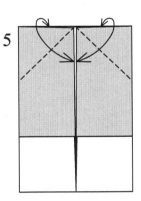
Valley-fold edge-to-edge and unfold.

6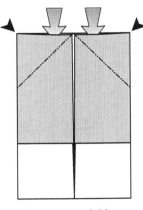
Reverse-fold.

7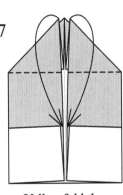
Valley-fold the two flaps down.

8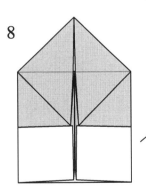
Turn over.

9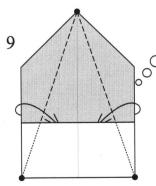
Valley-fold on the black dots shaded layers only, overlapping the flaps. This requires reaching underneath the top layer. For extra help, look up into the cloud.

9a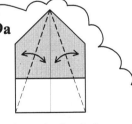
If you don't mind an extra crease on the card, you can make step 9 easier, by first valley-folding and unfolding on all layers and then attempting step 9.

10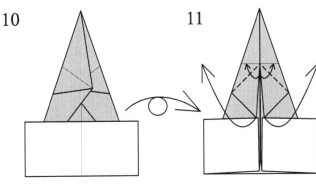
Turn over.

11
Valley-fold the two flaps edge-to-crease.

Star Bird Pop-up Card **27**

12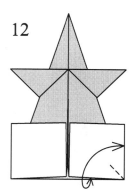

Valley-fold the flap edge-to-edge and unfold, creasing only where indicated.

13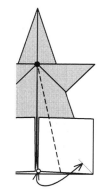

Valley-fold the white flap dot-to-creasemark and unfold. This crease originates at the black dot.

14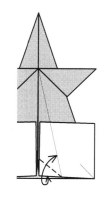

Valley-fold the flap edge-to-crease and unfold.

15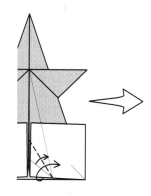

Valley-fold the flap crease-to-crease and **don't** unfold!

16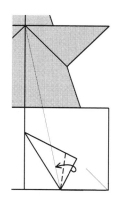

Valley-fold the flap edge-to-crease and **don't** unfold!

17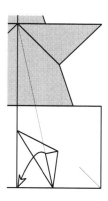

OK, now unfold the entire flap.

18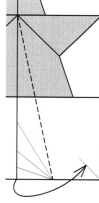

Valley-fold the flap on the existing crease and **don't** unfold.

19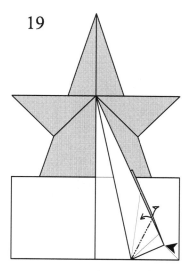

Squash the flap.

20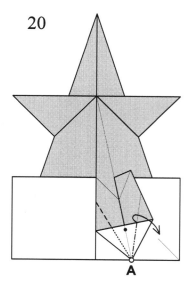

Rotate the top layer clockwise about point **A** and flatten on existing creases. Watch the black dot.

21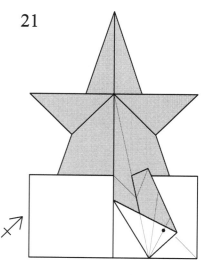

Repeat steps 12-20 on the left side.

28 *Origami Pop-ups*

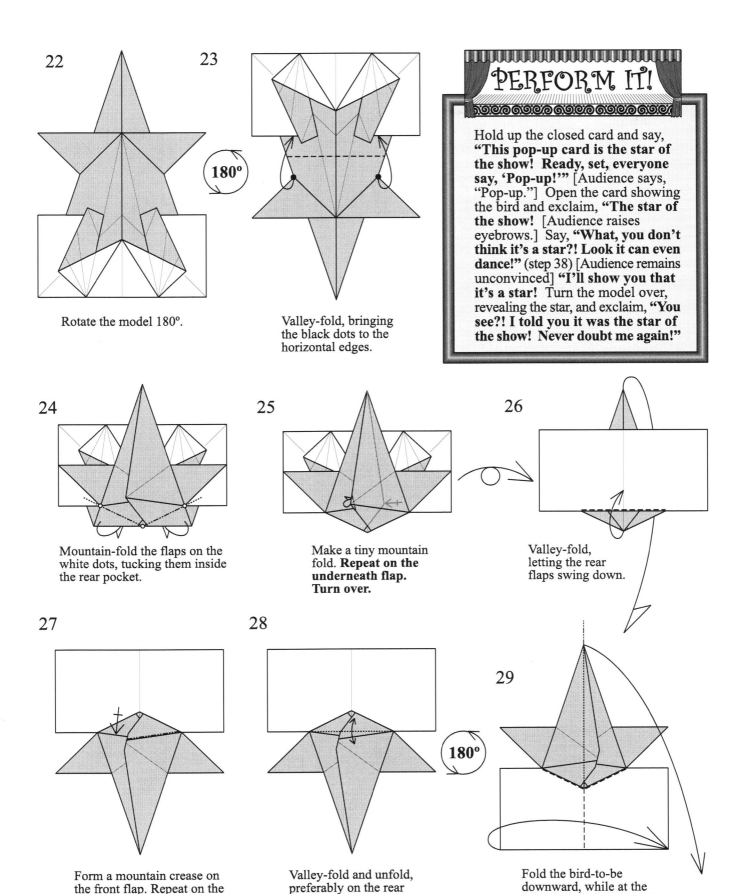

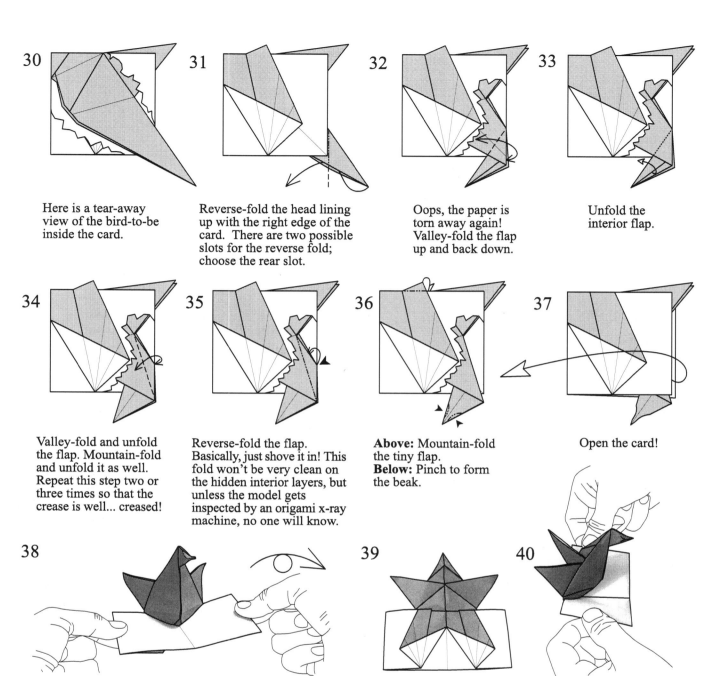

30. Here is a tear-away view of the bird-to-be inside the card.

31. Reverse-fold the head lining up with the right edge of the card. There are two possible slots for the reverse fold; choose the rear slot.

32. Oops, the paper is torn away again! Valley-fold the flap up and back down.

33. Unfold the interior flap.

34. Valley-fold and unfold the flap. Mountain-fold and unfold it as well. Repeat this step two or three times so that the crease is well... creased!

35. Reverse-fold the flap. Basically, just shove it in! This fold won't be very clean on the hidden interior layers, but unless the model gets inspected by an origami x-ray machine, no one will know.

36. Above: Mountain-fold the tiny flap.
Below: Pinch to form the beak.

37. Open the card!

38. The Star Bird has popped up and is waiting for the chance to dance. Repeatedly open and close the card and the bird will do a dance. To transform the bird into a star, open the card, pulling it as wide as possible, and, in a sudden motion, **turn the model over.**

39. The Starbird is a Star!

40. Side View.

PERFORM IT!

Open the card and ask, **"What's this?** [Audience says, "A bird."] Respond, "No, it's a starfish. [Audience raises eyebrows.] Turn it around so that the audience sees the star, and say, **"Well, I guess it does look like a bird. I don't know why I thought it was a starfish. I must be going crazy!** [Audience says, "Because it IS a star"] Say, **"Oh no! Now YOU all are going crazy! I better put this model away!"**

Origami Pop-ups

Crane Pop-up Card

By Jeremy Shafer ©2011

Inside this pop-up card is a crane that flaps its wings as the card is opened, making this model a special and thoughtful gift for any occasion, and you don't even need to fold a thousand!

1. Colored side up, valley-fold in half diagonally in both directions.

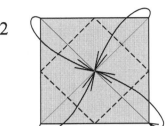
2. Valley-fold the four corners to the middle. Unfold one corner.

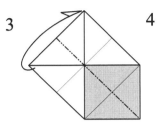
3. Mountain-fold the model in half.

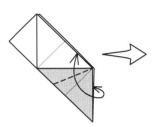
4. Valley-fold edge-to-edge and unfold.

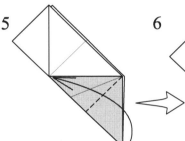
5. Valley-fold point-to-point.

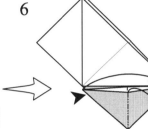
6. Squash.

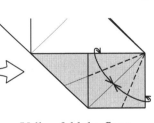
7. Valley-fold the flaps edge-to-crease and unfold.

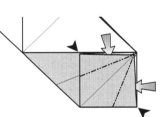
8. Reverse-fold.

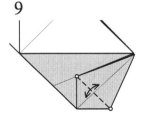
9. Valley-fold between the white dots (all layers) and unfold.

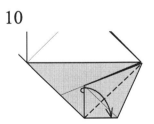
10. Valley-fold the flap down.

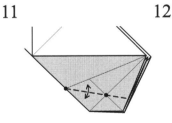
11. Valley-fold on the black dots (all layers).

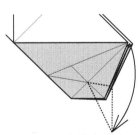
12. Reverse-fold the middle flap on the existing crease.

PERFORM IT!

Hold up the closed card and say, **"Inside this card is a super scary venomous razor-clawed prehistoric pterodactyl monster! You wanna see it?"** [Audience says, "Ya!"] **"Ready, set, everyone say, 'Pop-up!'"** [Audience says, "Pop-up."] Close your eyes and pretend to tremble in fear as you slowly open the card and show it the audience. Say, **"Isn't it so scary!!!** [Audience says, "No, it's just a bird."] Answer, **"It's just a bird??? Hmm, where'd the monster go? I'll bet it was so scary that it scared itself away! Well, say 'Bye bye birdie.'"** [Audience says, "Bye, bye birdie."] Close it and quip, **"That card was for the birds!"**

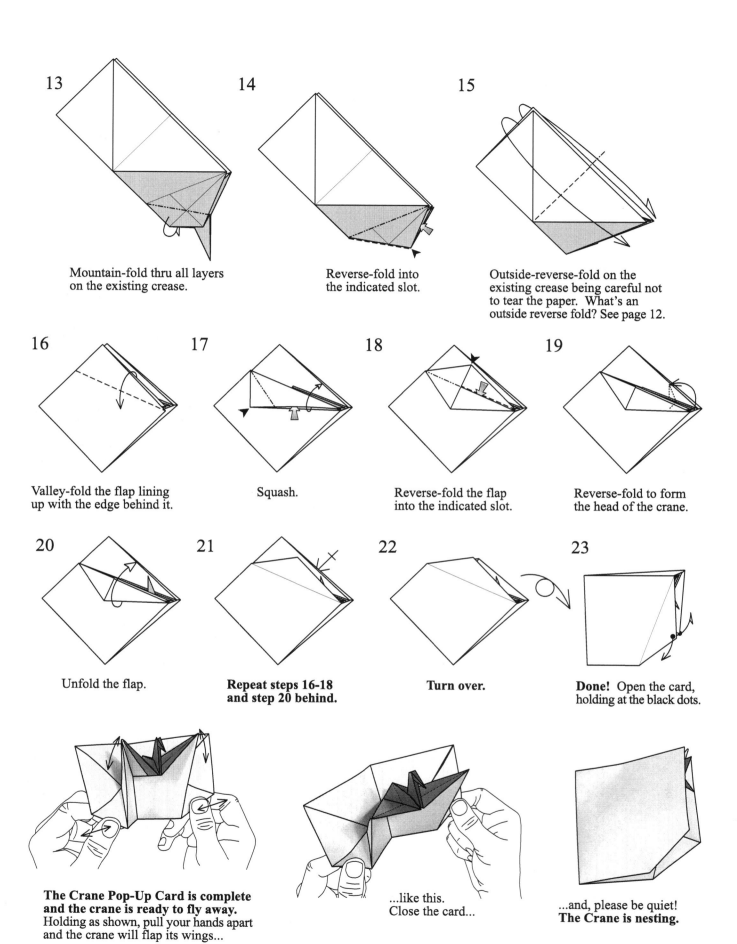

Kissing Love Birds Pop-up Card

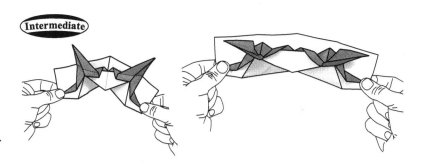

Kissing and flapping their wings, these birds put on a big show of affection!

1

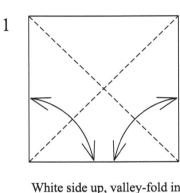

White side up, valley-fold in half diagonally and unfold in both directions.

2

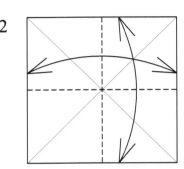

Valley-fold in half and unfold in both directions. **Turn over.**

3

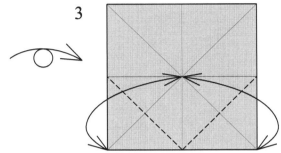

Valley-fold two corners to the center and unfold.

4

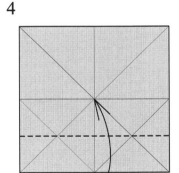

Valley-fold edge-to-crease.

5

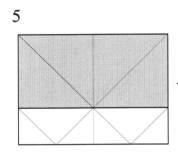

Turn over.

6

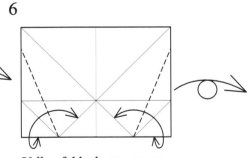

Valley-fold edge-to-crease and unfold. **Turn over.**

7

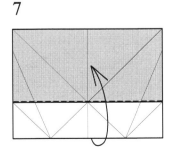

Valley-fold on the edge (but stay safe!).

8

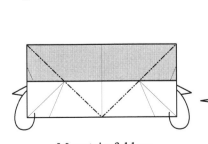

Mountain-fold on existing creases.

9

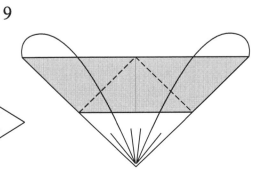

Valley-fold the two flaps to the bottom.

Kissing Love Birds Pop-up Card 33

10

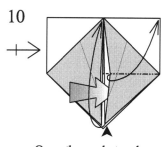

Open the pocket and squash. Repeat on the left side.

11

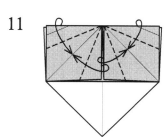

Valley-fold the flaps edge-to-crease.

12

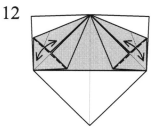

Make two valley creases **on all layers.**

13

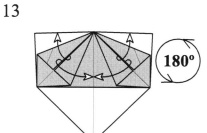

Unfold the four flaps. Rotate 180°.

14

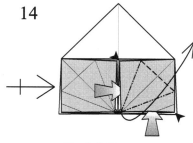

Petal-fold. What's a petal fold? See page 15.

15

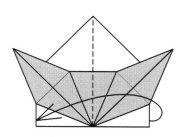

Valley-fold the model in half.

16

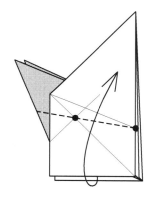

Valley-fold the front flap on the black dots.

17

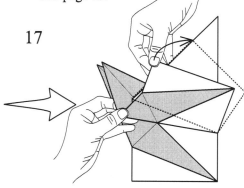

Holding as shown, pull the white corner out until it rests on the edge behind it and flatten.

18

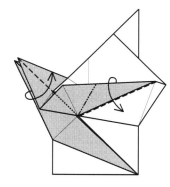

Make the indicated valley folds at the same time and flatten.

19

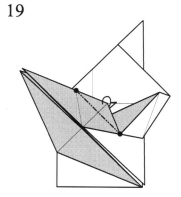

Mountain-fold the flap on the black dots.

20

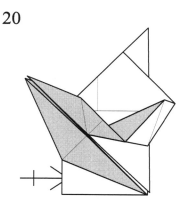

Repeat steps 16-19 behind.

21

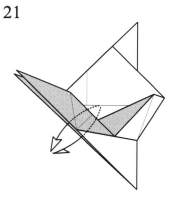

Pull the two colored flaps out from inside the model.

34 *Origami Pop-ups*

22

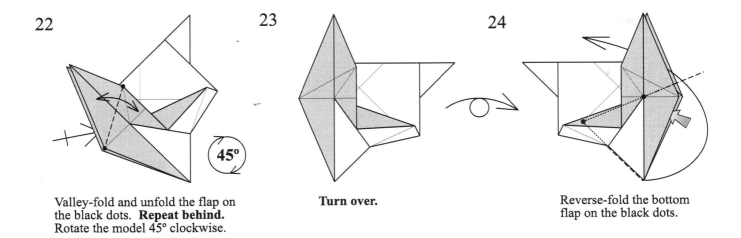

Valley-fold and unfold the flap on the black dots. **Repeat behind.** Rotate the model 45° clockwise.

23

Turn over.

24

Reverse-fold the bottom flap on the black dots.

25

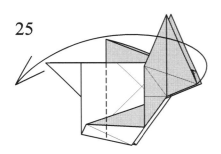

Valley-fold, opening like a book; crease lightly, or, preferably, not at all, because this is an extra crease.

26

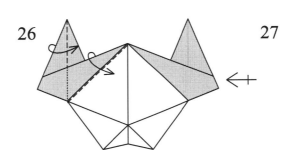

Make the indicated valley folds at the same time. Repeat on the right side.

27

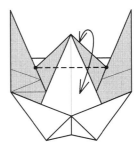

Valley-fold flap on the black dots and unfold.

28

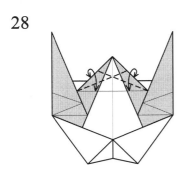

Valley-fold edge-to-crease and unfold.

29

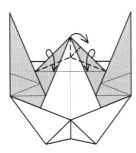

Rabbit-ear the flap. What's a rabbit ear? See page 13.

30

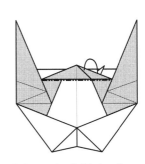

Mountain-fold the flap.

Kissing Love Birds Pop-up Card **35**

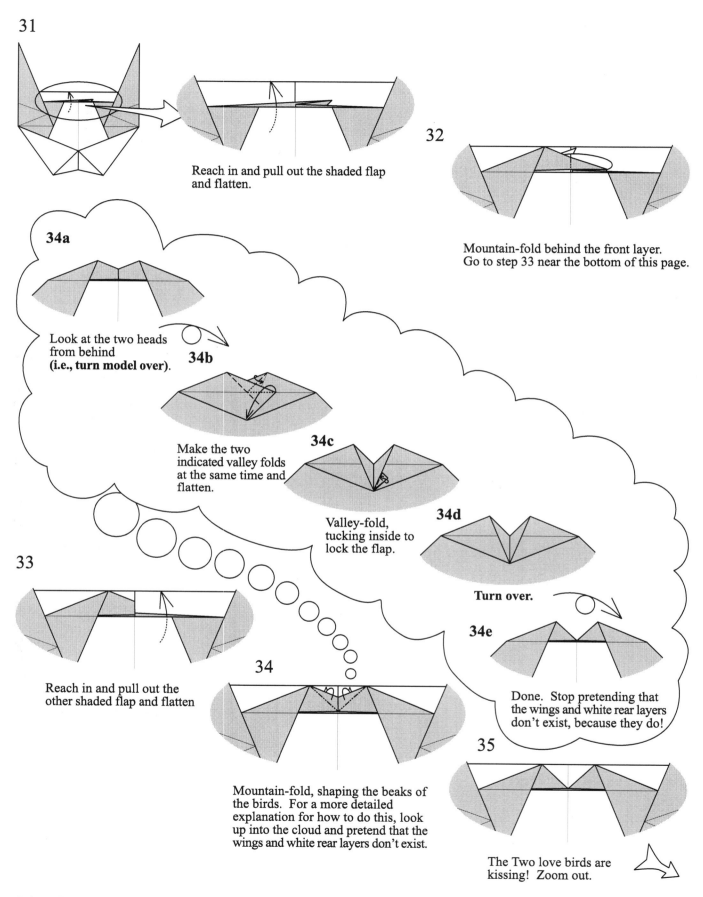

36

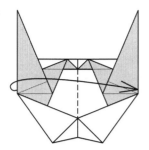

Valley-fold, like closing a book.

37

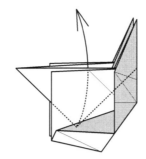

Reach into the middle pocket and pull out the triangular white flap; partly unfolding the model makes this much easier.

38

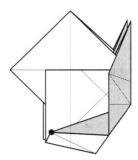

Pick up the model, one hand holding at the black dot and the other hand holding the same place behind and pull your hands apart.

39

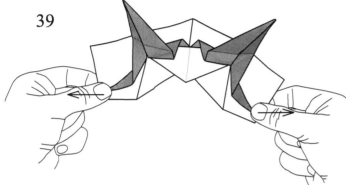

The Kissing Love Birds are complete and completely in love! In order to avoid tearing the paper, first ensure that you can make each bird flap individually before trying to make them flap at the same time. The action is similar to the Traditional Flapping Bird (page 15) except that it is caused by pulling each bird's head instead of by pulling its tail. When each bird can flap individually, hold the model as shown above and pull your hands apart and the birds will simultaneously flap their wings. Since the heads remain stationary, the action really amounts to pulling the bodies away from the heads rather than pulling the heads from the bodies. It's a lot less gruesome than it sounds!

PERFORM IT!

Hold up the closed card, look at it, and quickly put it back in the box a say, **"Oh I can't show you that one. It's a PG13 model and you guys are only 10 years old.** [Audience says, "Please show it to us!"] Say, **"Sorry, it's too sexy"** [Audience yells, "SHOW IT TO US!"] **"Alright I'll show it to you, but you have to close your eyes."** [Audience closes their eyes] **"OK, I showed it to you. Next model!"** [Audience yells, "SHOW IT TO US!"] **"OK! Ready, set, everyone say, 'Pop-up!'"** [Audience says, "Pop-up."] Open and show the model and say, **"You see, it's two flapping birds KISSING! Everyone say, 'Eewww!'"** [Audience says, "Eewww!"] Answer, **"See? I told you you're too young to see it and you didn't listen!**

40

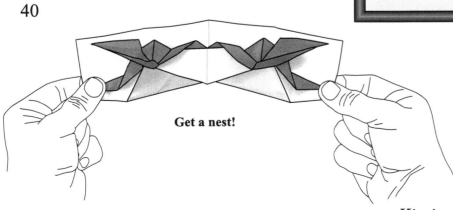

Get a nest!

Peacock Pop-up Card

by Jeremy Shafer ©2001 (Intermediate)

This card really struts its stuff! And, it also doubles as an intricate paper fan!

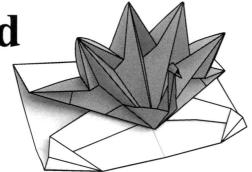

1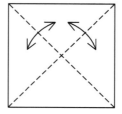

Valley-fold diagonally and unfold in both directions.

2

Valley-fold each edge to the center diagonal crease and unfold. **Turn over.**

3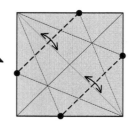

Valley-fold and unfold connecting the black dots as shown.

4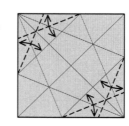

Valley-fold edge-to-crease and unfold.

5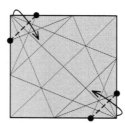

Valley-fold and unfold connecting the black dots.

6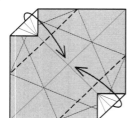

Valley-fold on the existing creases. Rotate the model 45° counterclockwise.

7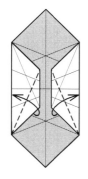

Valley-fold edge-to-edge letting the two hidden corners swing into view.

8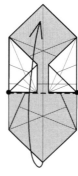

Valley-fold on the black dots.

9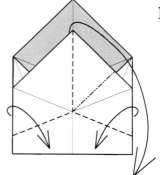

Rabbit-ear flattening the flap rightward. The valleys are on existing creases.

10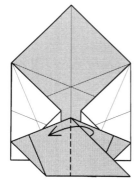

Valley-fold the flap over to the left.

11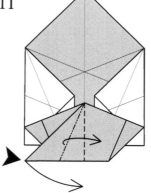

Squash!
(Don't sweet potato.)

12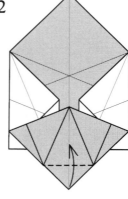

Valley-fold.

38 *Origami Pop-ups*

13 Unfold the flap and insert it into the pocket.

14 Mountain-fold, swinging the two hidden flaps apart.

15 Valley-fold the flaps further apart. Think Jacob's Ladder.

16 Valley-fold in half pleating the front layer. These pleats will become the peacock's tail feathers.

17 Like this.

18 Tear-away view. Reverse-fold the central five points, starting with the middle point; the folds are horizontal.

19 Reverse-fold the five flaps back the other way (edge-to-edge).

20 Open the card and flatten the tail feathers bringing the model back to how it looked in step 16.

21 Valley-fold point-to-point.

22 Valley-fold the front layer edge-to-edge and unfold; these creases should extend a little beyond the existing creases.

23 Valley-fold and unfold on the front layer. These creases should extend at least to the creases made in the previous step. Rotate the model 180°.

PERFORM IT!

Hold up the closed card and say, **"Ready, set, everyone say, 'Pop-up!'"** [Audience says, "Pop-up!"]. Ask, **"What is it?"** [Audience says, "A peacock."] Answer, **"That's right! Everyone make the sound of a peacock!"** To anyone who makes a sound, say, **"Oh, I didn't know that's how they sound. Well, ya' learn something everyday!"** If no one makes a sound, say, **"Wow, you peacocks sure are quiet!"**

Peacock Pop-up Card 39

24

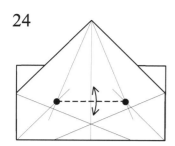

Valley-fold and unfold between the black dots on the front layer only.

25

Remake the existing valley folds while folding the flap down and flattening it. The two mountain folds get formed naturally when you flatten it.

26

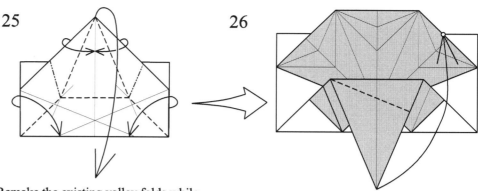

Valley-fold the flap to the white dot.

27

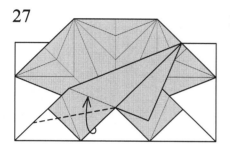

Valley-fold front flap edge-to-crease. The model will not lie flat.

28

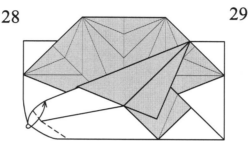

Valley-fold the corner on to the indicated edge and flatten.

29

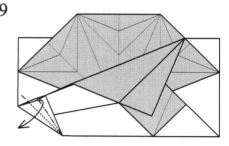

Pull the white dot downward and to the left as far as it will go and squash.

30

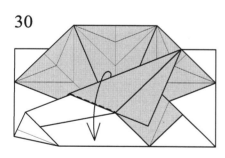

I see the folds made in steps 27-30 as the shadow of the peacock's head and neck. Think alter ego and unthink. Valley-fold the flap downward.

31

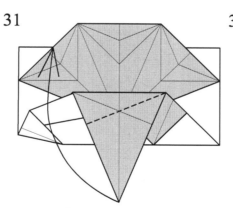

Repeat steps 26-30 on the other side.

32

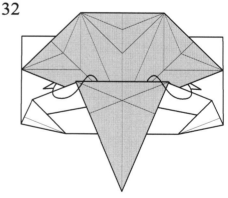

Another alter ego has been identified. Put the front layers behind the tail feathers.

Thoughts Behind the Folds

As with many of the other models in this book, I had the idea of folding a Peacock Pop-up Card before I started folding. I decided to make the head and neck from one of the corners, and the rest of the design gradually fell into place, but the hardest part was to find a good, well-guidelined method for attaching the head and neck to the rest of the body. My solution underwent extensive evolution. The original version was quite rough but, nevertheless, I decided to teach it at the OrigamiUSA Convention 2000 on the assumption that I would be able to refine it in time. But it was much harder than I had anticipated and I found myself banging my head on the problem all the way to New York and even while teaching the class itself, which, just my luck, was soldout! I told everyone I would find a nicer version and diagram and publish it. So, now, more than a decade later, here it is!

33

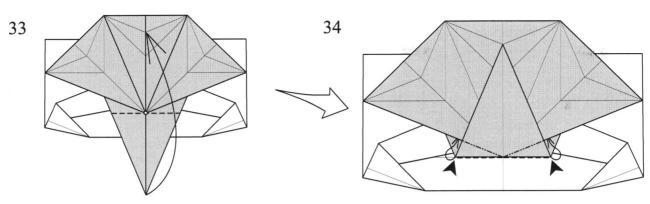

Valley-fold the flap on the white dot.

34

Reverse-fold the flaps inserting them into the pockets.

35

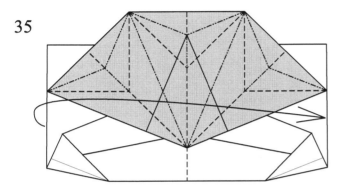

Fold the card in half, refolding the tail feathers as they were in step 20, but this time make the folds go through the top flap too as if it were part of the same layer.

36

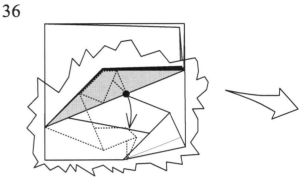

Cut-away view. Pull the peacock's beak downward.

37

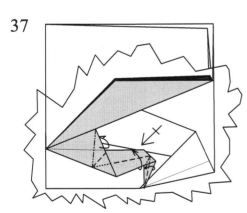

Narrow the neck and head with swivel folds (edge-to-edge). **Repeat behind.**

38

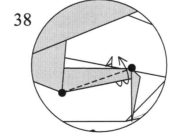

Outside-reverse-fold the neck. This fold extends between black dots on both sides. Let the folds on the head open and redefine themselves.

39

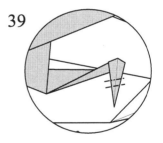

Crimp to form the beak.

Note: There are many much more intricate pleat patterns that can be applied to the tail feathers to enhance their appearance.

40

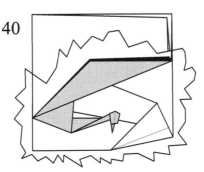

The Peacock Card is complete. Open it so the peacock can strut its stuff!

41

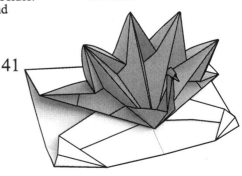

The Peacock is open, single, and available, and looking to impress some hot peachicks.

Peacock Pop-up Card

Bat Pop-up Card

By Jeremy Shafer ©2002

This card would make a good wedding invitation for Batman, though he might not find time in his busy schedule to fold it or even get married for that matter!

Intermediate

1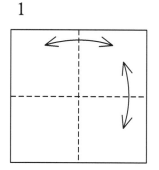
Valley-fold in half and unfold in both directions.

2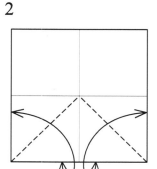
Valley-fold in half diagonally in both directions but crease only on the bottom half.

3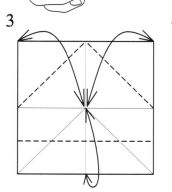
Above: Valley-fold the corners to the center and unfold.
Below: Valley-fold edge-to-crease and unfold.

4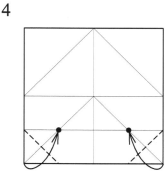
Valley-fold the corners to the black dots.

5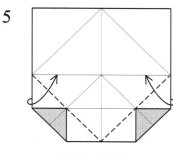
Valley-fold edge-to-crease.

6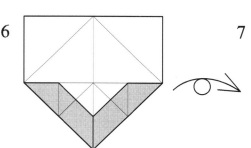
Turn over.

7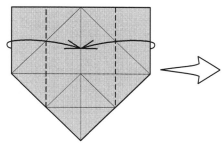
Valley-fold edge-to-crease.

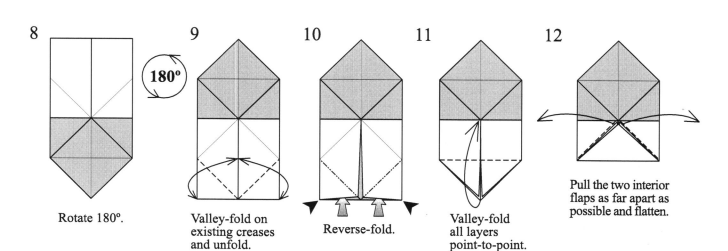

8 Rotate 180°.

9 Valley-fold on existing creases and unfold.

10 Reverse-fold.

11 Valley-fold all layers point-to-point.

12 Pull the two interior flaps as far apart as possible and flatten.

42 *Origami Pop-ups*

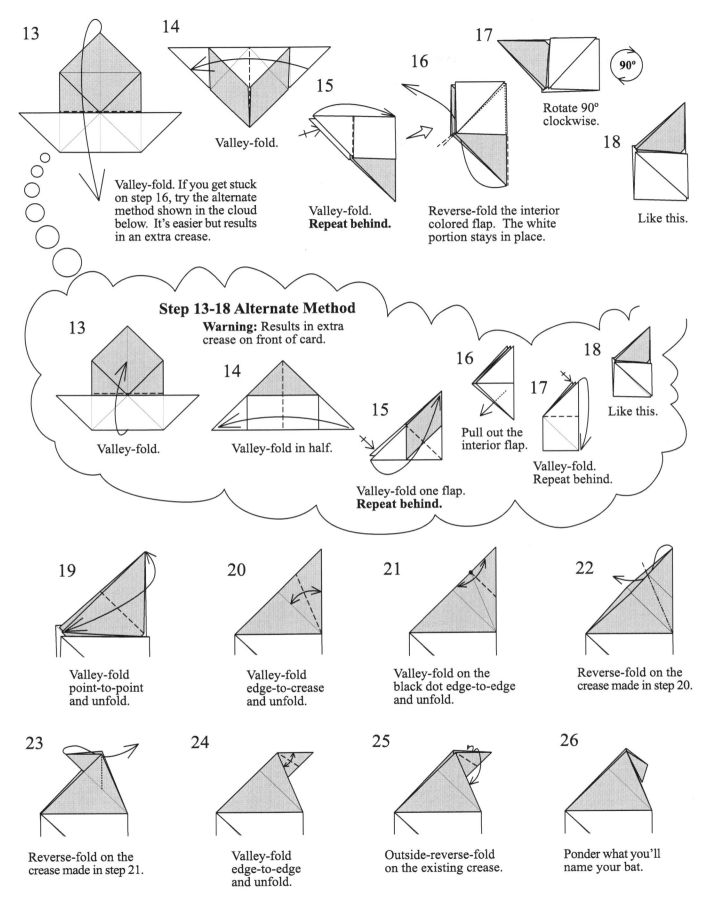

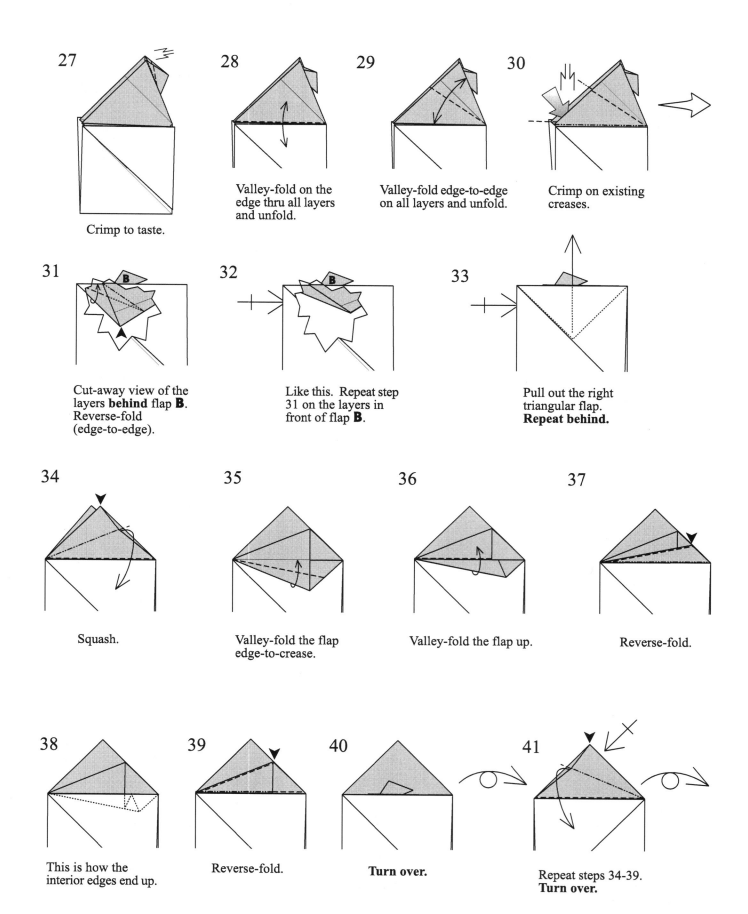

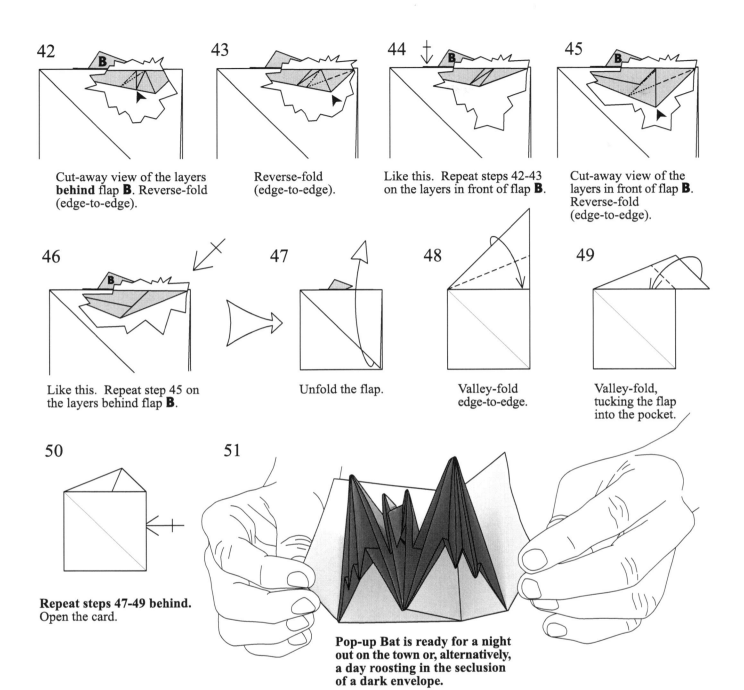

42 Cut-away view of the layers **behind** flap **B**. Reverse-fold (edge-to-edge).

43 Reverse-fold (edge-to-edge).

44 Like this. Repeat steps 42-43 on the layers in front of flap **B**.

45 Cut-away view of the layers in front of flap **B**. Reverse-fold (edge-to-edge).

46 Like this. Repeat step 45 on the layers behind flap **B**.

47 Unfold the flap.

48 Valley-fold edge-to-edge.

49 Valley-fold, tucking the flap into the pocket.

50 **Repeat steps 47-49 behind.** Open the card.

51 Pop-up Bat is ready for a night out on the town or, alternatively, a day roosting in the seclusion of a dark envelope.

PERFORM IT!

I usually perform this model following the Pop-up Housewife (page 114) and Pop-up Househusband (page 118). Hold up the closed card and say, **"What kind of house is this?"** To whatever the audience says, respond, **"No, this is Batman's house. Should we open it?"** [Audience says, "Ya."] **"I think we'd better knock on the door first. Ready, set, everyone say, 'Knock, knock!'"** [Knock on the house as the audience says, "Knock, Knock!"] Peek into the closed card and say, **"Hmm, looks like he's not home. Well, then, lets open it. Ready set everyone say, 'Pop-up!'"** [Audience says, "Pop-up!"] Open the card and exclaim, **"It's Batman! But the MAN left, so now it's just the BAT! Everyone flap your wings like a bat!"**

Bat Pop-up Card **45**

Bat

Designed by Peter Engel ©2004
Diagrammed in 2005 by
Jeremy Shafer from
Peter Engel's sketches

Designed for "Bat Day" at the Oakland Museum of California.

A 10" square makes a bat with a 7 1/4" wingspan and a body 3 5/8" tall.

1

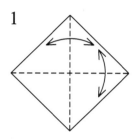

White side up, valley-fold and unfold diagonally in half in both directions.

2

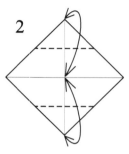

Valley-fold the top and bottom corners to center and unfold.

3

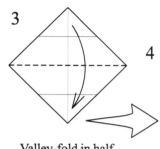

Valley-fold in half.

4

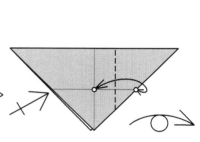

Valley-fold dot-to-dot and unfold. Repeat on the left side. **Turn over.**

5

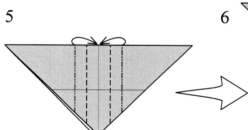

Pleat. The mountain folds are on the creases made in step 4. The valley folds are new.

6

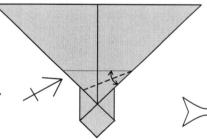

Valley fold edge-to-crease and unfold, making sure to crease firmly in the middle. Repeat on the left side.

7

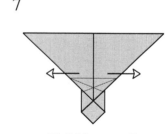

Unfold to step 5.

8

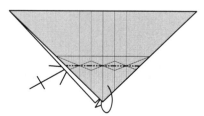

Mountain-fold on the front layer on the intersections of the creases. **Repeat behind.**

9

Refold the pleats.

10

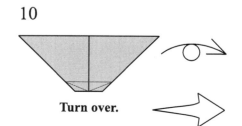

Turn over.

46 *Origami Pop-ups*

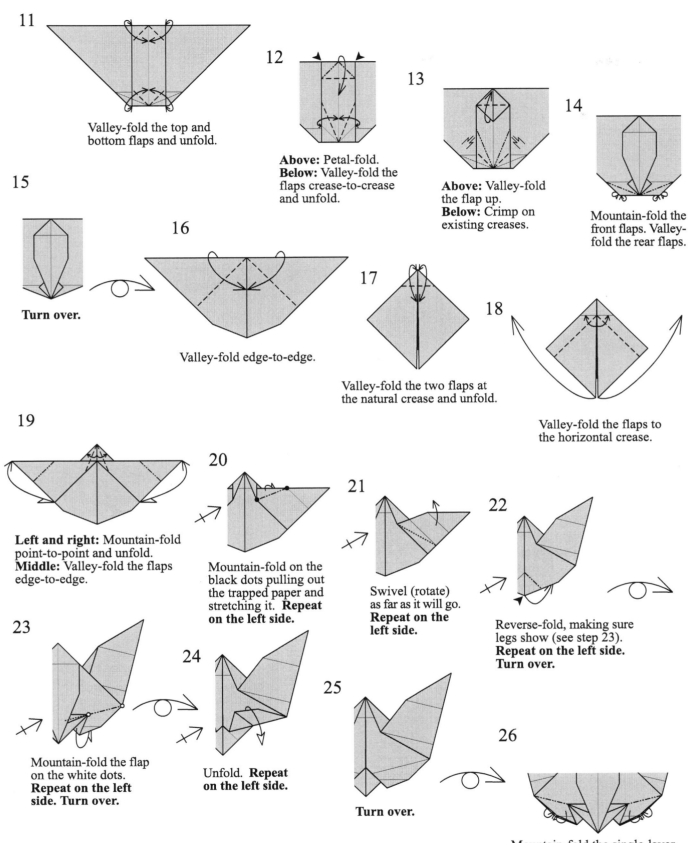

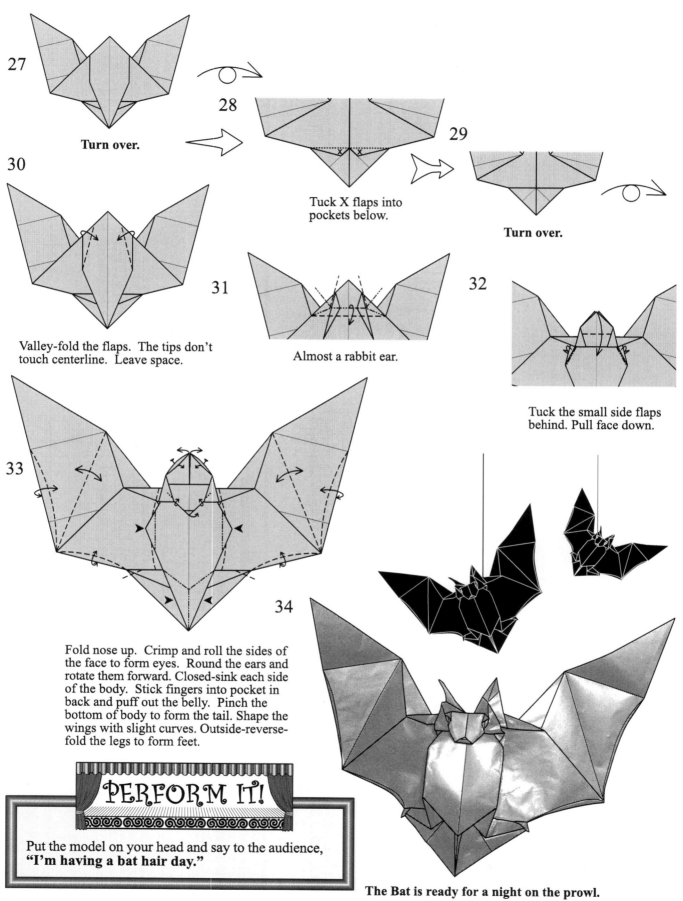

28 Tuck X flaps into pockets below.

27 Turn over.

29 Turn over.

30 Valley-fold the flaps. The tips don't touch centerline. Leave space.

31 Almost a rabbit ear.

32 Tuck the small side flaps behind. Pull face down.

34 Fold nose up. Crimp and roll the sides of the face to form eyes. Round the ears and rotate them forward. Closed-sink each side of the body. Stick fingers into pocket in back and puff out the belly. Pinch the bottom of body to form the tail. Shape the wings with slight curves. Outside-reverse-fold the legs to form feet.

PERFORM IT!

Put the model on your head and say to the audience, **"I'm having a bat hair day."**

The Bat is ready for a night on the prowl.

48 *Origami Pop-ups*

Flapping Bat By Jeremy Shafer ©2011

I got the idea to design a flapping bat after happening upon Tom Hull's Flapping Bat on YouTube. My original idea was to try to make a simpler flapping bat than his, but, obviously, that ambition did not come to fruition!

1

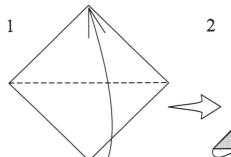

White side up, valley-fold in half diagonally.

2

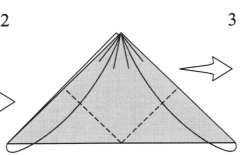

Valley-fold corner-to-corner.

3

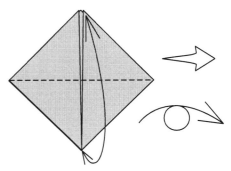

Valley-fold in half thru all layers and unfold. **Turn over.**

4

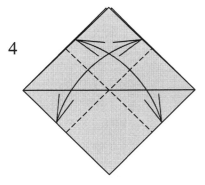

Valley-fold in half thru all layers and unfold in both directions.

5

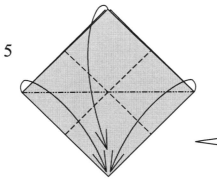

Fold a Square Base (fold thru all layers). What's a Square Base? See Page 15.

6

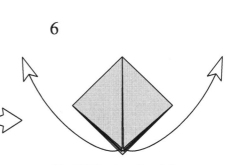

Unfold the two front flaps.

7

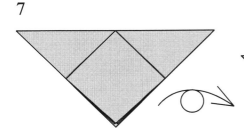

Turn over.

8

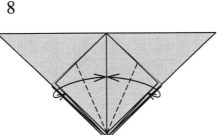

Valley-fold the two front flaps edge-to-crease and unfold.

9

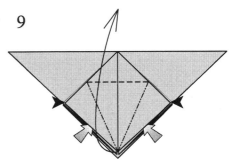

Petal-fold.

Flapping Bat **49**

10

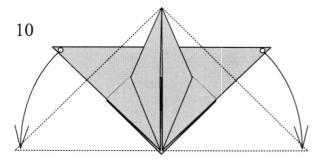

Pull the two corners down, releasing the trapped paper.

11

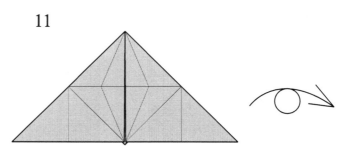

Turn over.

12

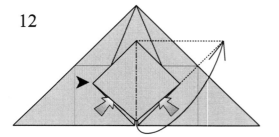

Lift the flap up and squash it to the right.

13

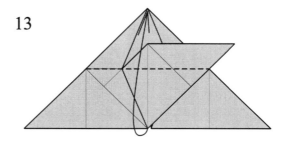

Valley-fold the front flap point-to-point.

14

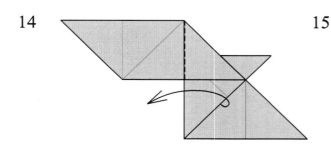

Valley-fold the right flap to the left.

15

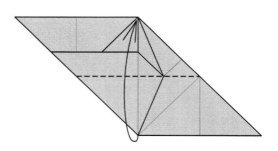

Valley-fold all layers point-to-point.

16

Turn over.

17

Unfold.

50 *Origami Pop-ups*

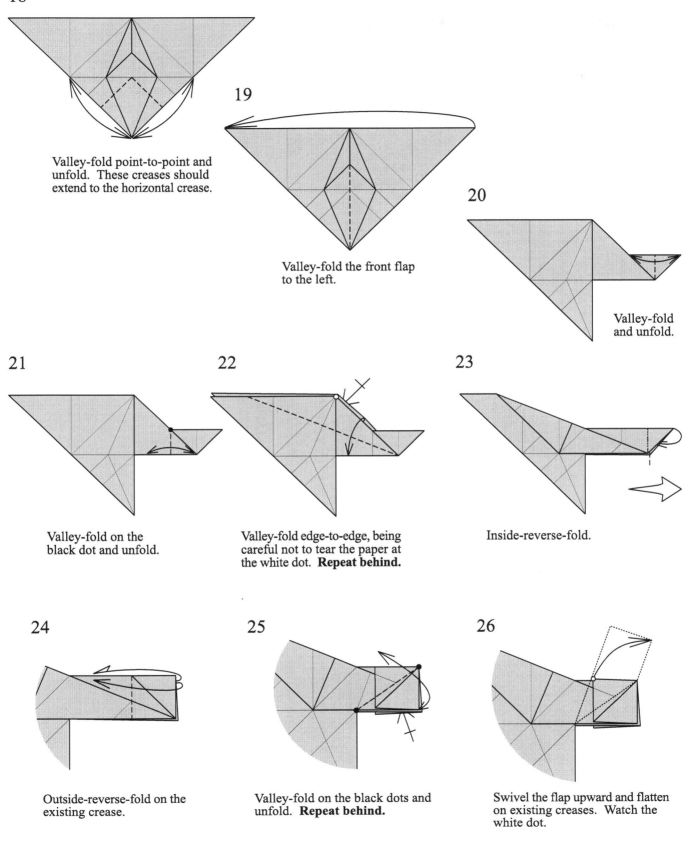

Flapping Bat 51

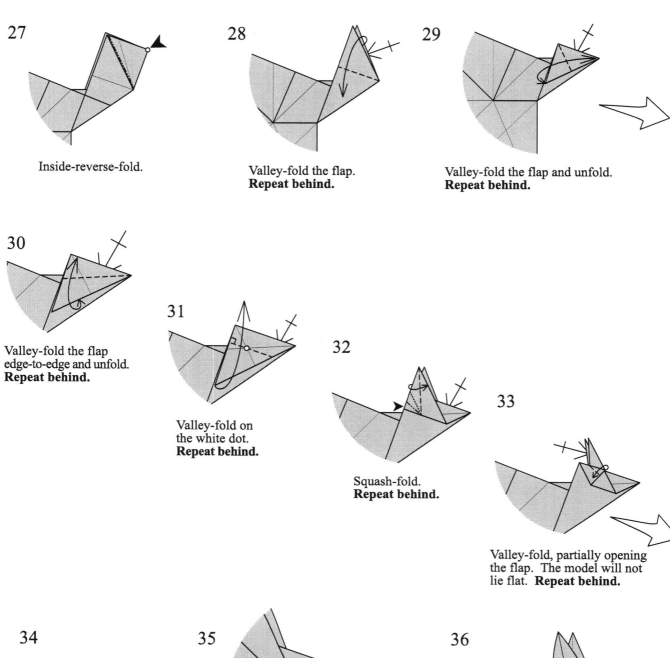

27. Inside-reverse-fold.

28. Valley-fold the flap. **Repeat behind.**

29. Valley-fold the flap and unfold. **Repeat behind.**

30. Valley-fold the flap edge-to-edge and unfold. **Repeat behind.**

31. Valley-fold on the white dot. **Repeat behind.**

32. Squash-fold. **Repeat behind.**

33. Valley-fold, partially opening the flap. The model will not lie flat. **Repeat behind.**

34. Outside-reverse-fold the two raw corners.

35. Outside-reverse-fold.

36. Inside-reverse-fold.

52 *Origami Pop-ups*

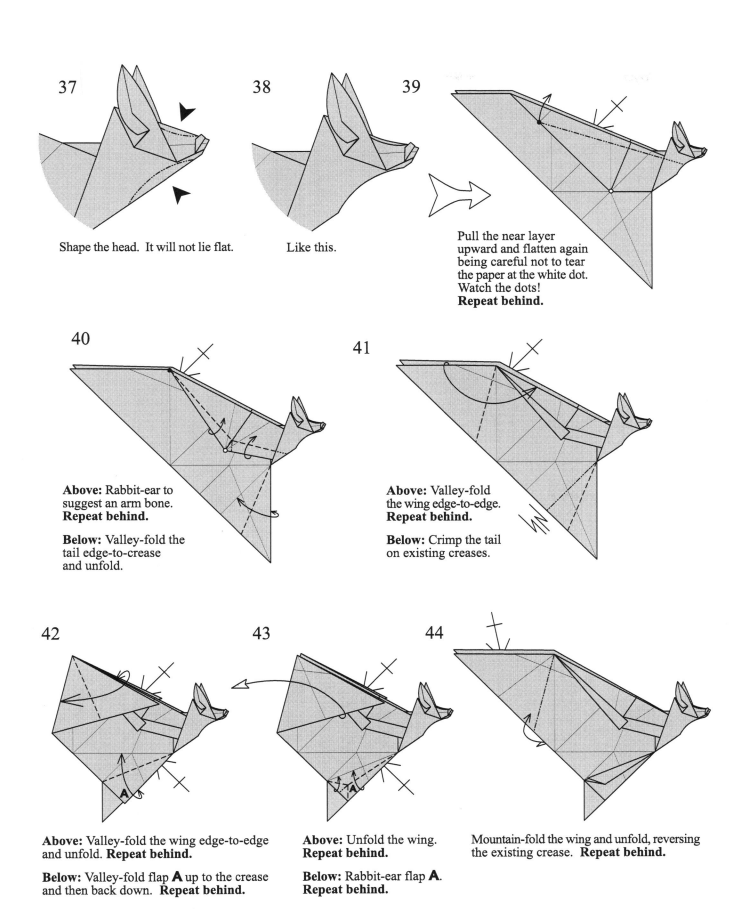

Flapping Bat 53

45

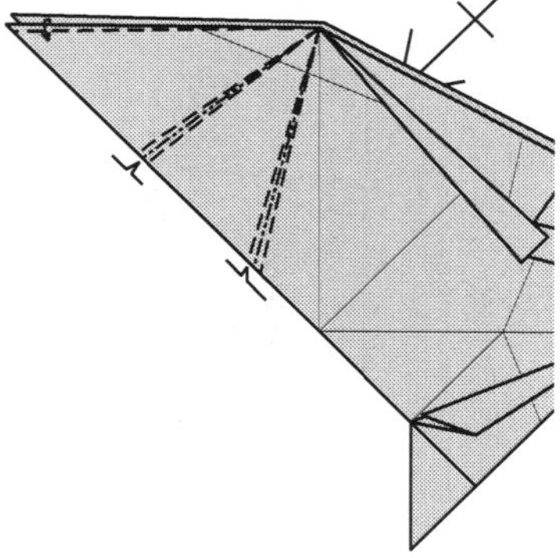

Make the two mountain folds stick up by putting valley folds on either side. Valley-fold the top edge making it stick up too. **Repeat behind.**

46

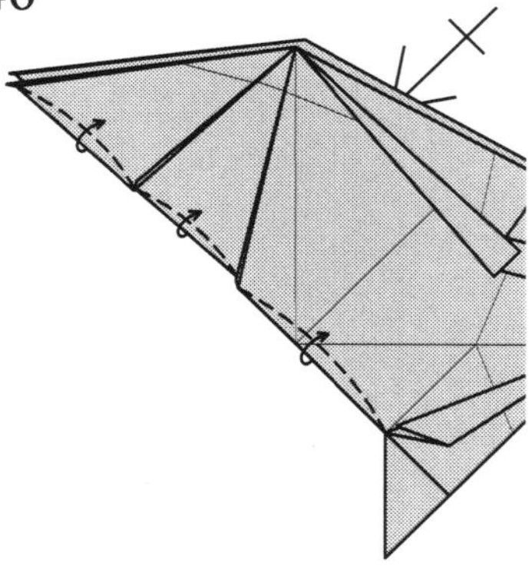

Make curved valley folds on the lower edge of the wing **Repeat behind.**

47

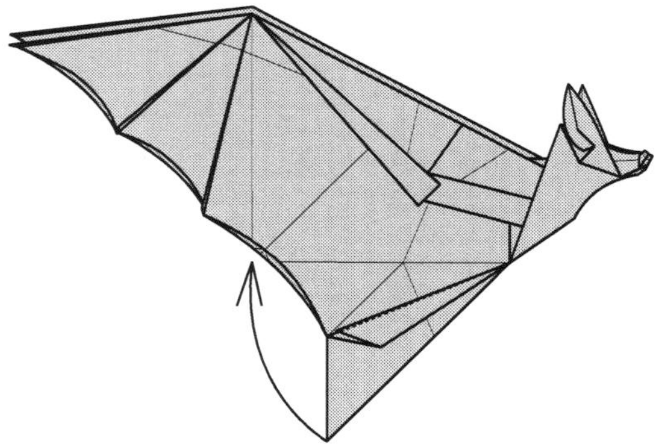

Reverse-fold the tail.

48

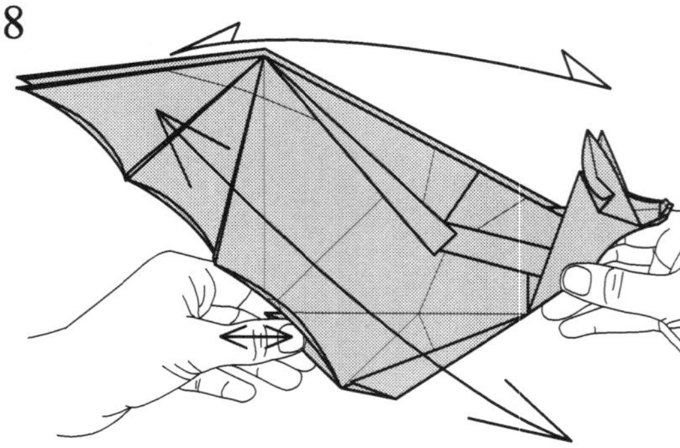

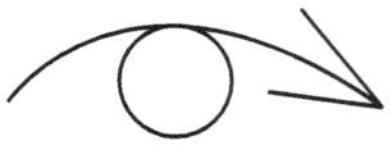

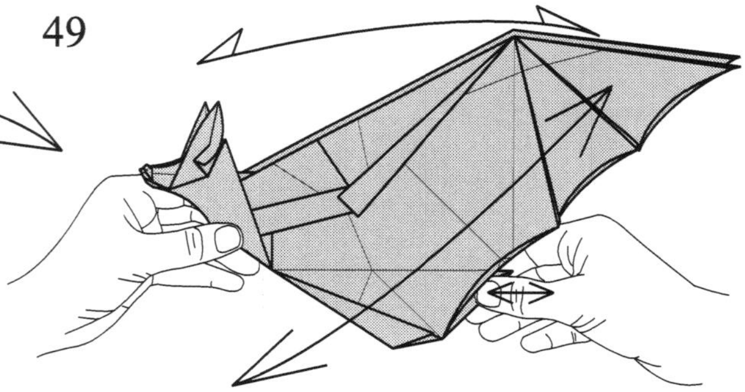

The Flapping Bat is ready to flap. If you are right-handed, **turn over.** If you are left-handed, hold it as shown above and pull the tail to make the wings flap. It uses the same mechanism as the traditional Flapping Bird (page 15). Once you can make the wings flap holding the tail as shown above, open the wings and tail as shown below and try to make it flap.

49

Right-handed Flappers: Hold as shown above and pull the tail to make the wings flap like the traditional Flapping Bird (page 15). Once you can make the wings flap holding the tail as shown above, open the wings and tail as shown below and try to make it flap.

50

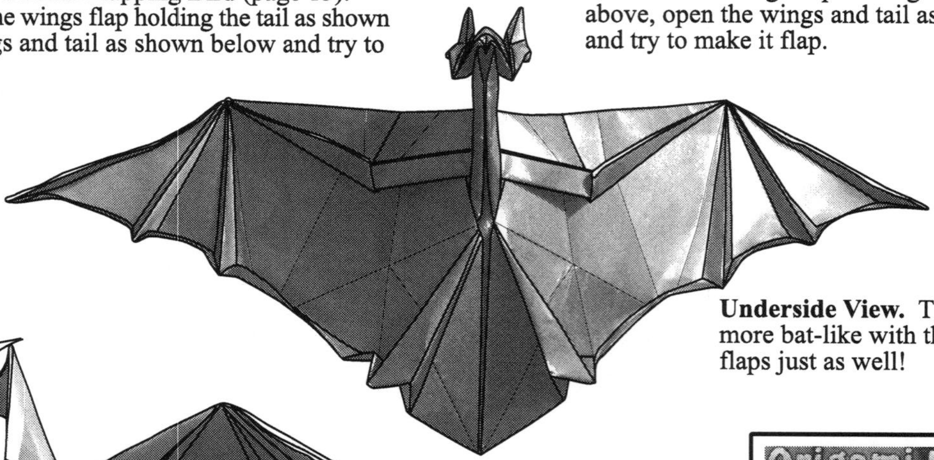

Underside View. The model looks more bat-like with the tail open and flaps just as well!

51

The Flapping Bat making a big flap about it.

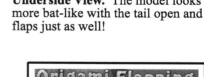

Video tutorial on youtube.com! **Search:** youtube shafer flapping bat

54 *Origami Pop-ups*

52

Mid-Flight: Wings Up

53

Mid-Flight: Wings Down

54

Top View (a.k.a. bird's eye view)

Headshot

PERFORM IT!

Hold up the model and ask the audience, **"What is this?"** [Audience says, "A bat."] Say, **"But not just any bat, it's a flapping bat! You want to see it flap?"** [Audience says, "Yes."] Make the bat flap and say, **"But it's not just a flapping bat, it's a pooping bat too. You want to see it poop?"** [Audience says, "Yes."] Release the tiny wad of black paper you have hidden in your right hand, catch it in your left hand, look at it and exclaim, **"Yuck!"** as you throw it into the audience. If you don't have a tiny wad of black paper, then simply say, **"Sorry, it looks like the bat is constipated today."**

Challenge: What other flapping creatures can you make using the same flapping mechanism? **Ideas:** dragon, dragonfly, hummingbird, teradactyl, conductor, person stranded on an desert isle waving at a passing airplane.

Flapping Bat **55**

Flapping Butterfly Pop-up Card

By Jeremy Shafer ©2008

Butterfly fanatics will flock to this model! You don't need a butterfly net to catch this specimen. And you don't need pins to attach it either!

1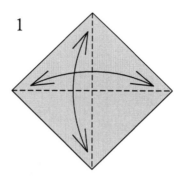

Colored side up, valley-fold and unfold diagonally in half in both directions.

2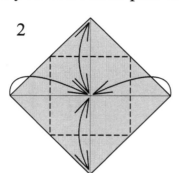

Valley-fold all four corners to the center and unfold the top and bottom corners.

3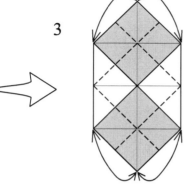

Valley-fold corner-to-corner and unfold.

4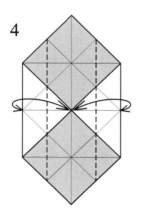

Valley-fold edge-to-crease and unfold.

5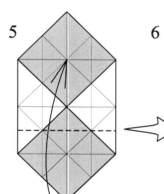

Valley-fold corner-to-crease.

6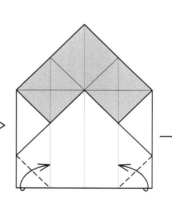

Valley-fold edge-to-crease.

7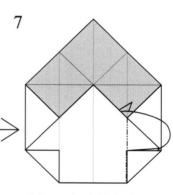

Mountain-fold the interior flap behind the front layer on the existing crease. Repeat on the left side.

8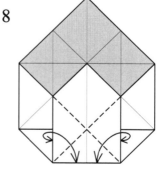

Valley-fold and unfold on the front flap only.

9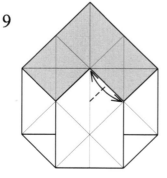

Valley-fold the flap point-to-point and unfold.

10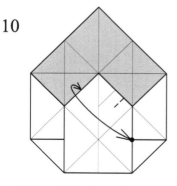

Valley-fold edge-to-black-dot and unfold, making a crease mark on the edge.

56 *Origami Pop-ups*

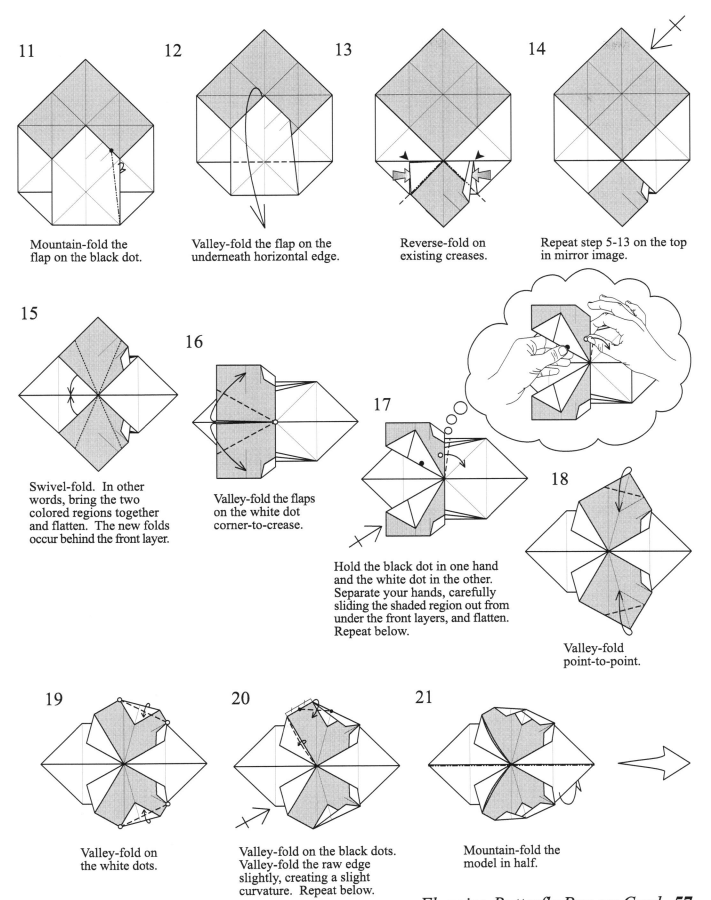

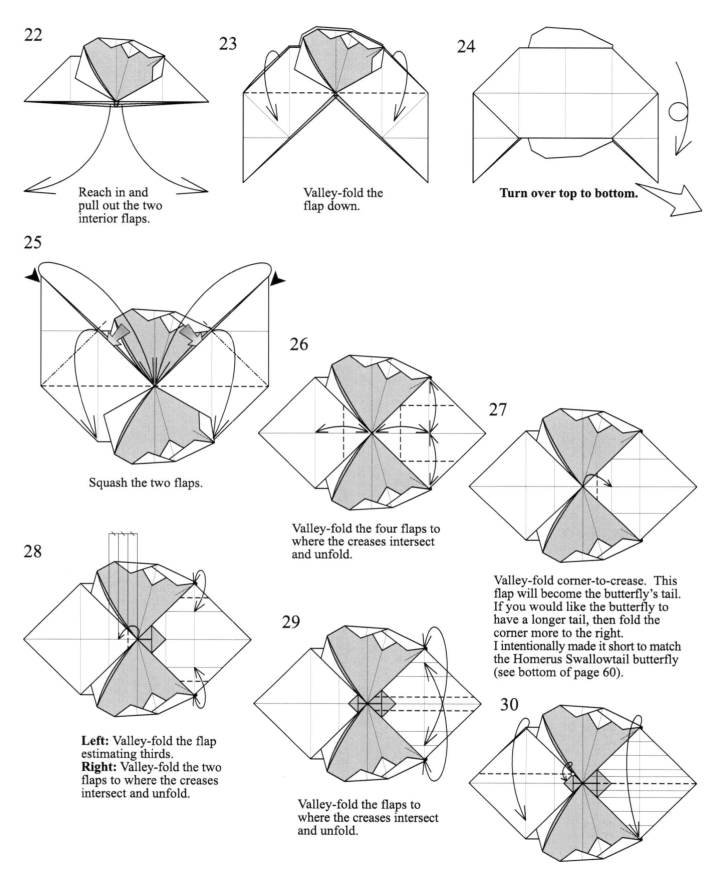

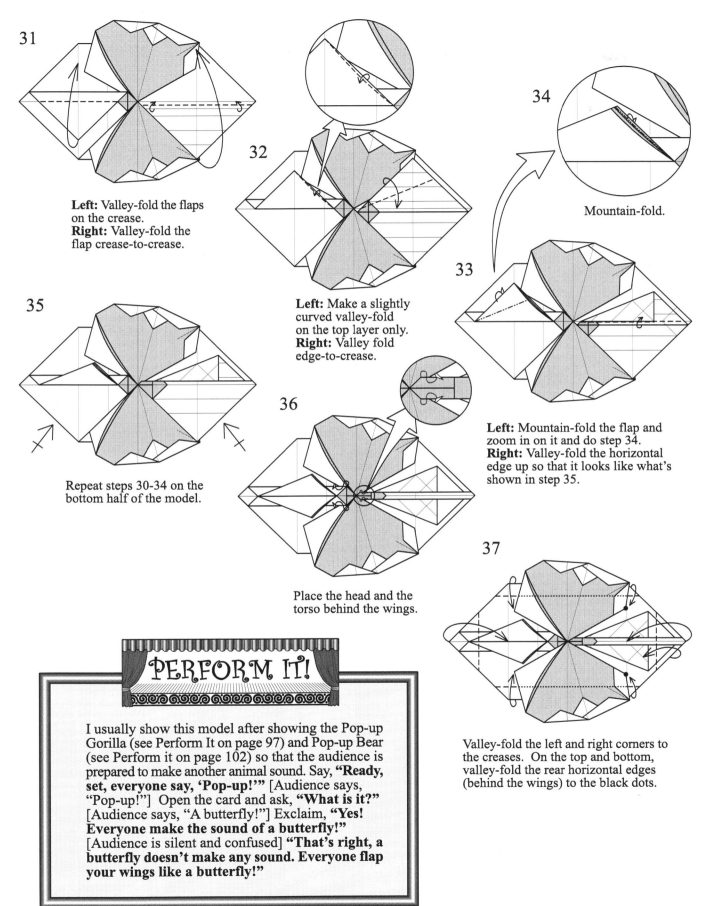

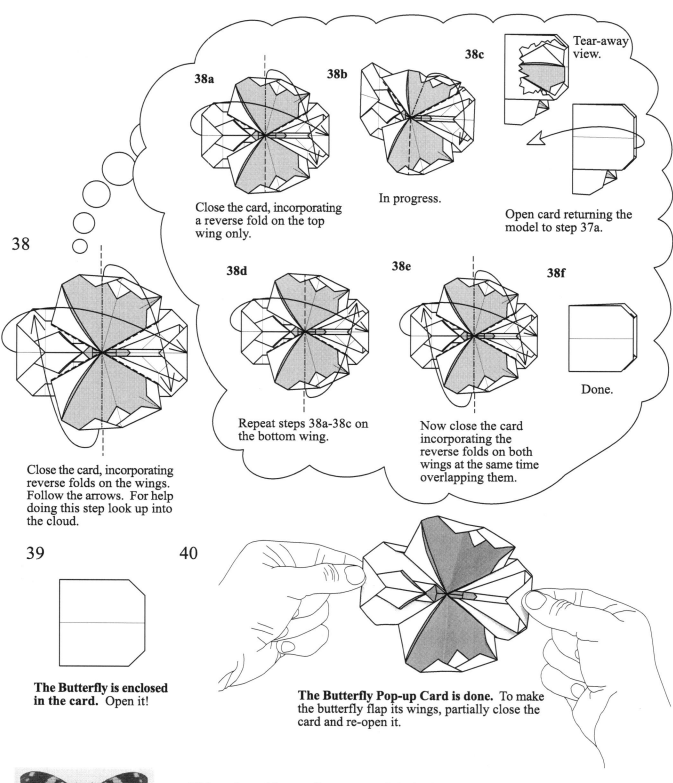

38 Close the card, incorporating reverse folds on the wings. Follow the arrows. For help doing this step look up into the cloud.

38a Close the card, incorporating a reverse fold on the top wing only.

38b In progress.

38c Tear-away view. Open card returning the model to step 37a.

38d Repeat steps 38a-38c on the bottom wing.

38e Now close the card incorporating the reverse folds on both wings at the same time overlapping them.

38f Done.

39 The Butterfly is enclosed in the card. Open it!

40 The Butterfly Pop-up Card is done. To make the butterfly flap its wings, partially close the card and re-open it.

Homerus Swallowtail

This origami butterfly was modeled after the **Homerus swallowtail**, *Papilio homerus*, which is the largest butterfly in the western hemisphere. It belongs to the (Tribus: papilionini) and is often placed in the Subgenus *Pterourus*, considered a genus by some authors. It is found only in Jamaica (The Blue mountains in eastern Jamaica and some forests in the west of the island) and is under significant pressure from commercial agriculture, as is most other wildlife. (source: Wikipedia)

60 *Origami Pop-ups*

Flapping Dragonfly Pop-up Card

By Jeremy Shafer ©2008

Rather Complex

Although this dragonfly is missing all six legs, its four flapping wings make it a fine additon to our pop-up card collection. It's not as hard as most insect models, but beware there is one step (step 24) that requires the skill of a seasoned folder to do cleanly.

1

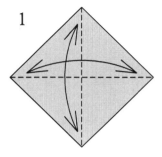

Colored side up, valley-fold in half diagonally and unfold in both directions.

2

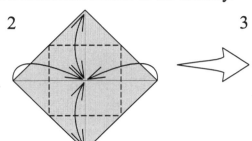

Valley-fold all four corners to the center and unfold the top and bottom corners.

3

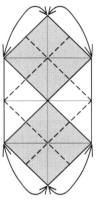

Valley-fold corner-to-corner and unfold.

4

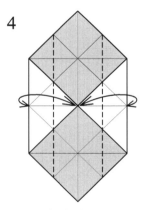

Valley-fold edge-to-crease and unfold.

5

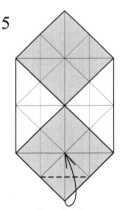

Valley-fold corner-to-crease.

6

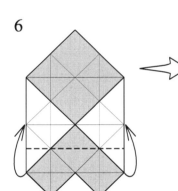

Valley-fold corner-to-crease.

7

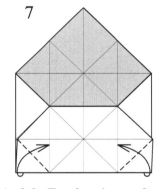

And the Envelope is complete! Oh, that's not what we're making? Well then, valley-fold edge-to-crease.

8

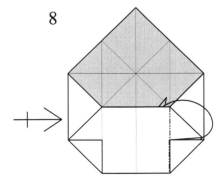

Mountain-fold the interior flap behind the front layer on the existing crease. Repeat on the left side.

9

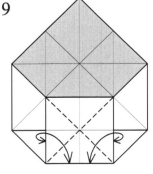

Valley-fold edge-to-edge (front layer only) and unfold in both directions.

10

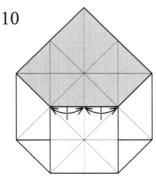

Valley-fold the flap and unfold, making a crease mark on the edge.

Flapping Dragonfly Pop-up Card

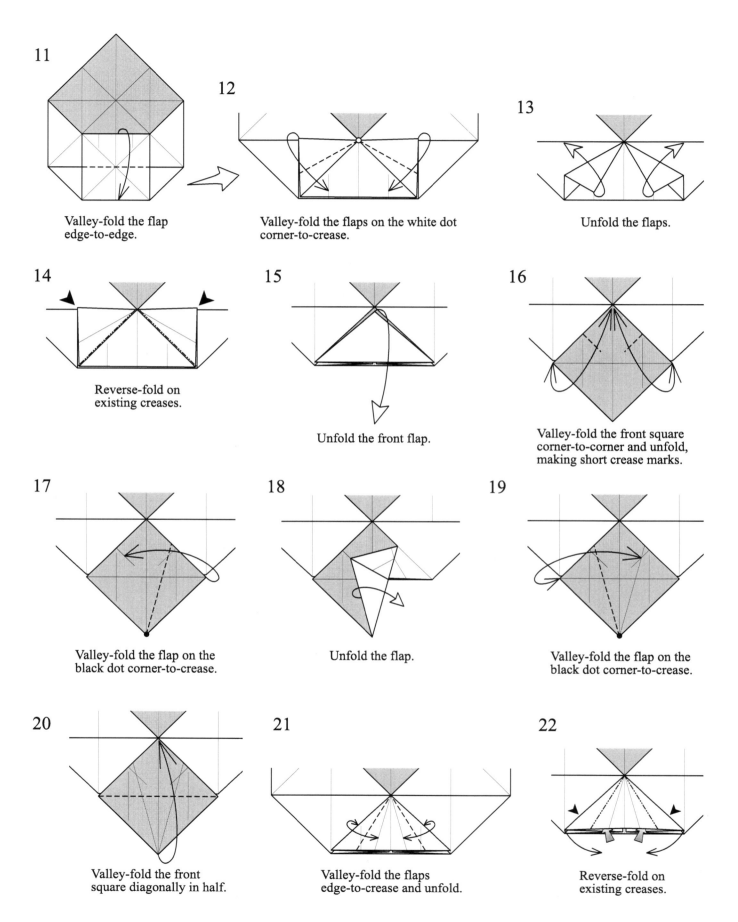

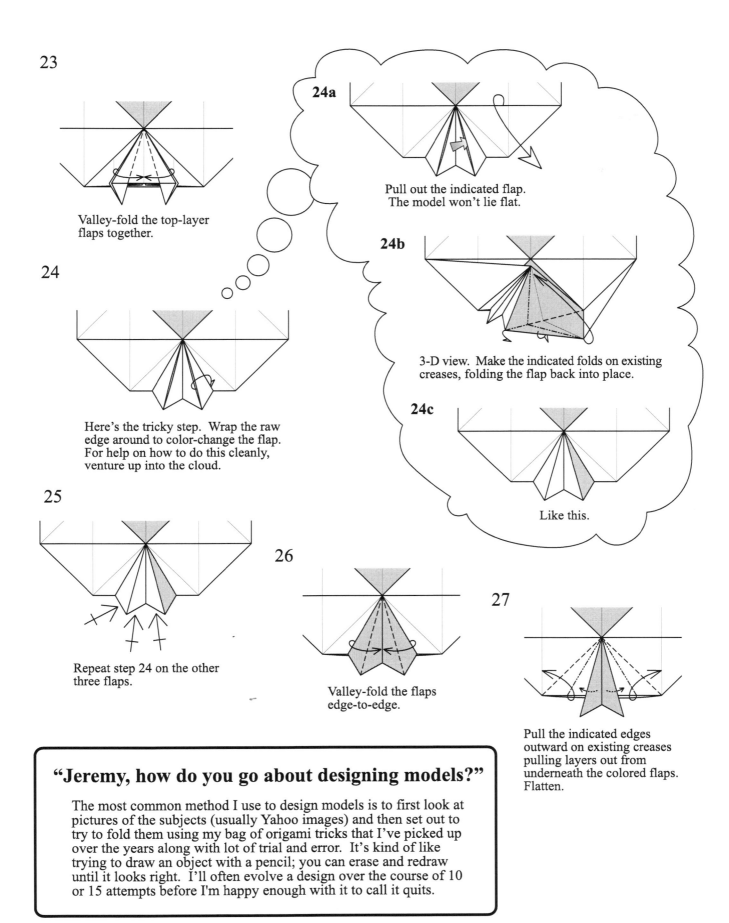

23 Valley-fold the top-layer flaps together.

24 Here's the tricky step. Wrap the raw edge around to color-change the flap. For help on how to do this cleanly, venture up into the cloud.

24a Pull out the indicated flap. The model won't lie flat.

24b 3-D view. Make the indicated folds on existing creases, folding the flap back into place.

24c Like this.

25 Repeat step 24 on the other three flaps.

26 Valley-fold the flaps edge-to-edge.

27 Pull the indicated edges outward on existing creases pulling layers out from underneath the colored flaps. Flatten.

"Jeremy, how do you go about designing models?"

The most common method I use to design models is to first look at pictures of the subjects (usually Yahoo images) and then set out to try to fold them using my bag of origami tricks that I've picked up over the years along with lot of trial and error. It's kind of like trying to draw an object with a pencil; you can erase and redraw until it looks right. I'll often evolve a design over the course of 10 or 15 attempts before I'm happy enough with it to call it quits.

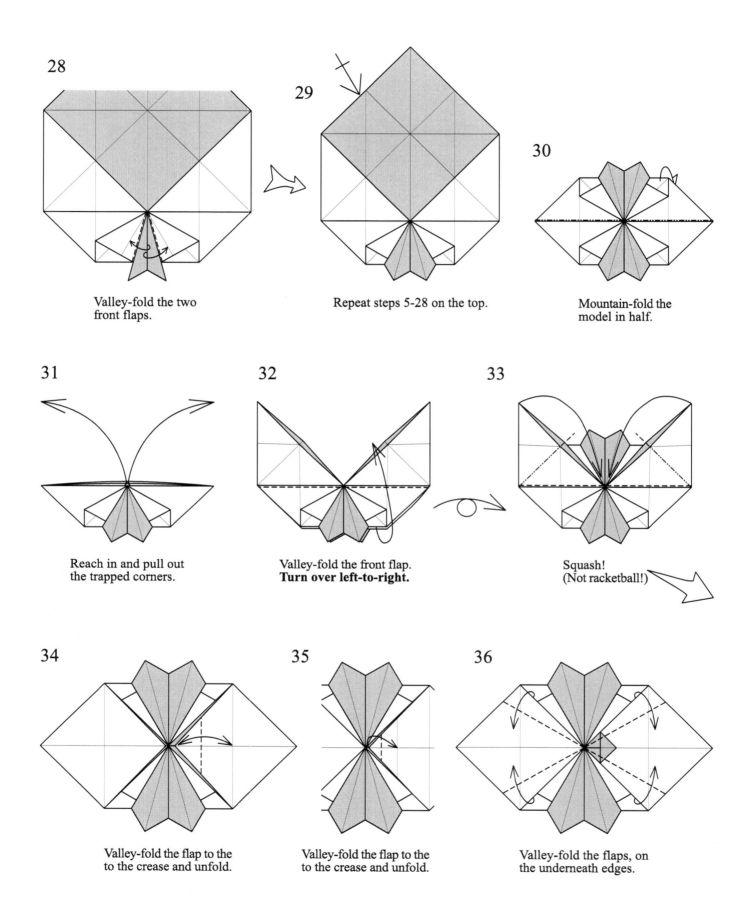

64 *Origami Pop-ups*

37. Valley-fold between the black dot and the indicated midpoint. Repeat on the other three corners.

38. Valley-fold the rear flap on the black dots, inserting it into the pocket. Repeat on the top.

39. Unfold the four flaps.

40. **Left:** Valley-fold on the black dots. **Right:** Mountain-fold on the existing creases.

41. Valley-fold the single-layer flap edge-to-edge.

42. Unfold the two flaps.

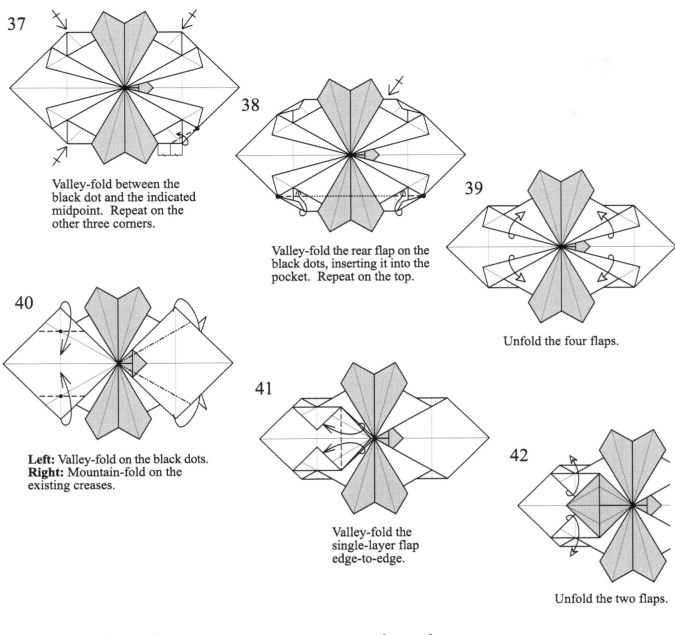

43. Valley-fold the flap down...

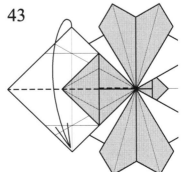

44. ...and valley-fold the same flap to the horizontal edge and unfold.

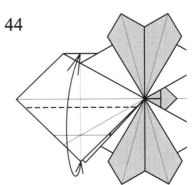

Flapping Dragonfly Pop-up Card **65**

45

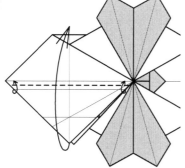

Valley-fold the flap, crease-to-crease.

46

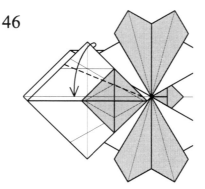

Valley-fold the flap edge-to-crease.

47

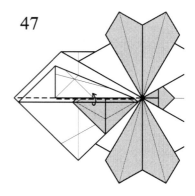

Valley-fold the horizontal edge up.

48

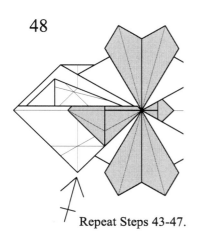

Repeat Steps 43–47.

49

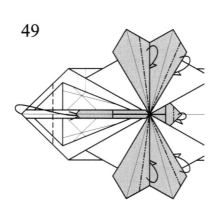

Left: Valley-fold the corner, tucking the tip into the small pocket at the end of the tail.
Middle: Mountain-fold the four wings edge-to-edge.
Right: Mountain-fold the tip of the head to taste.

50

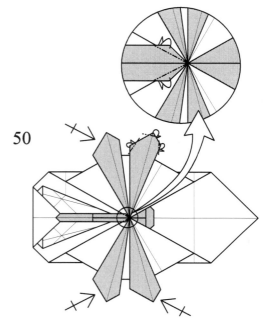

Round the wings with mountain folds. Make tiny mountain folds on the abdomen.

51

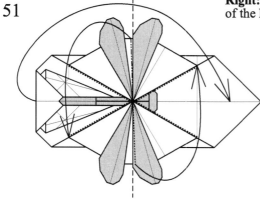

Close the card while lifting the top and bottom pairs of wings and making them pass by each other as shown above (passing to the right). One way to do this is to hold the card by the left and right sides and slightly rotate your hands in opposite directions (in a wringing motion) as you close the card.

52

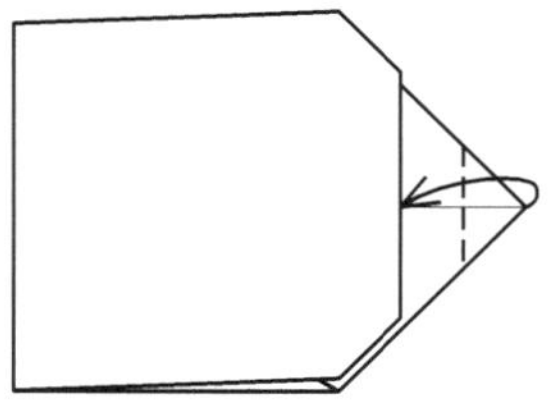

Valley-fold corner-to-edge.

53

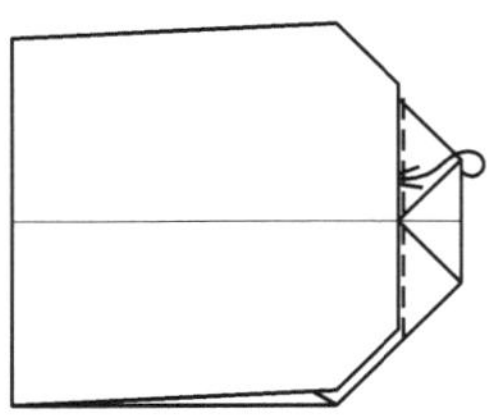

Valley-fold on the vertical edge tucking the flap inside the card.

54

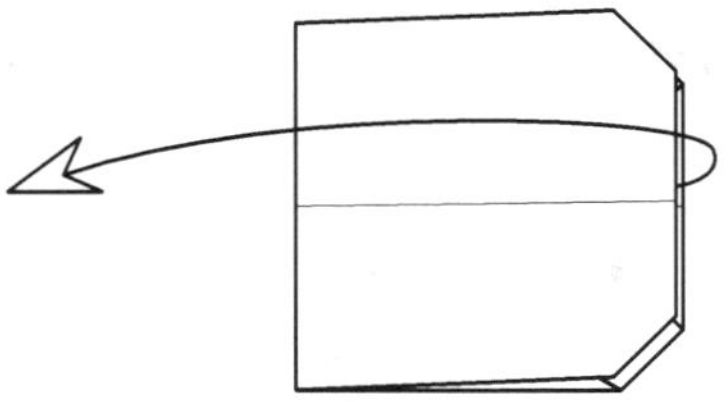

Like this. Now, open the card again (to look like step 51).

55

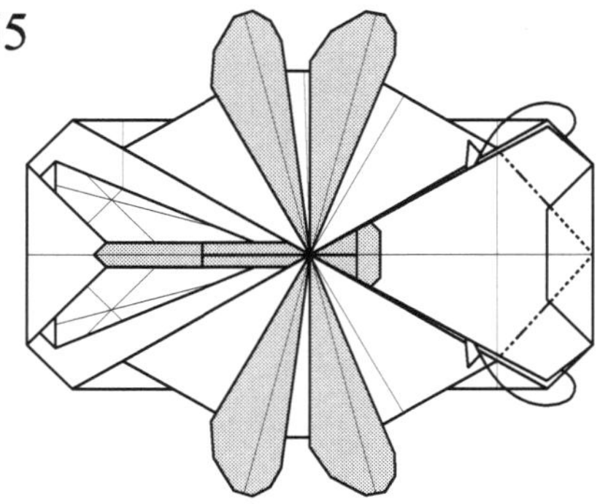

Mountain-fold the interior flaps. This will keep the right side of the model from unfolding.

56

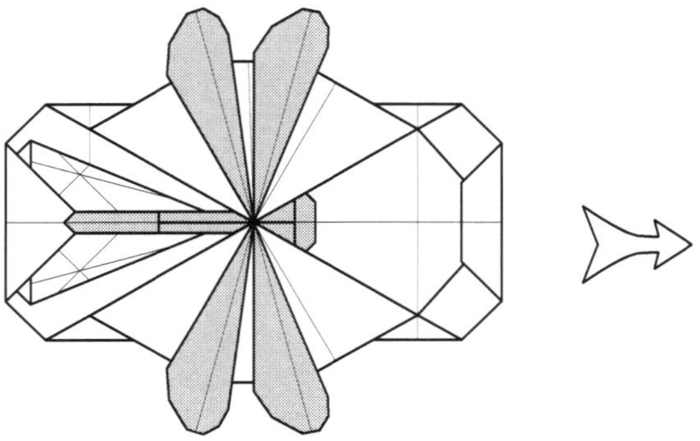

Done! The dragonfly is ready for flight.

57

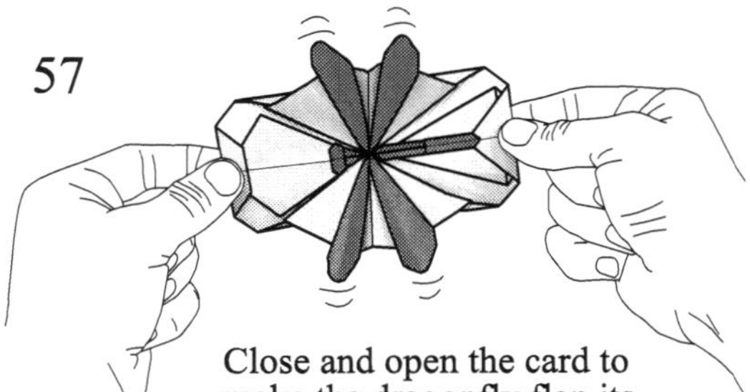

Close and open the card to make the dragonfly flap its wings. Throw it up in the air to make the dragonfly fly!

58

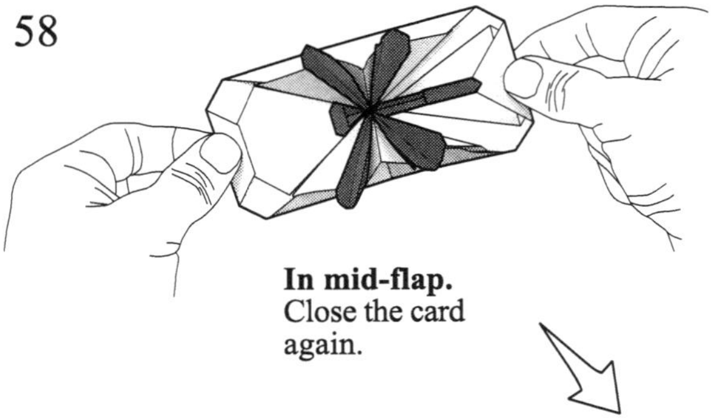

In mid-flap. Close the card again.

59

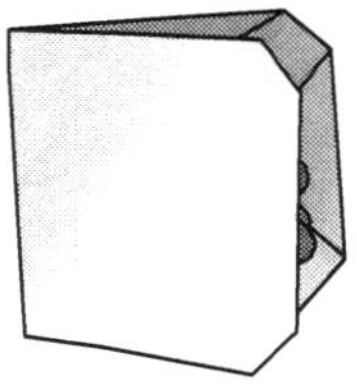

The Dragonfly is safely tucked in for the night.

PERFORM IT!

Hold up the closed card and say, **"Inside here is a Dragon and it can fly! Ready, set, everyone say, 'Pop-up!'"** [Audience says, "Pop-up."]. Open the card and ask, **"Can you tell what it is?"** [Audience says, "A dragonfly."]. Answer, **"You see? Like I said, it's a dragon..."** and as you make the wings flap say, **"...fly!"**

Flapping Dragonfly Pop-up Card

Land Animal Pop-up Cards

Many people just don't have space for animals in their homes, but I'll bet they have space for the animals in this chapter! These folded animals make wonderful pets not only because they don't take up much space – they also don't need to be fed or taken to the vet, and they don't poop or pee on the carpet! In addition, these pop-up cards make for wonderful and convenient gifts because **A:** They have to do with animals and people love animals, **B:** They are hand made by you, which is automatically special, **C:** They are made from inexpensive material – a single uncut sheet of paper, **D:** They come with their own card, and **E:** All of the above!

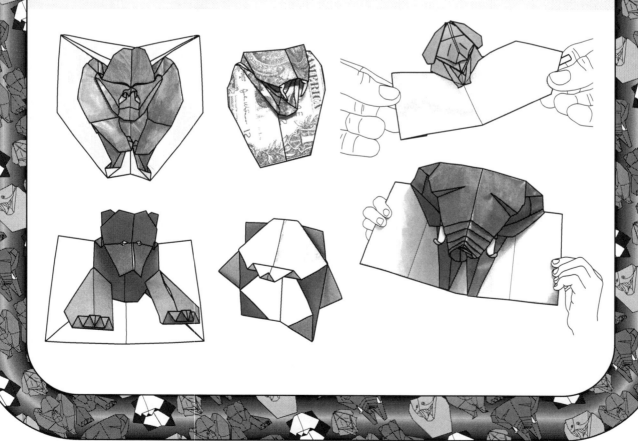

68 *Origami Pop-ups*

Giant Panda (Super Simple)

Designed by Sy Chen ©2001

So simple, you can fold a thousand in no time. At least this variety of giant panda will never go extinct!

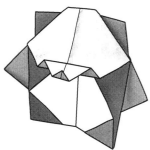

1
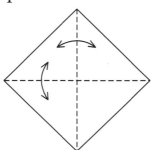

White side up, valley-fold in half diagonally and unfold in both directions.

2
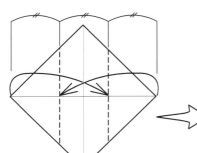

Fold in thirds making vertical valley folds. You do not need to be super exact.

3
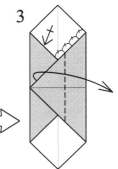

Valley-fold the front flap on the imaginary fourths mark. Again precision is not so important here. Repeat on the other flap.

4
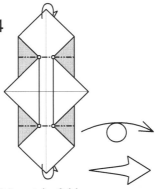

Mountain-fold on the white dots. **Turn over.**

5
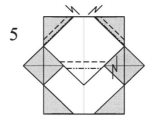

Top: Pleat to taste to form the ears.
Middle: Pleat the front flap to taste to form the eyes.

6
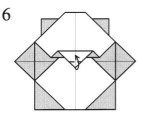

Valley-fold the front flap to form the snout.

7
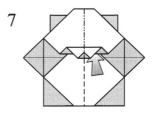

Finished Panda. To make the model stand up, partially valley-fold the body and mountain-fold the head.

8
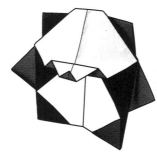

Really Finished Panda.

PERFORM IT!

Hold up the completed model and ask the audience, **"What's this?"** [Audience says, "A panda bear."]
Say, **"Yes! And it's also an action model. Wanna see?"** [Audience says, "Yes!"] Fold the model in half and carefully place it back it the box. Look up at the audience and ask, **"Can you see the action?"** [Audience says, "No!"]. Exclaim, **"Can't you see? It's hibernating!"** (And if the smart kid says, "Pandas don't hibernate," then reply, **"Ya, which makes THIS panda extra special, because it DOES!"**)

Simple Bunny Pop-up Card

By Jeremy Shafer ©2005

Here's how you can pull a bunny out of a hat. Write the word, *HAT* on this card. Open it and, VOILA! Out comes a bunny from the HAT!

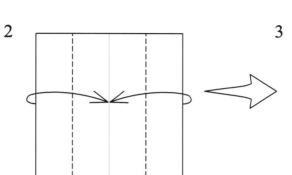

1

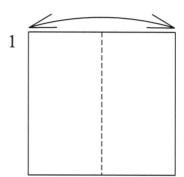

A 16-inch square will make a 4-inch by 6-inch card (when closed). White side up, valley-fold in half and unfold.

2

Valley-fold edge-to-crease.

3

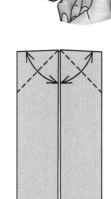

Valley-fold (all layers) edge-to-edge and unfold.

4

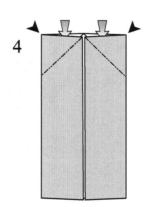

Reverse-fold on existing creases.

5

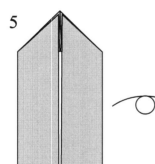

Turn over.

6

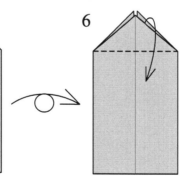

Valley-fold the front flap.

7

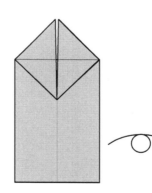

Turn over.

8

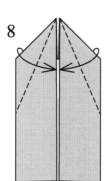

Valley-fold edge-to-edge.

9

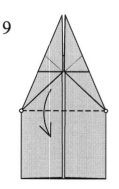

Valley-fold on the white dots.

10

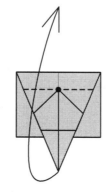

Valley-fold the flap on the black dot.

11

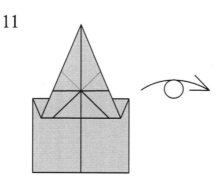

Turn over.

70 *Origami Pop-ups*

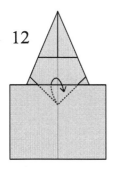

12

Pull out the hidden flap.

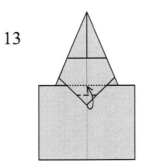

13

Valley-fold the tip up to the dotted line.

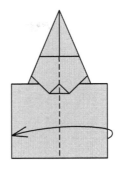

14

Valley-fold the model in half.

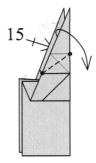

15

Valley-fold the flap dot-to-dot being careful not to tear the paper. **Repeat behind.**

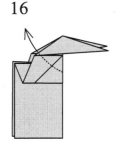

16

Pull out the interior flap and flatten.

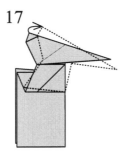

17

Rotate the head and neck clockwise.

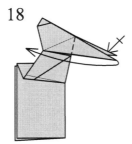

18

Valley-fold the flap on the edge. **Repeat behind.**

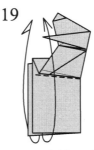

19

Outside-reverse-fold on the edge; **Note:** If you can do step 19 and 20 in one move, you can avoid making an extra crease on the cover.

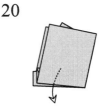

20

Pull out the interior layers.

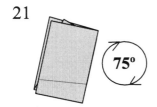

21

Rotate the model clockwise.

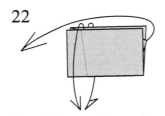

22

The Simple Bunny Pop-up is ready to pop out! Open the card, letting the bunny's head swing to the left. Close the front and back covers downward, reversing the spine of the card.

23

To make the model look slightly more like a bunny, unfold the ears upward.

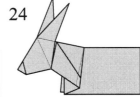

24

The bunny is sitting patiently, waiting to eat.

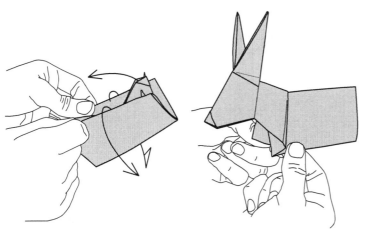

Simple Bunny Pop-up in Action

PERFORM IT!

Hold up the closed card and say to the audience, **"This used to be the body of a rabbit but I guess its head must have fallen off and rolled away. Has anyone seen it?"** Look around the room as you open the card. When the audience says, "There it is!," close the card, look at it, and ask, **"Where?"** Repeat, but stop before the joke gets old. Finish by exclaiming, **"There IS no rabbit head!,"** and as you put the card away, say, **"Well, at least you all have a very good imagination!"**

Simple Bunny Pop-up Card

Bouncing Bunny Pop-Up Card

By Jeremy Shafer ©2005

Intermediate

An Easter favorite... with a basket full of variations!

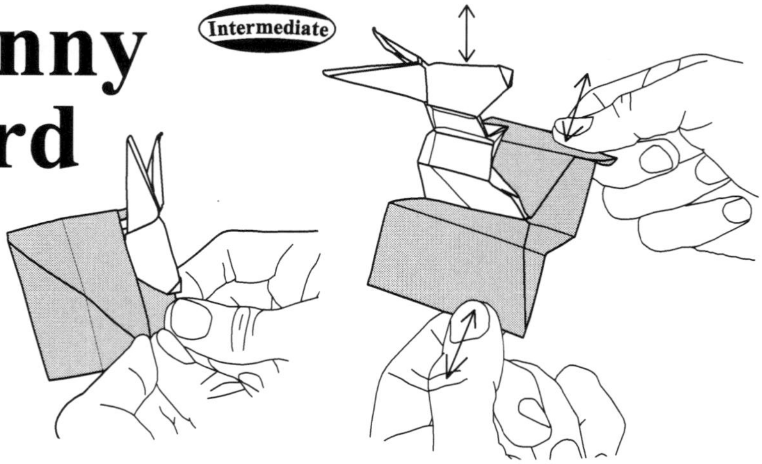

1. 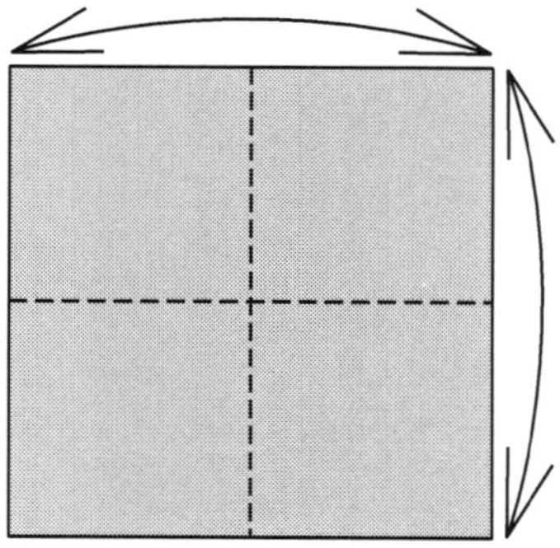 A 16-inch square will make a 4-inch square card (when closed). Colored side up, valley-fold in half and unfold in both directions.

2. Valley-fold and unfold edge-to-crease. **Turn over left-to-right.**

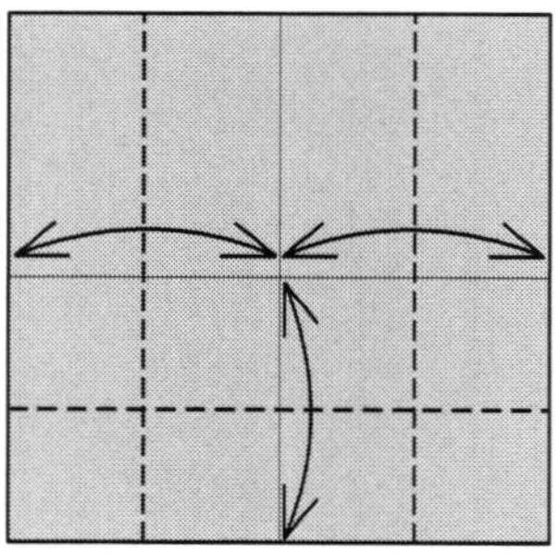

3. Valley-fold edge-to-crease.

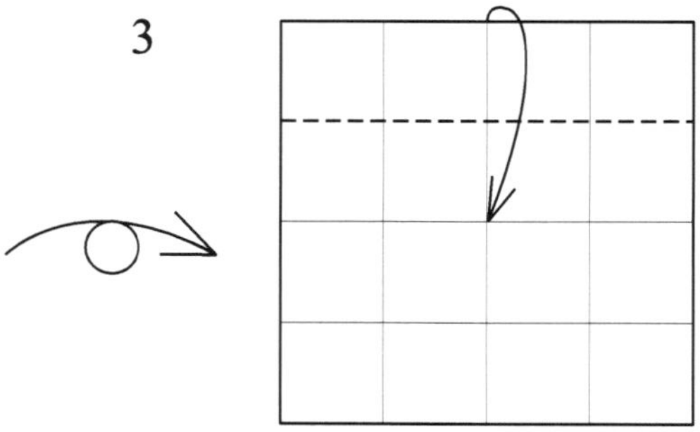

4. Turn over left-to-right.

5. Valley-fold edge-to-crease.

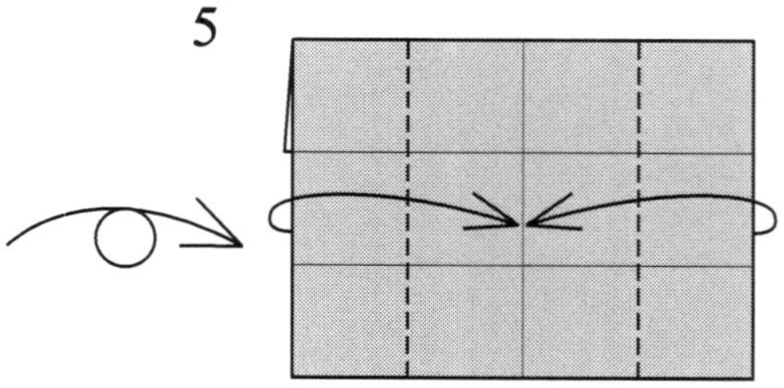

6. Valley-fold point-to-point and unfold.

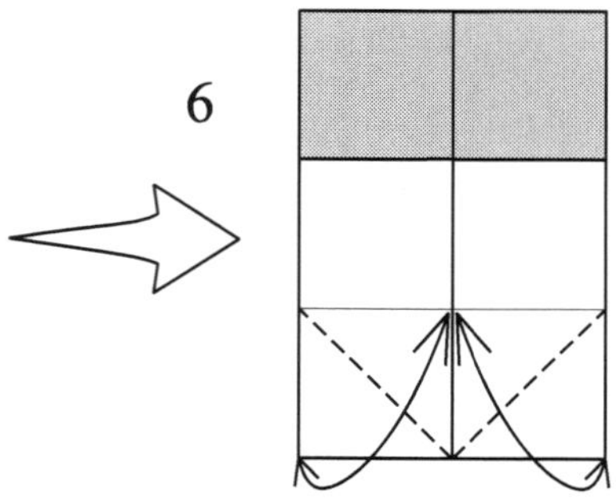

7. Reverse-fold the corners.

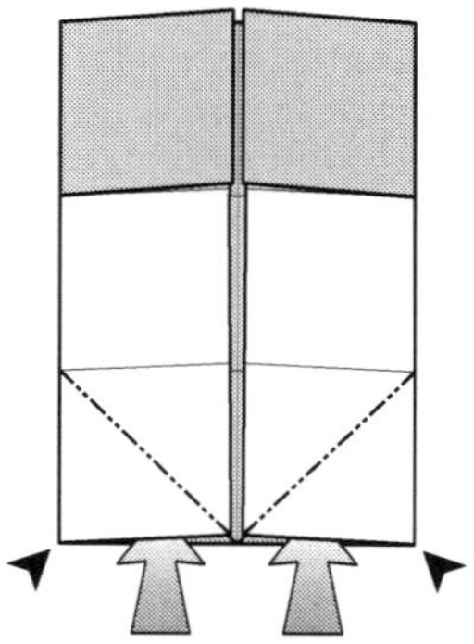

8. Turn over.

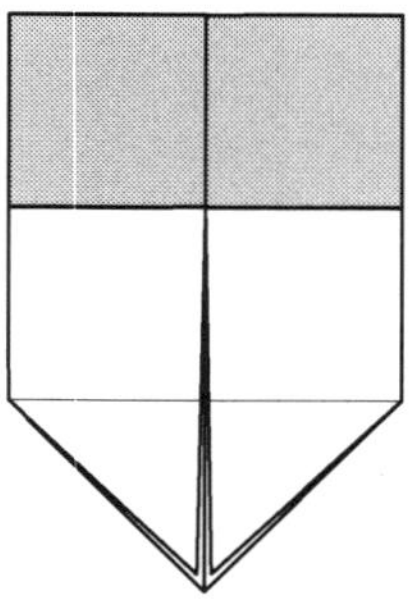

9. Valley-fold the front flap edge-to-crease and unfold.

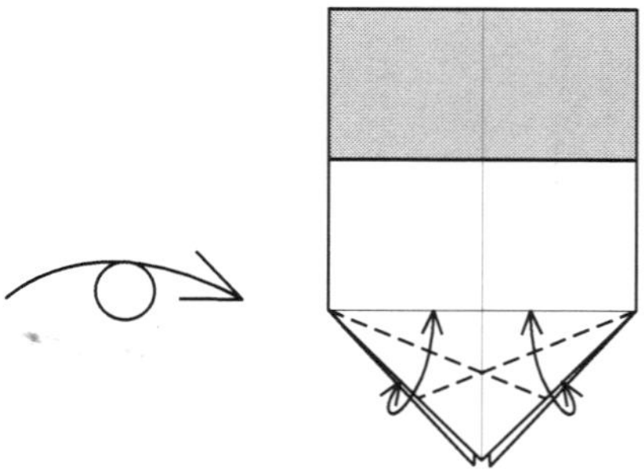

10. Valley-fold the front flap on the intersection of creases.

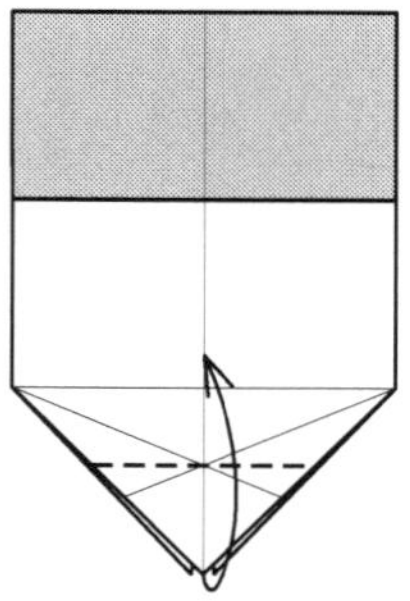

72 *Origami Pop-ups*

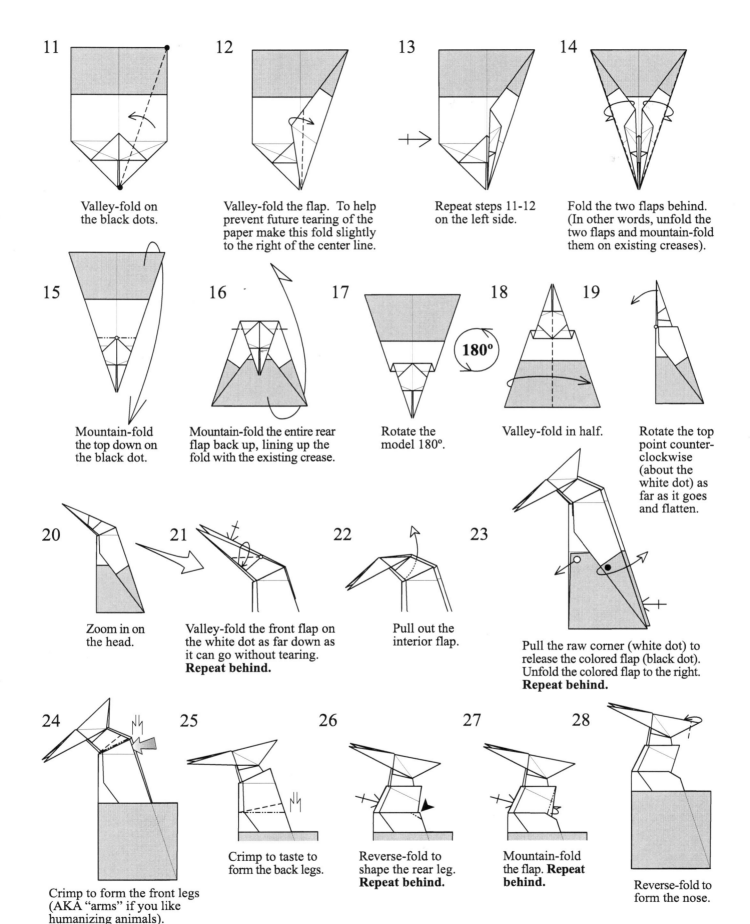

Bouncing Bunny Pop-up Card

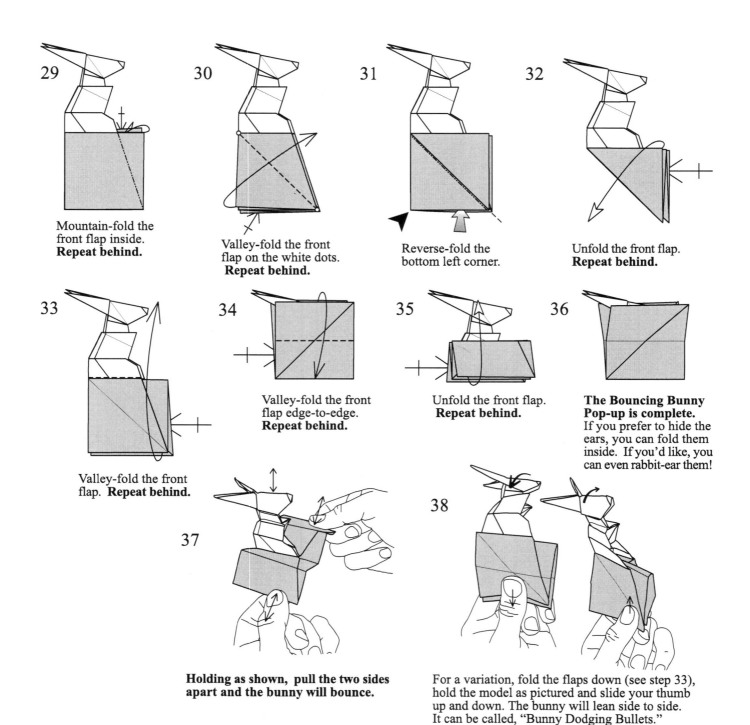

29 Mountain-fold the front flap inside. **Repeat behind.**

30 Valley-fold the front flap on the white dots. **Repeat behind.**

31 Reverse-fold the bottom left corner.

32 Unfold the front flap. **Repeat behind.**

33 Valley-fold the front flap. **Repeat behind.**

34 Valley-fold the front flap edge-to-edge. **Repeat behind.**

35 Unfold the front flap. **Repeat behind.**

36 **The Bouncing Bunny Pop-up is complete.** If you prefer to hide the ears, you can fold them inside. If you'd like, you can even rabbit-ear them!

37 **Holding as shown, pull the two sides apart and the bunny will bounce.**

38 For a variation, fold the flaps down (see step 33), hold the model as pictured and slide your thumb up and down. The bunny will lean side to side. It can be called, "Bunny Dodging Bullets."

PERFORM IT!

Hold up the closed card and quickly put it away, saying to the audience, **"I can't show you that one... It's too crazy!"** After the audience insists say, **"OK, I'll show it to you; everyone yell, 'Pop-up!'"** [Audience yells, "Pop-up!"] Open the card and make the bunny bounce and say, **"You see, it's a bouncing bunny."** Say to the bunny, **"Ok, you can stop bouncing.... STOP BOUNCING!"** Continue bouncing, and finally throw the model back in the box and, in an upset voice, exclaim, **"I told you it was too crazy!"**

74 *Origami Pop-ups*

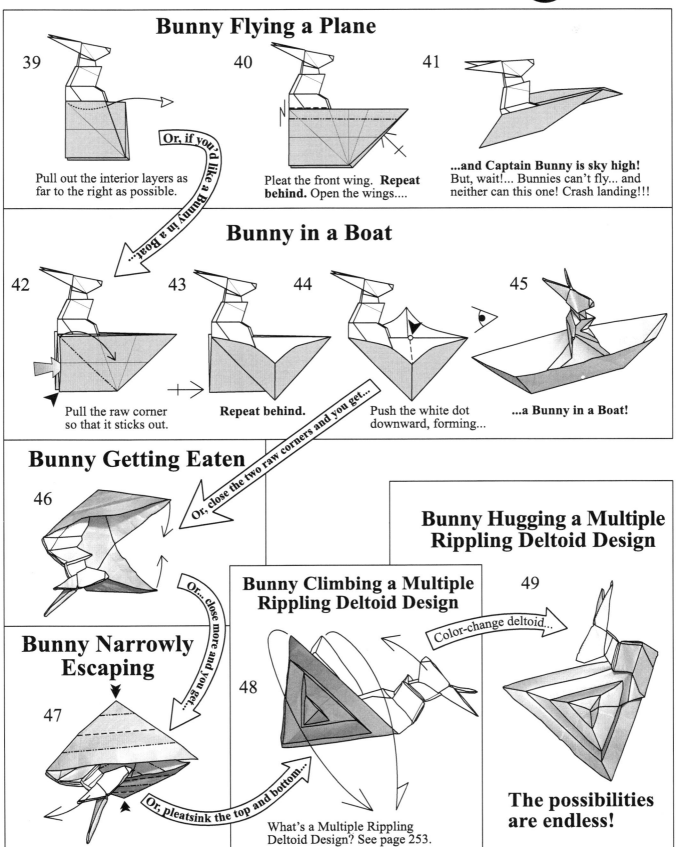

Magic Bunny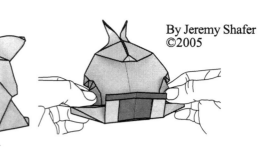

By Jeremy Shafer
©2005

Almost everyone has seen the old trick where the magician pulls a rabbit out of a hat. But have you ever seen a magician pull a hat out of a rabbit?!....

1
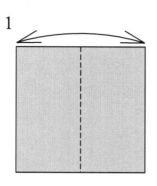

The bunny will be white and the hat will be colored. Use dark paper! Colored side up, valley-fold in half and unfold.

2
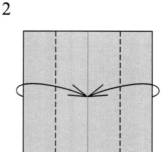

Valley-fold edge-to-crease.

3

Valley-fold edge-to-edge and unfold.

4
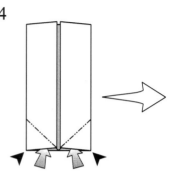

Reverse-fold on existing creases.

5
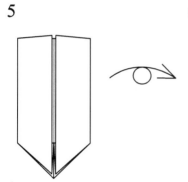

Turn over.

6
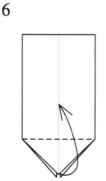

Valley-fold one flap up.

8

Turn over.

9
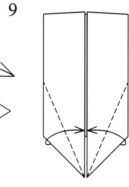

Valley-fold edge-to-edge.

10
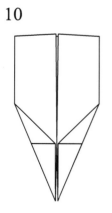

Turn over top to bottom.

11
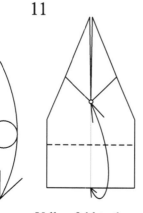

Valley-fold to the white dot and unfold.

12
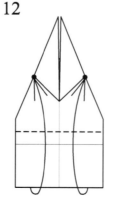

Valley-fold to the black dots.

13
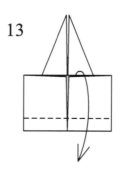

Valley-fold the flap on the existing crease.

14
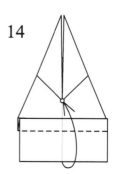

Valley-fold to the white dot.

15

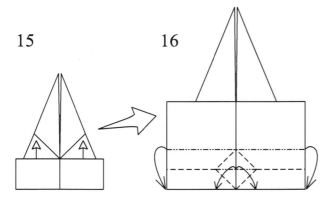

Unfold to step 13.

Refold to step 15, but, as you do this, reach in and pull out the middle raw edges and reverse-fold them (edge-to-edge).

17

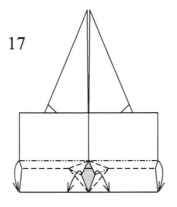

Step 16 in progress.

18

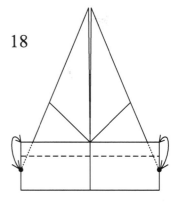

Valley-fold the flap to the black dots and unfold.

19

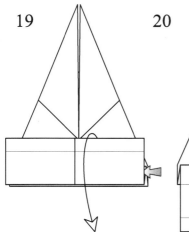

Unfold one flap only.

20

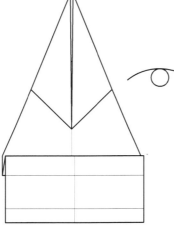

Turn over.

21

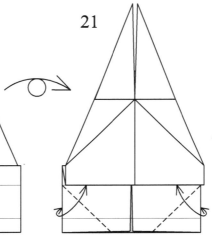

Valley-fold edge-to-edge and unfold.

22

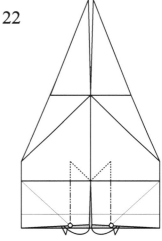

Mountain-fold the single layer vertically on the white dots. The fold extends underneath the horizontal folded edge.

23

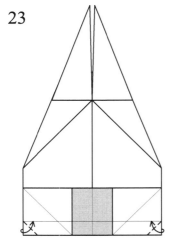

Valley-fold edge-to-crease.

24

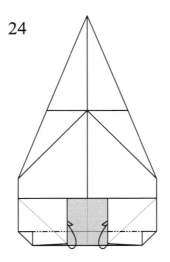

Mountain-fold the front flaps on the existing crease.

25

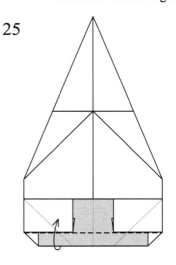

Valley-fold on the existing crease.

Magic Bunny **77**

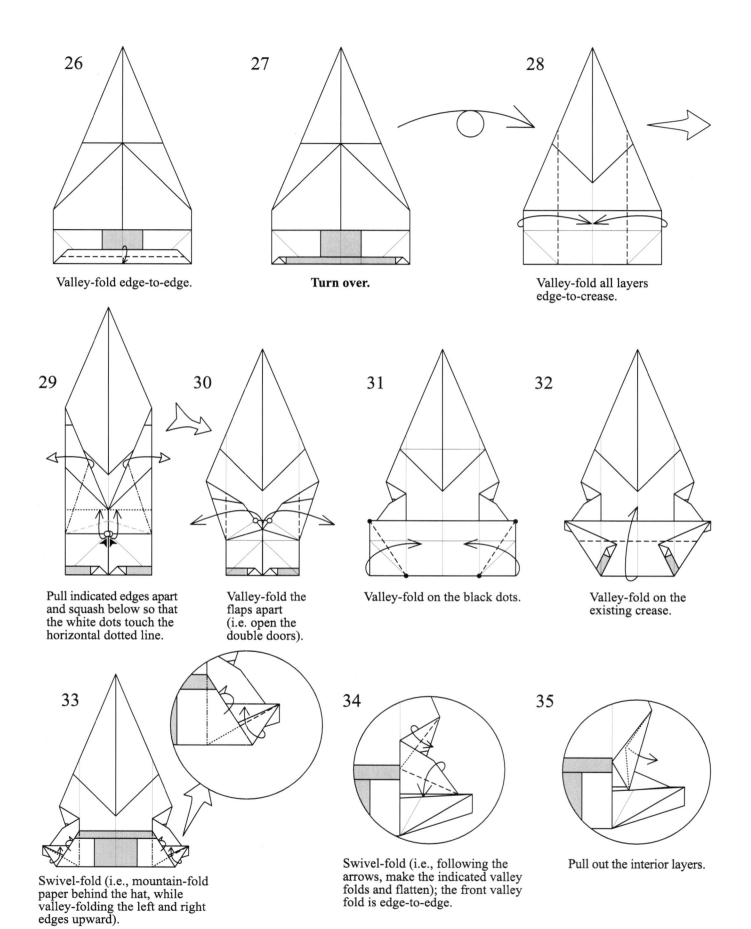

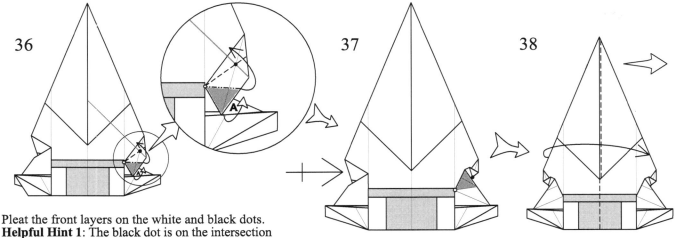

36. Pleat the front layers on the white and black dots.
Helpful Hint 1: The black dot is on the intersection of the crease and the rear edge.
Helpful Hint 2: Flap **A** gets unfolded.
Helpful Hint 3: The shaded triangle rotates counterclockwise about the white dot (see step 37).

37. Repeat steps 34-36 on the left side.

38. Valley-fold the model in half.

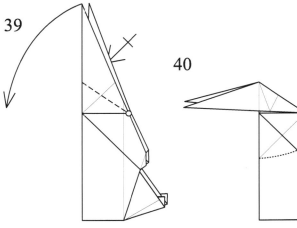

39. Valley-fold the front flap on the white dot as far down as it can go without tearing between the ears (because that would be animal cruelty!). **Repeat behind.**

40. Pull out the interior flap.

PERFORM IT!

Hold up the closed model and say to the audience, "**This is a magic rabbit! I will now pull it out of a hat. Oh wait, it's already out! Hmmm.... Ah! Then I will perform another trick; everyone say the magic words, 'Abracadabra!'**" [Audience says Abracadabra!] Open the model, show the hat and say, "**And amazingly, the hat has been pulled out of the rabbit!**" Finish by putting it on your head (so that the hat is visible and the rabbit is face down) and say, "**Even Houdini never did that!**"

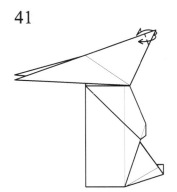
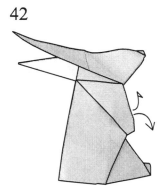
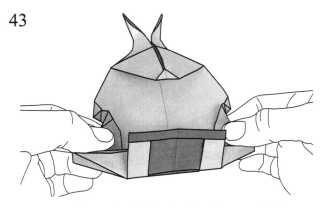

41. Outside-reverse-fold to form the nose, and sculpt the model to taste if desired.

42. The Magic Bunny is ready to perform prestidigitation. Say the magic words and open the bunny...

43. ...and, magically, the hat has been pulled out of the rabbit! No hats were injured in the performing of this magic trick.

Magic Bunny **79**

Puppy Pop-up Card

Alliteration Included!

By Jeremy Shafer ©2005

Here's one for all you dog lovers! Your very own puppy! You'll never need to feed it, walk it or take it to the vet, and it even comes with its very own dog house!

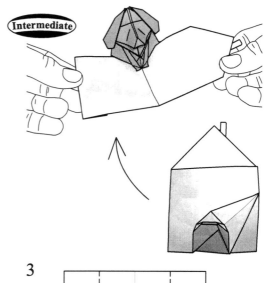

1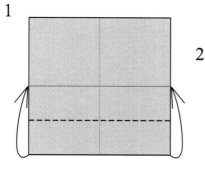

Valley-fold to the crease you made in the step 0 (not shown).

2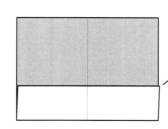

Turn over.

3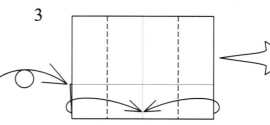

Valley-fold edge-to-crease.

4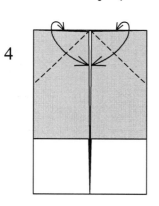

Valley-fold edge-to-crease and unfold.

5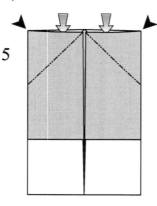

Reverse-fold on existing creases.

6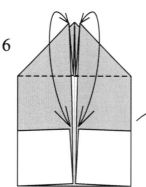

Valley-fold the two flaps down and back up again. **Turn over.**

7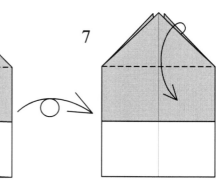

Valley-fold the single flap down.

8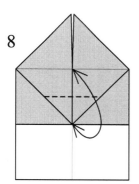

Valley-fold the flap to the crease and unfold.

9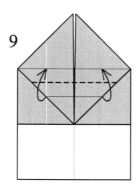

Valley-fold the flap, aligning the creases.

10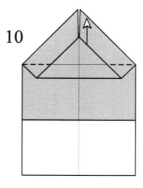

Pull the flap upward.

11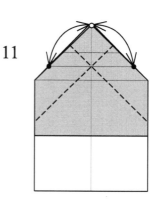

Valley-fold white-dot-to-black-dot thru all layers and unfold on both sides.

80 *Origami Pop-ups*

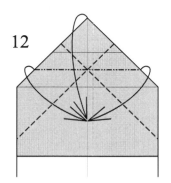

On existing creases, fold the top into a Square Base. What's a Square Base? See page 15.

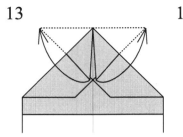

Unfold the front flaps.

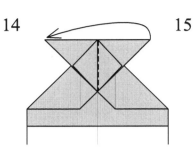

Valley-fold the flaps to the left.

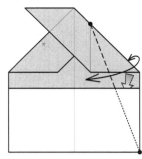

Valley-fold the colored flap on the black dots, folding underneath the white rectangle and unfold.

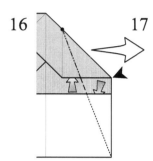

Reverse-fold the colored flap, once again folding it underneath the white rectangle.

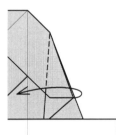

Valley-fold the flap.

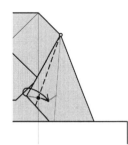

Valley-fold the flap on the dots; the black dot is on the folded edge (behind the front layer) and on the middle crease.

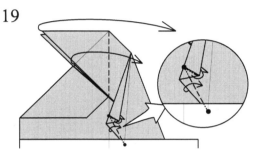

Reverse-fold on the black dots. The mountain fold is on edge, so please be sensitive.

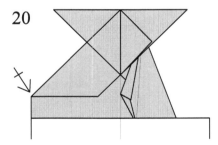

Repeat steps 14-19 on the left side.

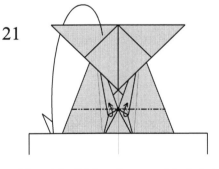

Mountain-fold on the same black dot. Let the two small flaps swing upward. These will be the paws.

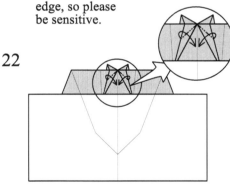

Pull the two folded edges together releasing paper from the paws.

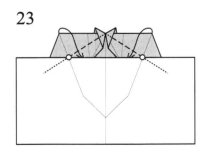

Valley-fold on the white dots, inserting the two corners under the top layer. The paws still point up.

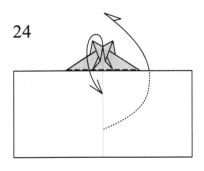

Now, valley-fold the paws down while swinging the rear flap upward.

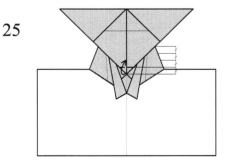

Valley-fold the tip of the nose.

Puppy Pop-up Card **81**

26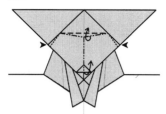
Squeeze the snout so that it sticks out. The valley fold is on an existing crease. The model will not lie flat.

27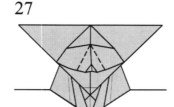
Form two valley folds to define the base of the nose.

28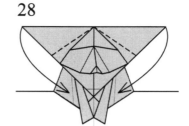
Valley-fold the ears to taste.

29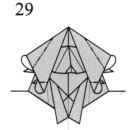
Shape the ears to taste with mountain folds.

30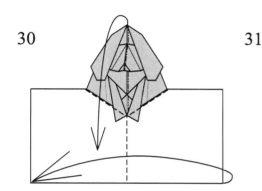
Close the card, incorporating a reverse fold to enclose the dog inside.

31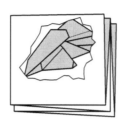
Cut-out view of the dog inside the card. Don't worry; she'll be fine.

32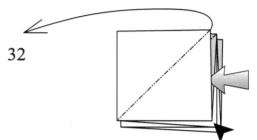
Pull the corner leftward and squash.

PERFORM IT!

Hold up the closed card and say to the audience, **"What's this?"** [Audience says, "A house."] Ask, **"But, what kind of house?"** To whatever they say, answer, **"It's a dog house! But, where do you think the dog is?"** [Audience says, "Inside."] Answer, **"Yes! Ready, set, everyone say, 'Pop-up!'"** [Audience says, "Pop-up!"]. Open the card and, making loud barking sounds, pretend to sic the dog on the audience. Before anybody gets hurt, forcibly pull the dog away and quickly close the card and say, **"I'm so sorry! I really need to put a BEWARE OF DOG sign on this house."**

33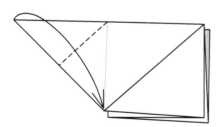
Now for the roof and chimney! Valley-fold point-to-point.

34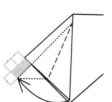
Valley-fold the flap so that the shaded rectangle is 2-by-1, or just fold it to taste!

35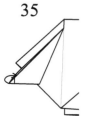
Reverse-fold the flap to taste.

36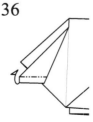
Mountain-fold the flap to taste.

37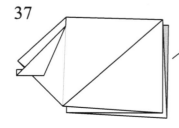
Turn over.

38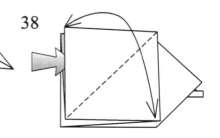
Valley-fold and unfold **on the front layer only.**

82 *Origami Pop-ups*

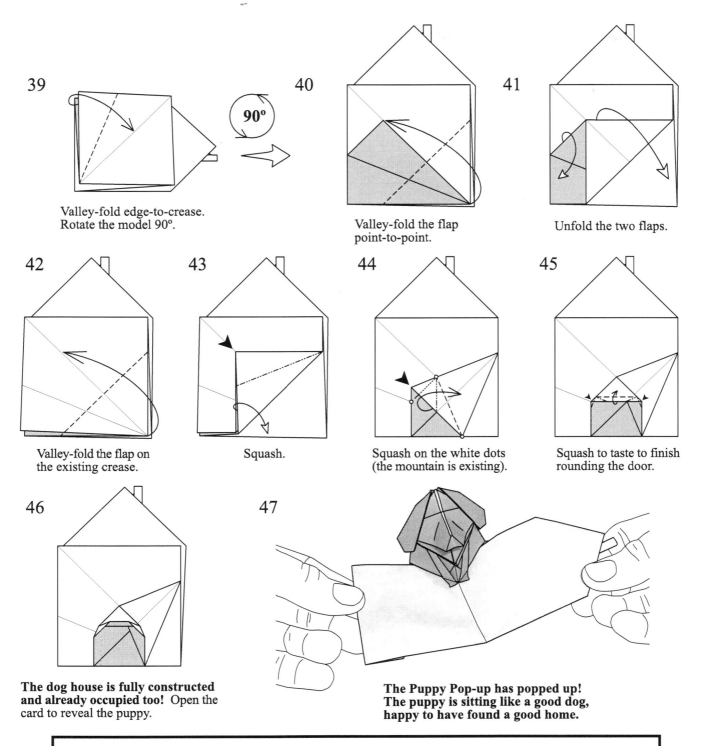

39 Valley-fold edge-to-crease. Rotate the model 90°.

40 Valley-fold the flap point-to-point.

41 Unfold the two flaps.

42 Valley-fold the flap on the existing crease.

43 Squash.

44 Squash on the white dots (the mountain is existing).

45 Squash to taste to finish rounding the door.

46 **The dog house is fully constructed and already occupied too!** Open the card to reveal the puppy.

47 **The Puppy Pop-up has popped up! The puppy is sitting like a good dog, happy to have found a good home.**

Thoughts Behind the Folds

The road to designing this model first included the discovery of a new origami pop-up mechanism (see steps 21-24), which I've used a lot since! Then I started thinking of what subject I should make pop up using the new mechanism, and a Puppy Pop-up came to mind. The evolution of the design spanned a couple of months, mostly trying to improve the puppy. Early versions resulted in two extra corner flaps of paper on the card which I simply sunk out of sight, but that wasted paper. So finally, I figured out a way to use the flaps: one flap became the dog house roof, and the other became a dog door. **Challenge:** What else can you pop-up? I believe almost any existing 2-D model can be adapted into a pop-up card. Simply keep the better half of your favorite origami model as it is, and unfold the worse half and transform it into a card. For subject matter, the animal kingdom is a good place to start, but the possibilities are endless!

Puppy Pop-up Card

Surprise Guest for Dinner

A.K.A. "Hello Kitty"

Here is a pop-up about a little bird that really did "tee a puddy tat." This model should appeal to both cat and bird lovers, for in this meeting, what happens next is in the hands of the folder or in the imagination of the viewer.

By Jeremy Shafer
©2007

Hello Kitty!

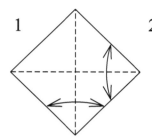

1. White side up, valley-fold in half diagonally and unfold in both directions.

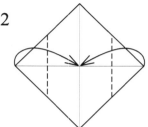

2. Valley-fold to the center.

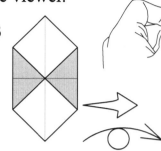

3. **Turn over.**

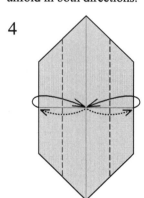

4. Valley-fold the left and right sides to the middle crease, letting the rear flaps swing apart.

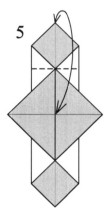

5. Valley-fold point-to-point and unfold.

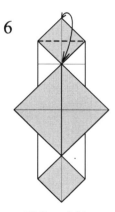

6. Valley-fold point-to-point and unfold.

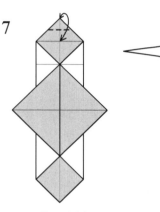

7. Valley-fold point-to-point and unfold.

8. Valley-fold point-to-point and **don't** unfold!

9. Valley-fold.

10. Valley-fold point-to-point and unfold, creasing on top.

11. Valley-fold edge-to-crease.

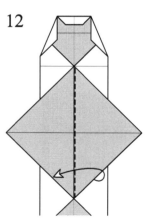

12. Unfold one flap to the left.

Open the finished model and say to the audience, **"This is a little bird that has invited a big cat for Thanksgiving dinner. What do you think is on the menu?"** [Audience says, "The bird!"] Reply, **"No! This cat messed with the wrong bird!"** Make the bird peck at the cat (see page 86, step 40) as you say in a birdy voice, **"Yum yum! Tastes like Kit Kat!"**

84 *Origami Pop-ups*

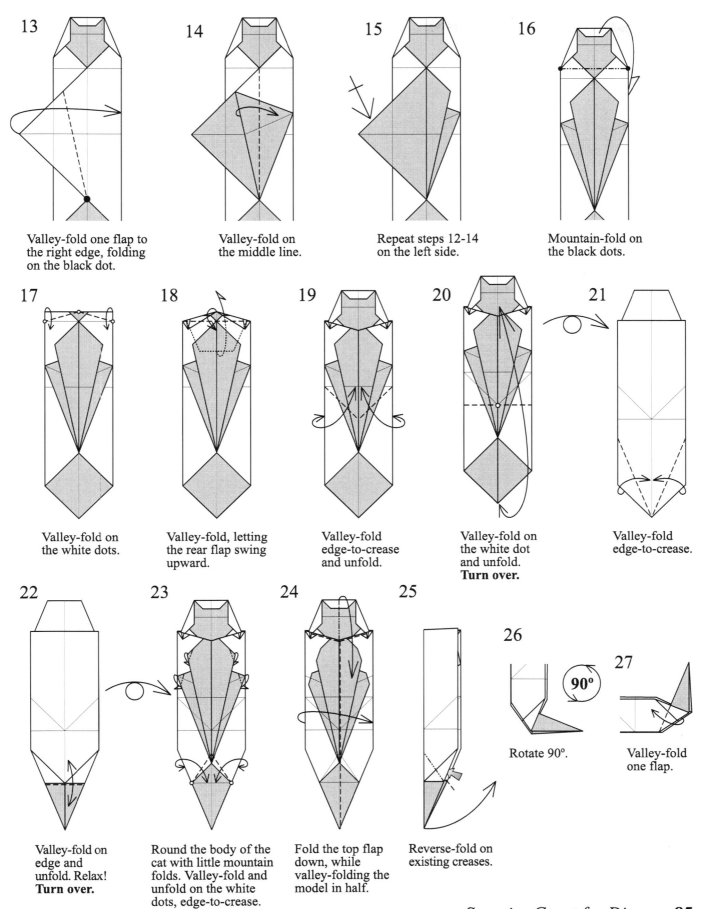

Surprise Guest for Dinner 85

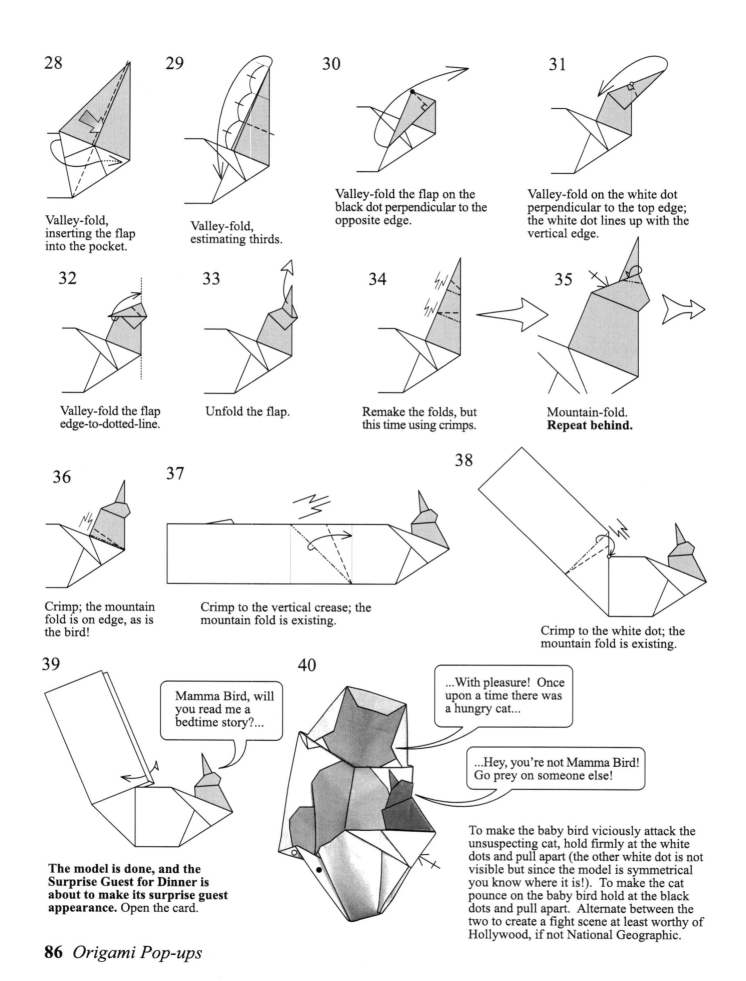

Elephant Pop-up Card

(Intermediate)

By Jeremy Shafer
©2005

Who needs to go to the circus to see elephants?! Fold this pop-up card, and you'll have your very own circus elephant at your fingertips!

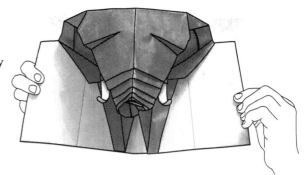

1

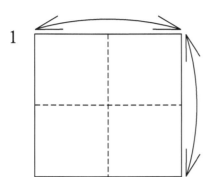

A 16-inch square will make a 4-inch square card (when closed). White side up, valley-fold in half and unfold in both directions.

2

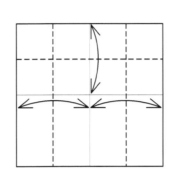

Valley-fold edge-to-crease and unfold.

3

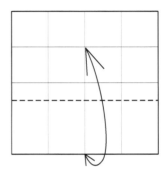

Valley-fold edge-to-crease and unfold.

4

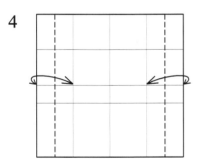

Valley-fold edge-to-crease and unfold.

5

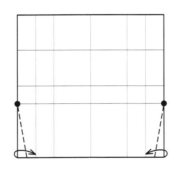

Valley-fold on the black dots corner-to-crease.

6

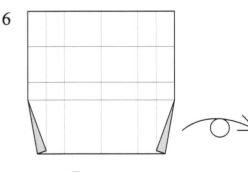

Turn over.

7

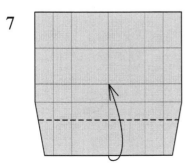

Valley-fold edge-to-crease.

8

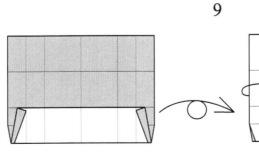

Turn over.

9

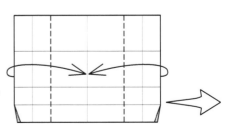

Valley-fold edge-to-crease.

Elephant Pop-up Card 87

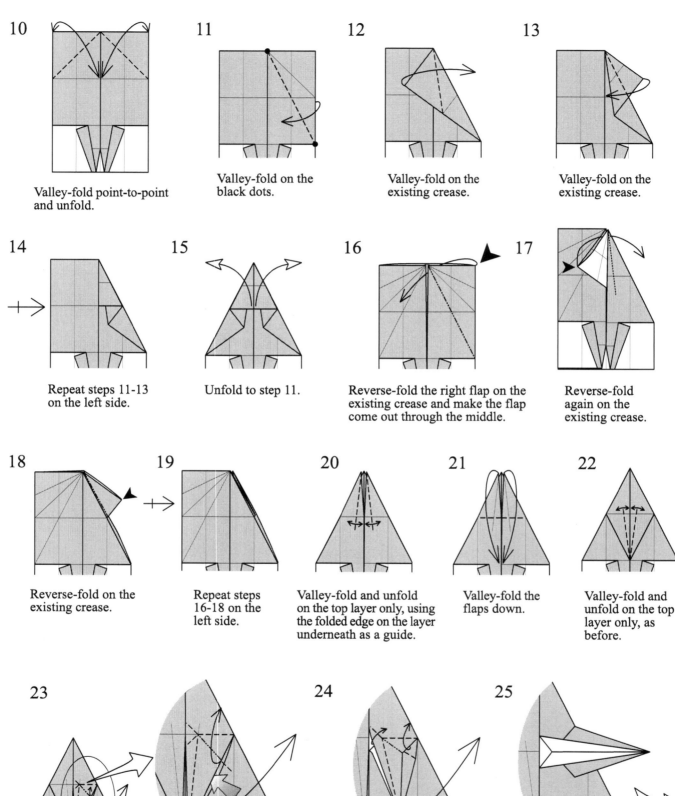

10 Valley-fold point-to-point and unfold.

11 Valley-fold on the black dots.

12 Valley-fold on the existing crease.

13 Valley-fold on the existing crease.

14 Repeat steps 11-13 on the left side.

15 Unfold to step 11.

16 Reverse-fold the right flap on the existing crease and make the flap come out through the middle.

17 Reverse-fold again on the existing crease.

18 Reverse-fold on the existing crease.

19 Repeat steps 16-18 on the left side.

20 Valley-fold and unfold on the top layer only, using the folded edge on the layer underneath as a guide.

21 Valley-fold the flaps down.

22 Valley-fold and unfold on the top layer only, as before.

23 Squash the flap to the right on the creases made in steps 20-22.

24 In progress.

25 Like this (and comment and subscribe too, please!).

88 *Origami Pop-ups*

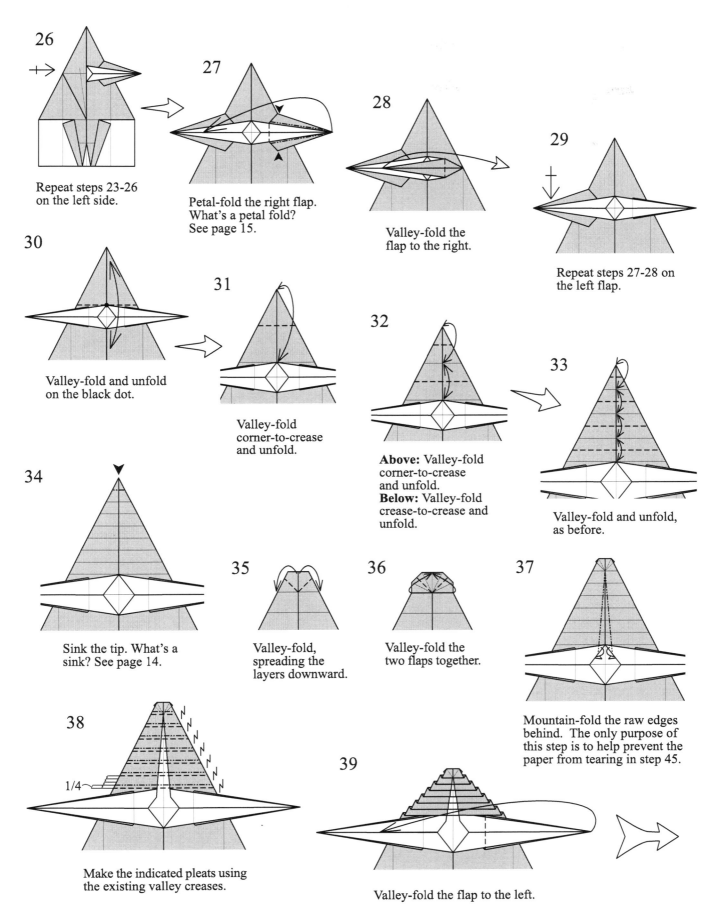

Elephant Pop-up Card

40

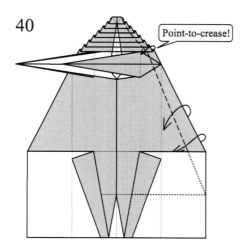

Valley-fold as shown; on the lower part of the model, the fold extends underneath the top layer and terminates at the horizontal hidden crease.

41

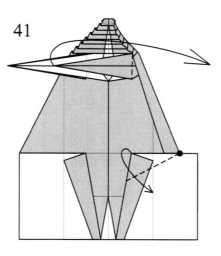

Above: Valley-fold the tusk to the right.
Below: Valley-fold on the black dot so that the corner touches the existing crease.

42

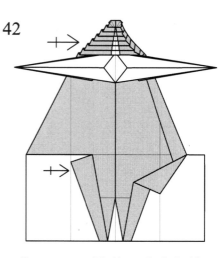

Repeat steps 39-41 on the left side.

43

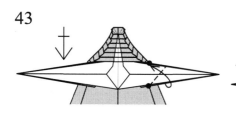

Valley-fold the flap so that its lower edge touches the two black dots. Repeat on the left side.

44

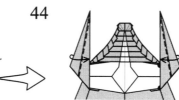

Valley-fold edge-to-edge.

45

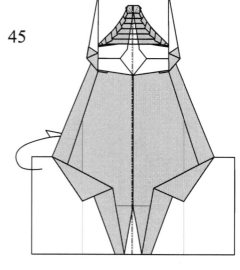

Mountain-fold the left side behind.

46

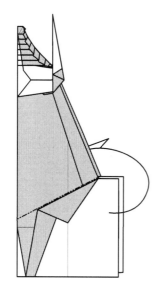

Mountain-fold on the edge through all layers.

47

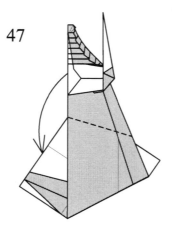

Valley-fold edge-to-edge.

48

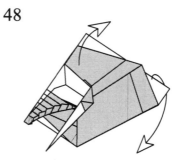

Unfold to step 46.

90 *Origami Pop-ups*

49

PERFORM IT!

Hold up the model and say to the audience, **"Ready, set, everyone say, 'Pop-up!'"** [Audience says, "Pop-up!"] Open the card and ask, **"What is it?"** [Audience says, "An Elephant!"] Say, **"Yes! Who wants to get bopped in the head by an elephant?!"** Go around gently bopping any willing volunteers (see step 56), and make the elephant bop you on the head too. Finish by having the elephant whisper a message in your ear. Relay the message, **"The elephant says he's tired of bopping people."**

Outside-reverse-fold on existing creases.

50

Bend the trunk upward, stretching the bottom edge. Be careful not to tear the paper!

51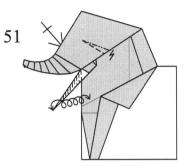

Above: Make a pleat to suggest the elephant's eye.
Below: Curve the tusk to taste by rolling and unrolling it (vertical valley creases). **Repeat behind.**

52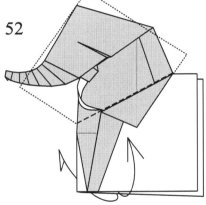

Outside-reverse-fold the card around the elephant on existing creases; pull out the interior flap to make the card whole.

53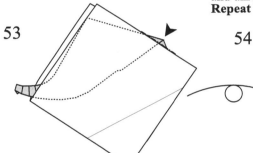

Reverse-fold the top of the ear so that it no longer protrudes. **Turn over.**

54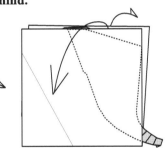

The Elephant Pop-up is ready to pop up. The trunk sticks out a bit to tantalize the viewer as to what will happen when we... **Open the card!**

55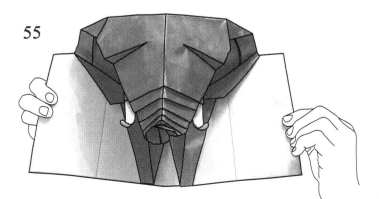

The Elephant popped out of nowhere and is staring right at you, about to charge. Run for your life!

56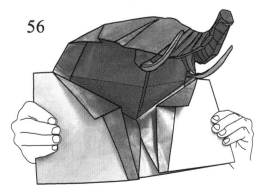

Pull left and right sides apart and elephant lifts its head!

WARNING: Maintain a safe distance from elephant or risk getting poked in eye.

Elephant Pop-up Card 91

$ Cobra Pop-Up Card   *Intermediate*

Although any 3 X 1 rectangle works, Using a U.S. One Dollar Bill is ideal because it results in a cobra with white fangs and spiral eyes!

By Jeremy Shafer ©2007

Note: If you use a 1-by-3 rectangle instead of a dollar, make sure the paper is the same color on both sides and begin at step 2.

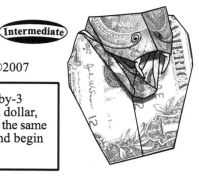

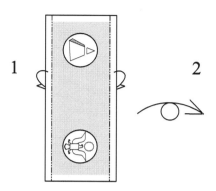 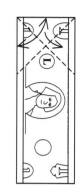 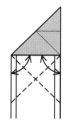  

1. Begin with a U.S. One Dollar Bill, eagle and pyramid side up. Mountain-fold the left and right borders (the white part), resulting in a roughly 1-by-3 rectangle. **Turn over.**

2. Valley-fold and unfold diagonally in one direction. In the other direction, valley-fold diagonally and don't unfold.

3. Valley-fold edge-to-edge and unfold in both directions.

4. Unfold.

5. Valley-fold and unfold.

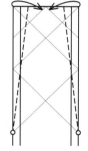 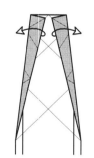   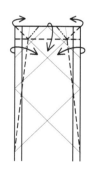

6. Valley-fold the corners to the existing diagonal creases; the folds originate at the white dots.

7. Unfold the flaps.

8. Valley-fold on the white dots and unfold.

9. Fold the three edges toward the middle on existing creases while rabbit-earing the two corners and folding them upward.

10. Valley-fold edge-to-edge.

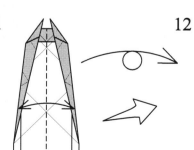 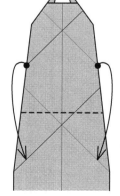 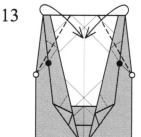 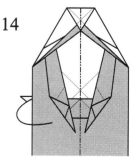

11. Valley-fold the model in half and unfold. **Turn over.**

12. Valley-fold the black dots to the diagonal creases.

13. Valley-fold the corners to the center line; the folds originate at the white dots.

14. Mountain-fold the model in half.

92 *Origami Pop-ups*

15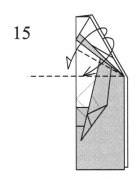
Outside-reverse-fold to the imaginary horizontal line.

16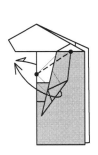
Outside-reverse-fold on the black dots.

17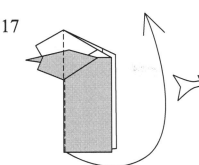
Pull the bottom flap out to the right, undoing the reverse fold.

18
Wrap the raw edge around to the interior of the model; the corner at the black dot needs to be turned inside out. **Repeat behind.**

19
Outside-reverse-fold the long flap on the white dot. The angle of this fold is to taste. The closer the fold is to being perpendicular to the top edge, the better the cobra's head will fit inside the card, but the less the head will "pop up" when the card is opened.

20
Valley-fold. This fold is also to taste.

21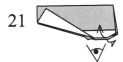
Open the card and look into the mouth like a dentist.

22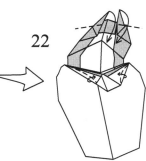
Perform oral surgery: Valley-fold the fangs downward and shape the lower jaw with two sharply creased, curved valley folds.

23 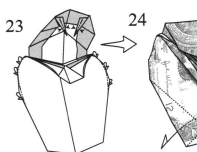 24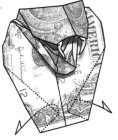

Round the left and right edges of the cobra with tiny mountain folds. Narrow and shape the fangs to taste... YUM!

Like this! To make the card stand, unfold the two rear flaps.

PERFORM IT!

Say to the audience, **"This is a scary dollar. Ready, set, everyone say 'Pop-up!'"** [Audience says, "Pop-up!"] Open the model and ask, **"What is it?"** [Audience says, "It's a snake."] **"But what kind of snake?"** [Audience says, "Cobra."] **"Who wants to get bitten by a cobra?"** Attack all willing victims and yell, **"Oh no, we have lots of snake bites! Does anyone have any anti-venom?"** Stick the model on your finger, shake it around, and shout, **"Aaah! It's got my finger!"**

Video tutorial on youtube.com!
Search: shafer cobra popup video

25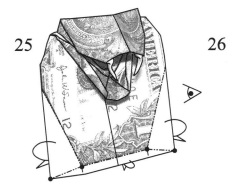
Pinch a mountain fold on the black dots, and then fold the two flaps behind again. This will enable the Cobra Card to stand.

26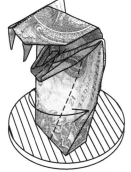
The Cobra Pop-up is poised to strike, or, perhaps, just striking a pose. Now, close the card.

27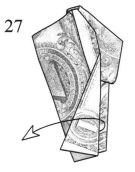
The Cobra Pop-up is closed. Open again.

28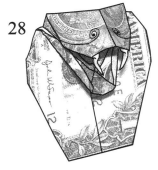
The Cobra Pop-up is finished, and waiting to snack on some pop-up mice.

$ Cobra Pop-up Card

Gorilla Pop-up Card *Intermediate*

By Jeremy Shafer ©2006

Now you can have a pet gorilla without having to get a zoo license, and you won't even need to feed it bananas.

1 White side up, fold a Square Base (page 15).

2 Valley-fold the front layers edge-to-crease.

3 Mountain-fold on the edge and unfold.

4 Valley-fold, reversing the crease.

5 Valley-fold, edge-to-edge.

6 Unfold to step 2.

9a Valley-fold edge-to-crease and unfold. Repeat behind.

9b Reverse-fold on the existing crease. Repeat behind.

9c Valley-fold the front flap. Repeat behind.

9d Color-change the left front flap by wrapping the raw edge behind the flap. To do this cleanly, partially unfold the model. Repeat behind.

9e Valley-fold.

9f Valley-fold.

9g Valley-fold.

9h Pull out the interior layers leftward.

9i Done.

7 Reverse-fold the front layers on existing creases.

8 Minor Miracle Fold: Fold flap **A** to the right and fold flap **B** behind to the left.

9 Here's a tricky step. Valley-fold the front and rear flaps up while incorporating outside reverse folds on the layers of the left side. Partially unfolding the model is necessary to complete this step cleanly. If you can't figure this step out, look up into the cloud for an easier but longer method of getting to step 10.

10 Minor Miracle Fold: Fold flap **A** to the left and fold flap **B** behind to the right.

Origami Pop-ups

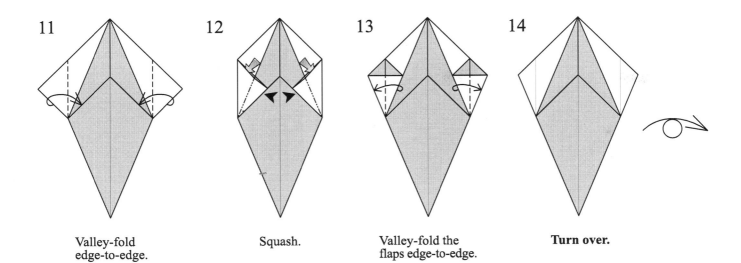

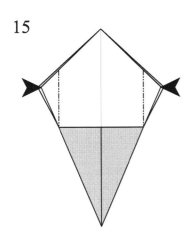

Reverse-fold the front flaps on existing creases.

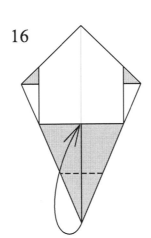

Valley-fold to the horizontal edge.

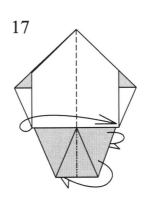

Minor Miracle Fold: Valley-fold the front left flap to the right and mountain-fold the rear right flap to the left.

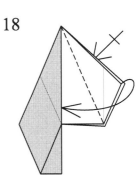

Valley-fold one flap. **Repeat behind.**

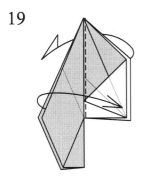

Minor Miracle Fold: Valley-fold the front left flap to the right and mountain-fold the rear right flap to the left.

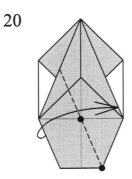

Valley-fold the flap on the black dots (edge-to-edge).

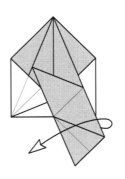

Unfold.

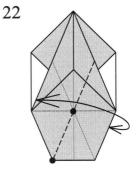

Valley-fold the flap on the black dots (edge-to-edge).

Gorilla Pop-up Card **95**

23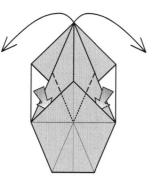
Valley-fold the two flaps behind the front layer on existing creases.

24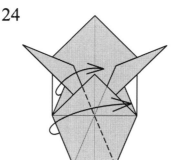
Valley-fold the flap on the existing crease.

25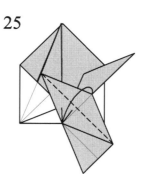
Valley-fold the flap point-to-point.

26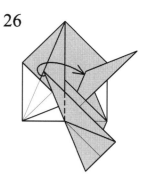
Valley-fold the flap to the right.

27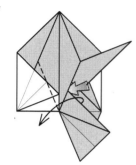
Valley-fold the flaps to the left.

28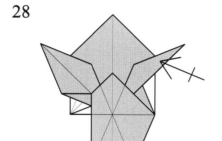
Repeat steps 24-27 on the right side.

29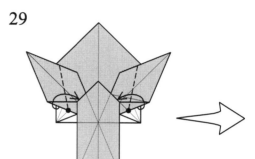
Valley-fold on the black dots edge-to-edge.

30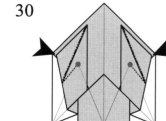
Reverse-fold: The hidden valley folds (dotted lines) terminate at the gray dots.

31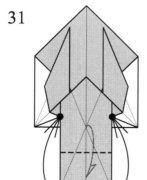
Valley-fold to the black dots, letting the rear flap swing downward.

32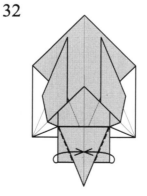
Valley-fold the flaps on the edges.

33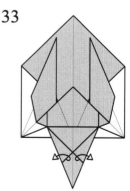
Unfold.

96 *Origami Pop-ups*

34. Reverse-fold the flaps on existing creases.

35. Valley-fold to the horizontal edge. Rotate the model 180°.

36. Valley-fold, inserting the flap under the front layers.

37. Valley-fold point-to-point and unfold.

38. Valley-fold the flap crease-to-crease and unfold.

39. Mountain-fold a "sliver" (a very thin flap).

40. Unfold the flap but don't unfold the tiny pleat.

41. Pleat: Form the mountain fold on the existing crease and valley fold it to the other existing crease.

42. Reverse-fold on the white dots.

43. Like this! (and favorite it too!)

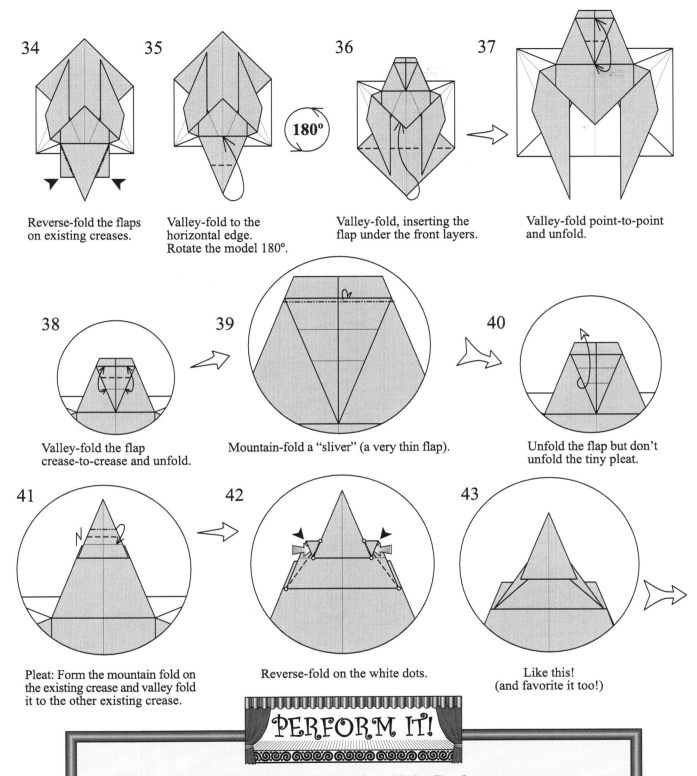

PERFORM IT!

Say to the audience, **"I'll bet you'll know what this is. Ready, set, everyone say, 'Pop-up!'"** [Audience says, "Pop-up"] Open the card and ask, **"What is it?"** [Audience says, "A gorilla."] Respond, **"A GIRL???"** Hold it up to the face of a boy and ask, **"Is she your girlfriend?!"** [Audience says, "No! A Gorilla!"] Reply, **"Oh! A gorilla! She's your gorilla girlfriend! Everybody make the sound of a gorilla!"** [Everybody makes gorilla sounds.] Exclaim, **"Wow, you guys are really Great Apes!"**

Gorilla Pop-up Card

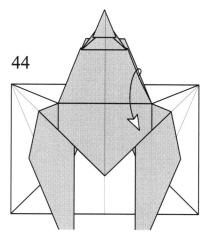

44

Swing the front flap down.

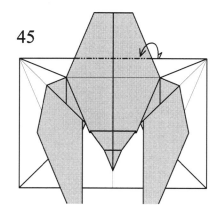

45

Mountain-fold and unfold.

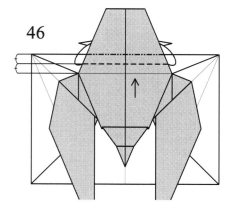

46

Pleat the front flap: the mountain is existing; the valley is new.

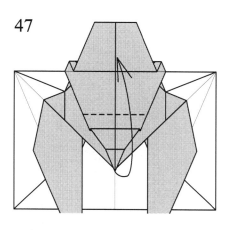

47

Valley-fold to taste.

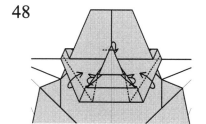

48

Shape the face to taste with reverse folds. Mountain-fold the tip of the nose.

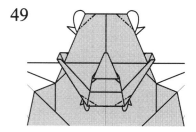

49

Round the head to taste with mountain folds.

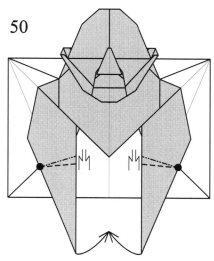

50

Crimp on the black dots so that the two corners come together.

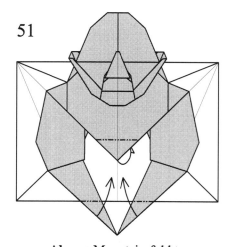

51

Above: Mountain-fold to form the chest.
Below: Reverse-fold on the edge to form the hands.

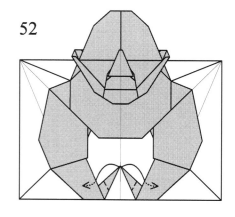

52

Valley-fold, inserting the flaps behind the front layers.

98 *Origami Pop-ups*

53

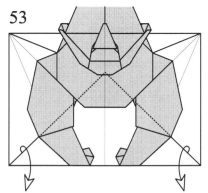

If you would prefer a rectangular greeting card and you don't mind just the upper torso showing, then skip to step 57. For the full-body Gorilla, unfold the interior white flap and proceed to step 54.

54

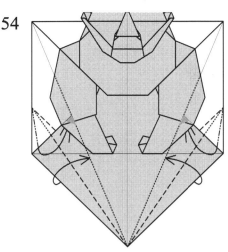

Valley-fold the raw edges to the dotted lines; this fold goes underneath the arms. Alter the folds slightly to cover up that annoying dark-shaded region that would be left if you were to do just an ordinary valley-fold.

55

Reverse-fold to taste to form the legs.

56

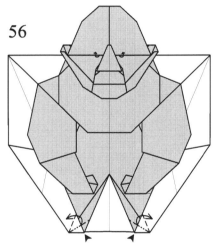

Above: Make tiny valley folds to suggest the eyes.
Below: Squash to form the feet.

57

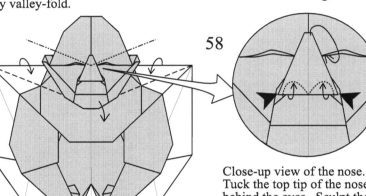

Closing the card partially, make a pleat on the neck so that the head does not stick out when the card is closed.

58

Close-up view of the nose. Tuck the top tip of the nose behind the eyes. Sculpt the bottom edge of the nose to form two large nostrils. Don't worry about guidelines... think paper sculpture, not origami! The nose does not have to lie perfectly flat. The nostrils should stick out from the face.

59

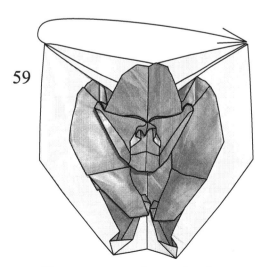

Shape to taste and your done!
That's a wild gorilla! Before it gets loose and hurts somebody, we'd better restrain it by closing the card!

60

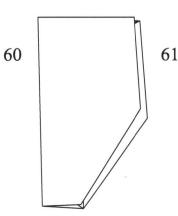

The gorilla is sufficiently restrained for now, but ready to pop-up at any moment to try out for the next Origami King Kong movie, or else play a part in some other upstart monkey business.

61

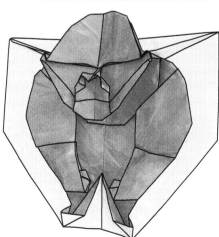

Pulling the left and right sides of the card apart will make the gorilla bob its head up and down. Isn't he a Great Ape?!

Gorilla Pop-up Card 99

Grizzly Bear Pop-up Card

By Jeremy Shafer ©2005 (Intermediate)

Here's a model that's greatly grizzly, and that's one pun that's bear-ly bear-able.

1. White side up, fold a Square Base (page 15).

2. Valley-fold on the front layers edge-to-crease.

3. Mountain-fold on the edge and unfold.

4. Valley-fold, reversing the crease.

5. Valley-fold, edge-to-edge.

6. Unfold to step 2.

9a. Valley-fold edge-to-crease and unfold. Repeat behind.

9b. Reverse-fold on the existing crease. Repeat behind.

9c. Valley-fold the front flap. Repeat behind.

9d. Color-change the left front flap by wrapping the raw edge behind the flap. To do this cleanly, partially unfold the model. Repeat behind.

9e. Valley-fold.

9f. Valley-fold.

9g. Valley-fold.

9h. Pull out the interior layers leftward.

9i. Done.

7. Reverse-fold the front layers on the existing creases.

8. Minor Miracle Fold: Fold flap **A** to the right and fold flap **B** behind to the left.

9. Here's a tricky step. Valley-fold the front and rear flaps up while incorporating outside reverse folds on the layers of the left side. Partially unfolding the model is necessary to complete this step cleanly. If you can't figure this step out, look up into the cloud for an easier but longer method of getting to step 10 (Warning: adds extra creases on cover of card).

10. Minor Miracle Fold: Fold flap **A** to the left and fold flap **B** behind to the right.

100 *Origami Pop-ups*

11

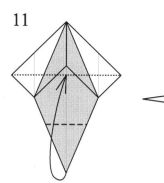

Valley-fold to the imaginary dotted line.

12

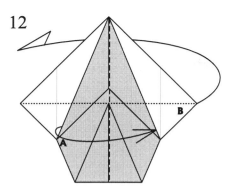

Minor Miracle Fold. I'm sure you know what that means by now! Three minor miracles in five steps makes you a minor miracle worker!

13

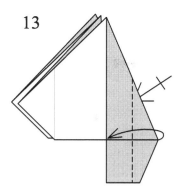

Valley-fold point-to-point. **Repeat behind.**

14

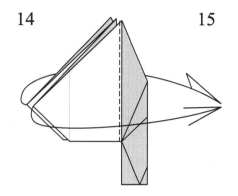

Valley-fold the front and rear flaps to the right. **Repeat behind.**

15

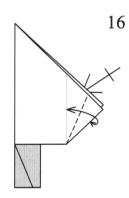

Valley-fold edge-to-edge and unfold. **Repeat behind.**

16

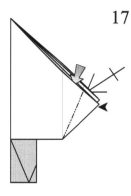

Reverse-fold the flap on the existing crease. **Repeat behind.**

17

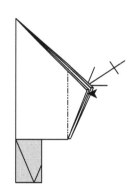

Reverse-fold the front flap on the existing crease. **Repeat behind.**

18

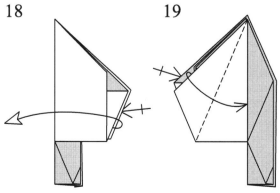

Unfold the front flap. **Repeat behind.**

19

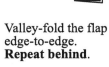

Valley-fold the flap edge-to-edge. **Repeat behind.**

20

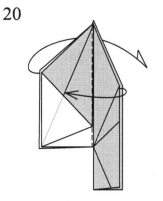

Minor miracle fold. The miracle is more and more minor by the minute. It no longer deserves to be capitalized!

21

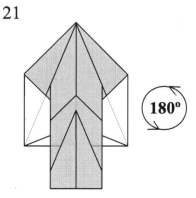

Rotate 180°.

Grizzly Bear Pop-up Card **101**

22

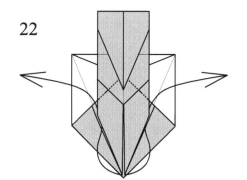

Reverse-fold apart the two middle flaps on the diagonal raw edges.

23

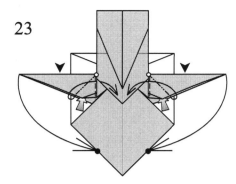

Squash the two flaps on the white dots so that their points touch the raw edges.

24

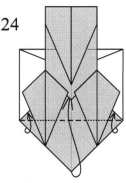

Valley-fold the bottom flap, inserting it behind the front layers.

25

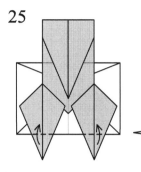

Valley-fold the flaps on the horizontal edge. Zoom in on the model.

26

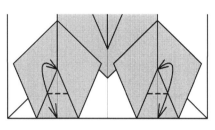

Valley-fold the flaps point-to-point and unfold.

27

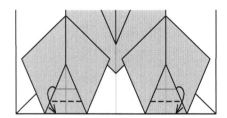

Valley-fold the flaps so that the existing crease touches the bottom edge.

28

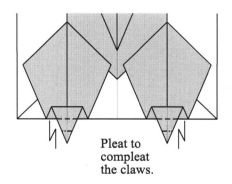

Pleat to compleat the claws.

29

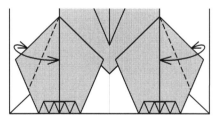

The claws are compleated! Valley-fold the flaps edge-to-edge and unfold.

30

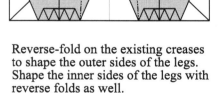

Reverse-fold on the existing creases to shape the outer sides of the legs. Shape the inner sides of the legs with reverse folds as well.

PERFORM IT!

Say to the audience, **"Ready, set, everyone say, 'Pop-up!"** [Audience says, "Pop-up"] Open the card and ask, **"What is it?"** [Audience says, "A bear!"] Respond, **"Everyone growl like a Bear!"** [Audience growls.] Exclaim, **"Stop! You're scaring me! I can't "bear" it anymore!** [Audience will probably start growling even more.] If so, say, **"Ok, that's it! You're all under arrest for being too scary!"**

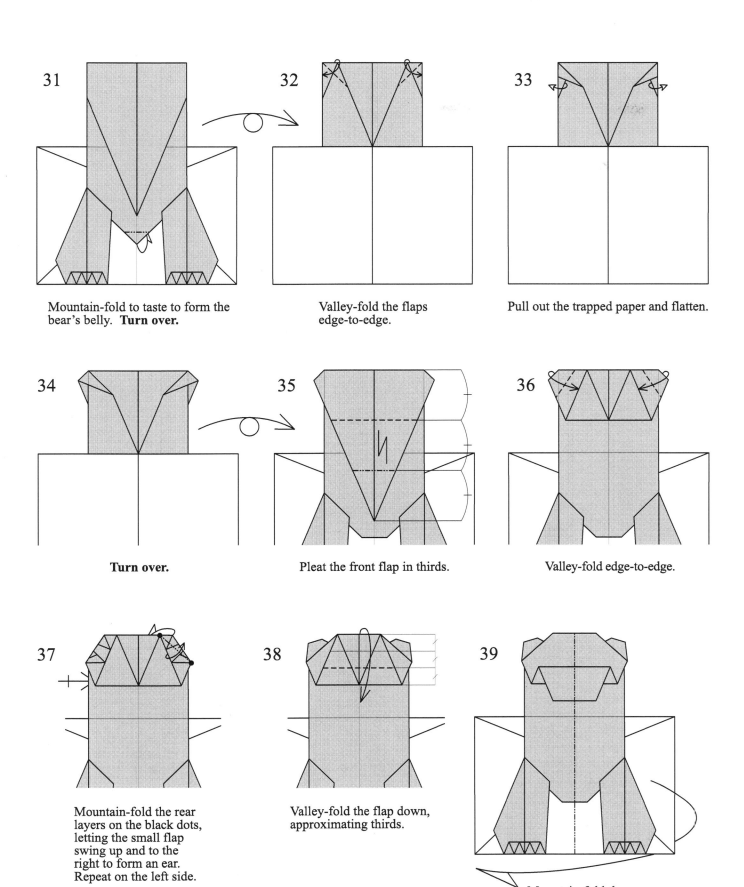

Grizzly Bear Pop-up Card

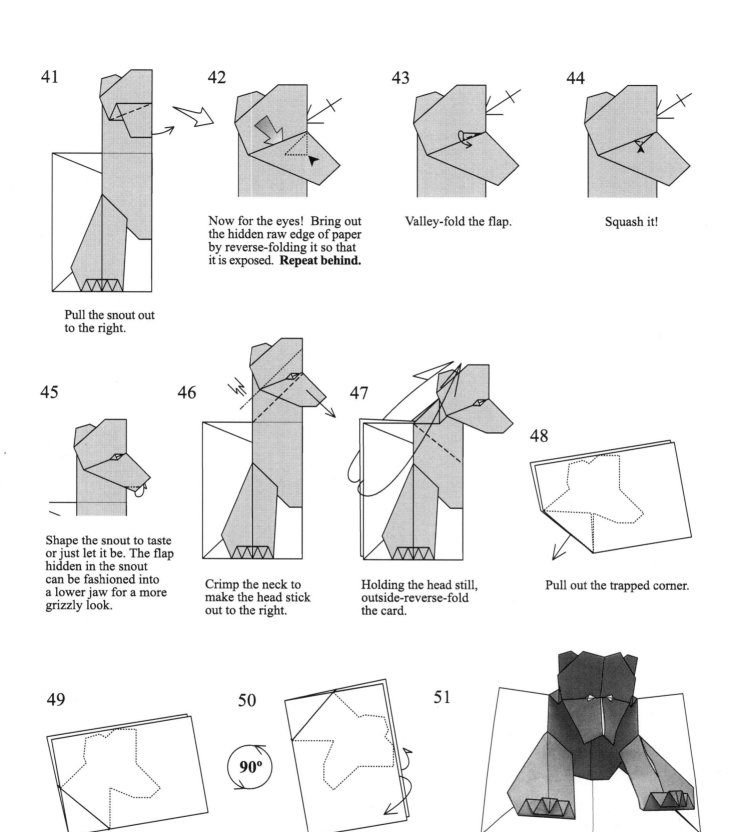

Fantasy Pop-Ups

This short chapter is devoted to creatures that don't really exist, or do they??? Folding origami fantasy creatures is a fantastic way to make them real! For example, if someone asks you, "Do dragons really exist?," you can hold up an origami dragon and reply, **"Yes, origami dragons really do exist!"** I always act like the origami models in my box are real, which opens the door for children's imaginations to run wild!

Now, time for a little performance Q&A!

Question: How can you keep an audience entertained by just showing them origami models?

Answer: As I mentioned in the intro, the key to keeping an audience engaged and entertained is to use these four elements: suspense, surprise, amazement and humor. The routines in the "Perform It!" boxes use these elements and they also get the audience to participate, not just watch, which is another key to a successful origami show. I recommend practicing the "Perform It!" routines on friends and family to get comfortable and confident using origami as a performance art. Try to come up with new acts too!

Another key to keeping the audience entertained by an origami show is to eliminate any dead time between models. That's why I like to show them in rapid succession; as I put one model back in the box, I'm already pulling out the next! I also like to bring audiences as close to me as practical, making the show up-close and personal and, that way, more captivating. And, lastly, I speak with excitement, which tends to be contagious!

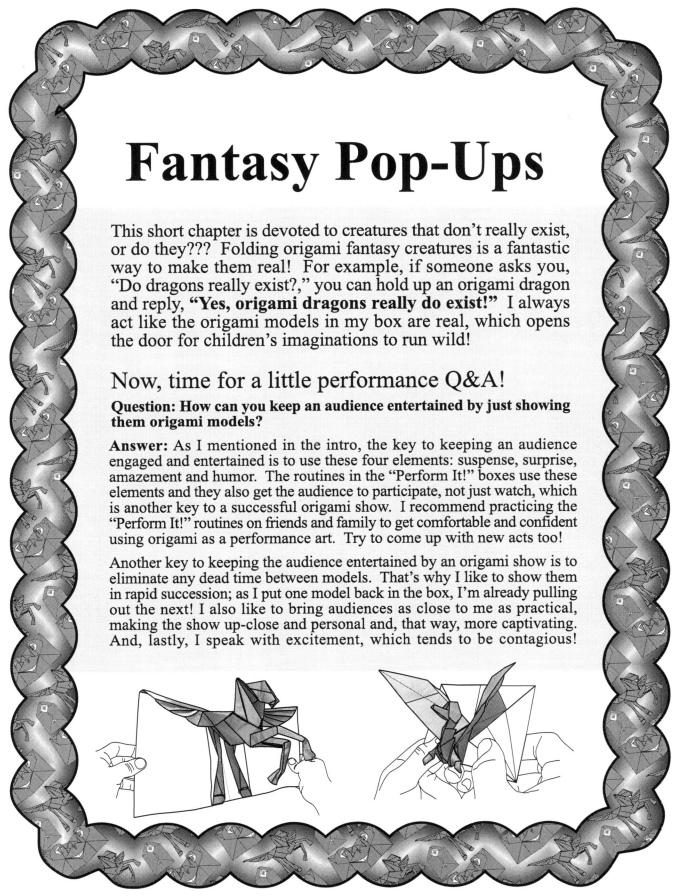

Pippy Cyclops Pop-up Card

By Jeremy Shafer ©2007

Everyone "k**nose**" why this model can be called a pop-up card, but did you know that Cyclopes can forge lightning bolts, helmets of invisibility and tridents of immense power? This one can't do all that, but it can open its mouth!

Super Simple

1. White side up, Valley-fold diagonally in half and unfold in both directions.

2. Valley-fold each edge to the horizontal diagonal and unfold.

3. Valley-fold on the black dots.

4. Valley-fold lining up with the vertical crease.

5. Repeat steps 3-4 on the right side.

6. Fold the flap to the left.

7. Valley-fold both layers and valley-fold again to ensure that the two flaps stay together. Make the folds sharp.

8. Valley-fold the united flaps to the right.

9. Valley-fold corner-to-point and unfold.

10. Valley-fold corner-to-point and unfold.

11. Valley-fold the white dots to the creases.

12. Valley-fold corner-to-corner.

13. Valley-fold on the white dot, point-to-edge.

106 *Origami Pop-ups*

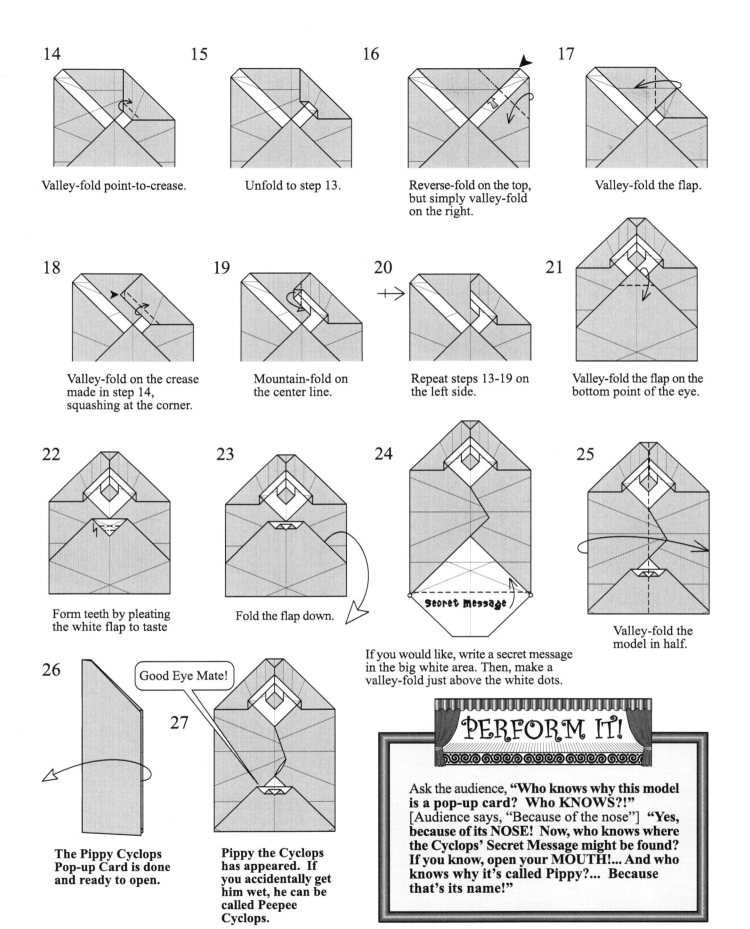

E.T. Pop-up Card

By Jeremy Shafer ©2002

Here's a great model to send to family members living in distant galaxies. Gray paper, not green, is recommended because otherwise many people will mistake it for a frog, but that might not be so bad if you are giving it as a birthday present to an amphibian.

1

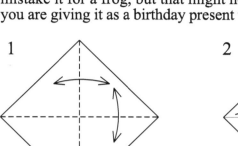

White side up, valley-fold in half diagonally and unfold in both directions.

2

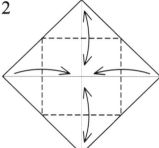

Valley-fold all four corners to the center. Unfold the top and bottom corners.

3

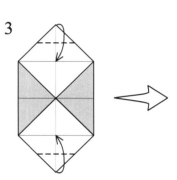

Valley-fold to the intersection of creases.

4

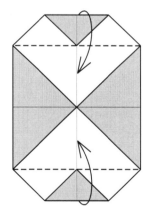

Look, it's a simple heart card! Valley-fold on existing creases.

5

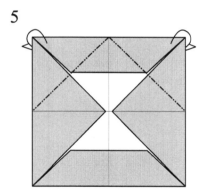

Mountain-fold the top corners to the center.

6

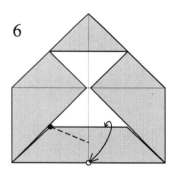

Valley-fold the flap on the black dot so that the edge touches the white dot and unfold; the crease extends from the black dot to the middle crease.

7

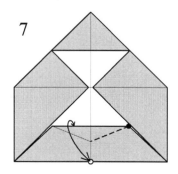

Repeat step 6 on the right side.

8

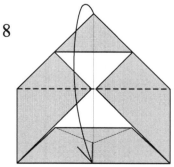

Valley-fold top-to-bottom.

9

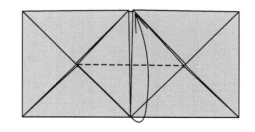

Valley-fold the flap to the top.

108 *Origami Pop-ups*

10

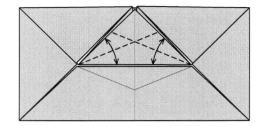

Valley-fold the front flap edge-to-edge and unfold on both sides.

11

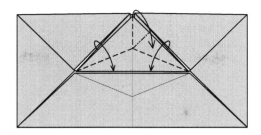

Rabbit-ear the flap. What's a rabbit ear? See page 13.

12

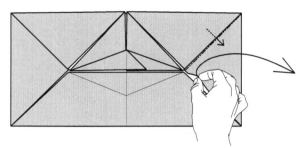

Pull the raw edge rightward, pulling paper out from under the front layer, and flatten.

13

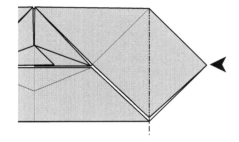

Reverse-fold on the existing creases.

14

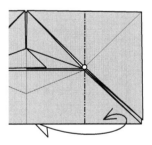

Mountain-fold vertically on the white dot and unfold.

15

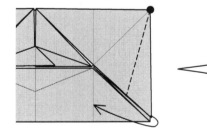

Valley-fold the flap on the black dot, corner-to-crease.

16

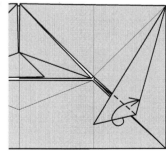

Valley-fold the flap edge-to-edge.

17

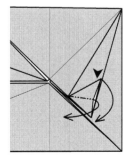

Squash it!
(or squish it but don't mush it or bullsh it!)

18

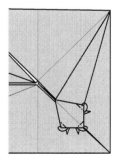

Mountain-fold the iris-to-be, rounding it to taste.

E.T. Pop-up Card **109**

19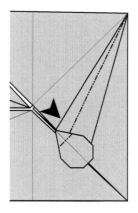

Open-sink to taste. This requires completely unfolding the flap. What's a sink? See page 14. If you can't manage this step, skipping it is much better than tearing up the model.

20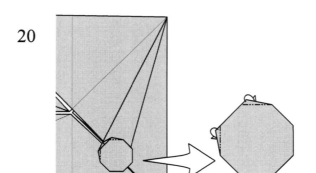

Mountain-fold to complete the octagon. Round it to taste. To me, perfect octagons are tasteful, but the last three steps were so unguidelined that any round shape you can achieve is quite alright!

21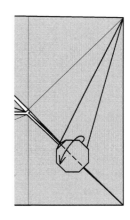

Valley-fold the flap.

22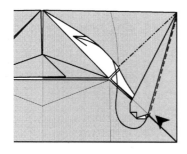

Reverse-fold.

23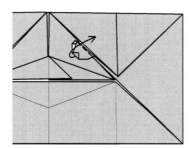

Valley-fold the flap, exposing the full iris.

24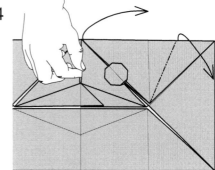

Rotate the flap rightward, so that it points straight up as pictured in the next step, and flatten.

25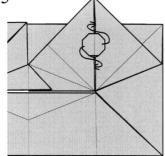

Hide the iris behind the front layer.

26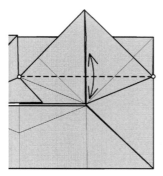

Valley-fold the flap on the white dots and unfold.

27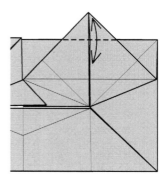

Valley-fold even with the top edge.

110 *Origami Pop-ups*

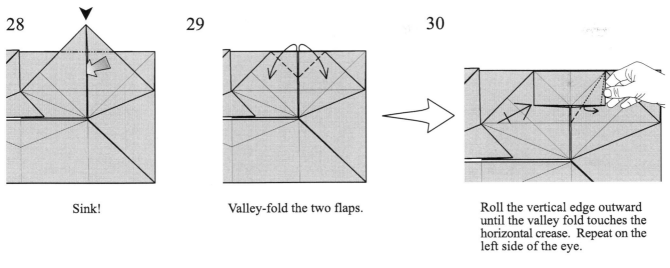

28 Sink!

29 Valley-fold the two flaps.

30 Roll the vertical edge outward until the valley fold touches the horizontal crease. Repeat on the left side of the eye.

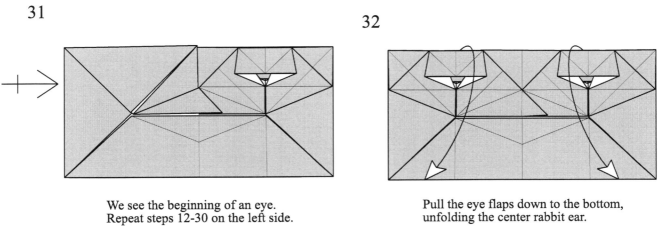

31 We see the beginning of an eye. Repeat steps 12-30 on the left side.

32 Pull the eye flaps down to the bottom, unfolding the center rabbit ear.

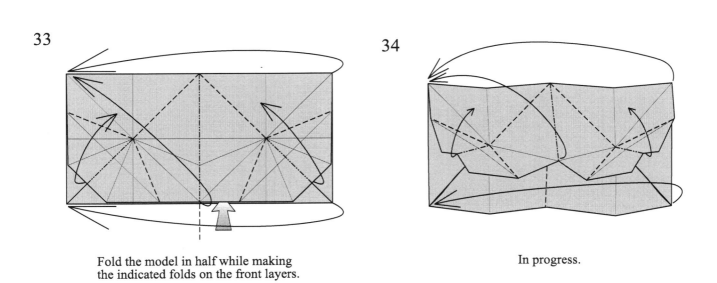

33 Fold the model in half while making the indicated folds on the front layers.

34 In progress.

E.T. Pop-up Card **111**

35

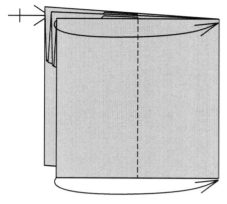

The card has taken shape.
Valley-fold corner-to-corner.
Repeat behind.

36

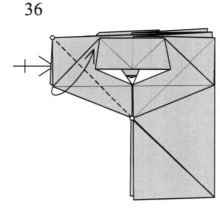

The model looks like a sleepy dragon's head. This is a good stopping place if it's nap time. Otherwise, valley-fold the flap on the white dots. **Repeat behind.**

37

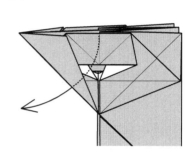

Pull out the flap from inside the model.

38

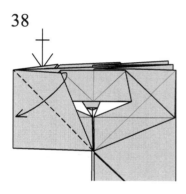

Valley-fold. **Repeat behind.**

39

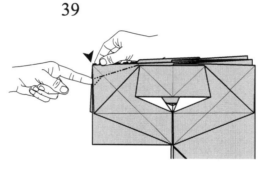

Reverse-fold the top to taste to form the nose; this requires applying force to the middle layer of the left side.

40

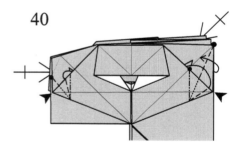

Make reverse folds on the black dots; the mountain folds are vertical; the valley fold on the right is edge-to-crease; the valley fold on the left is to taste. **Repeat behind.**

41

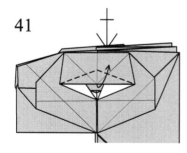

Valley-fold the raw edge to form the eyelid. Let the model take on a 3-D shape to avoid tearing the paper. **Repeat behind.**

42

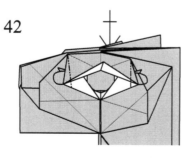

Mountain-fold to round the eye. Round further if desired. **Repeat behind.**

43

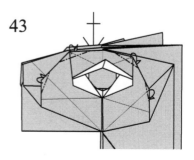

Mountain-fold to round the, shall we say, eyebrow? **Repeat behind.**

44

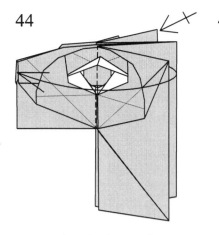

Swing the front and back flaps leftward. **Repeat behind.**

45

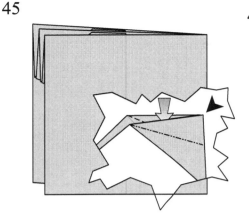

Tear-away view. Reverse-fold on existing creases (made in steps 6 and 7) to form the lower jaw.

46

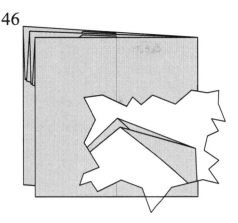

Like this!

47

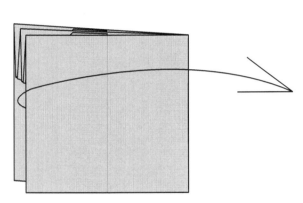

The ET Pop-up Card is ready to open...

PERFORM IT!

Hold up the closed card and say to the audience, **"Ready, set, everyone say, 'Pop-up!'"** [Audience says, "Pop-up!"] Open the model and say, **"What is it?"** [Audience says, "ET" or "Frog."] Reply, **"E.T.! Who want's to get eaten by E.T.?"** If you folded the model big enough, you can put it over their heads. Otherwise, you can have it just nibble on their fingers as you ventriloquistically say, **"Hmmm, your fingers are delicious! And nutritious!"**

48

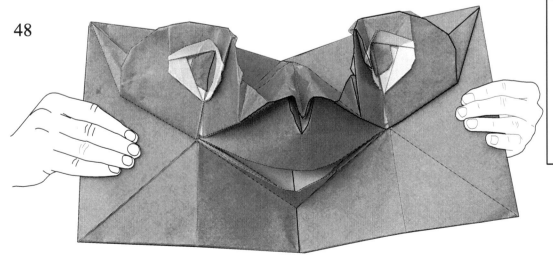

Note: I would have made this E.T. look a lot more like the one in the movie, but then I might have gotten sued by Universal Pictures. What? You don't believe me? Well, at least it's a fine excuse!

E.T. is popped up! Pull on the sides and he will talk. Made out of huge paper, E.T. can actually eat small origami models, though that really isn't part of his character. The E.T. in the above picture, made from a 28-inch square of paper, can even eat my head, well, at least enough of it to make for a good a hat!

E.T. Pop-up Card **113**

Flapping
Dragon Pop-up Card

By Jeremy Shafer ©2005 *Intermediate*

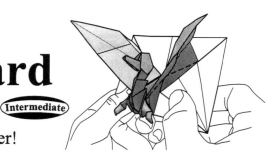

This is a great greeting card to give to a dragon slayer!

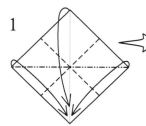
1. White side up, fold a Square Base (page 15).

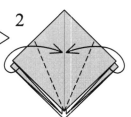
2. Valley-fold the front flaps edge-to-crease.

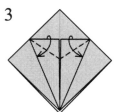
3. Valley-fold the flaps edge-to-edge.

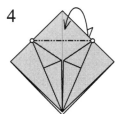
4. Mountain-fold on the white dots and unfold.

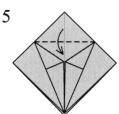
5. Valley-fold, reversing the crease.

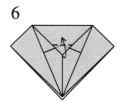
6. Valley-fold on the intersection of edges.

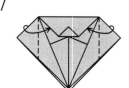
7. Valley-fold, edge-to-edge.

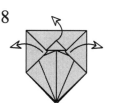
8. Unfold to step 2.

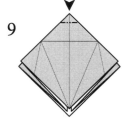
9. Sink. What's a sink? See page 14.

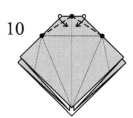
10. Valley-fold the front flaps on the dots. Go to step 11 at the bottom of the page.

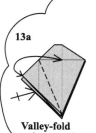
13a. Valley-fold point-to-point and unfold. Repeat behind.

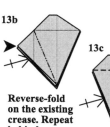
13b. Reverse-fold on the existing crease. Repeat behind.

13c. Valley-fold the front flap. Repeat behind.

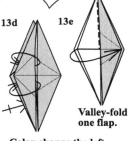
13d.

13e. Valley-fold one flap.

Color-change the left front flap by wrapping the raw edge behind the flap. To do this cleanly, partially unfold the model. Repeat behind.

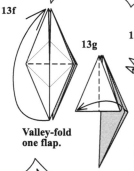
13f.

13g. Valley-fold one flap.

Valley-fold.

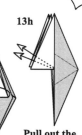
13h. Pull out the interior layers leftward.

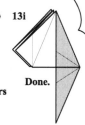
13i. Done.

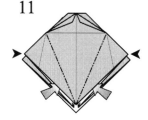
11. Reverse-fold the front flaps on the existing creases.

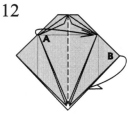
12. Minor Miracle Fold: Fold flap **A** to the right and fold flap **B** behind to the left.

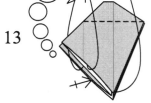
13. Here's a tricky step. Valley-fold the front and rear flaps up while incorporating outside reverse folds on the layers of the left side. Partially unfolding the model is necessary to complete this step cleanly. If you can't figure this step out, look up into the cloud for an easier but longer method of getting to step 14.

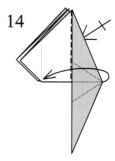
14. Valley-fold one flap to the left. **Repeat behind.**

114 *Origami Pop-ups*

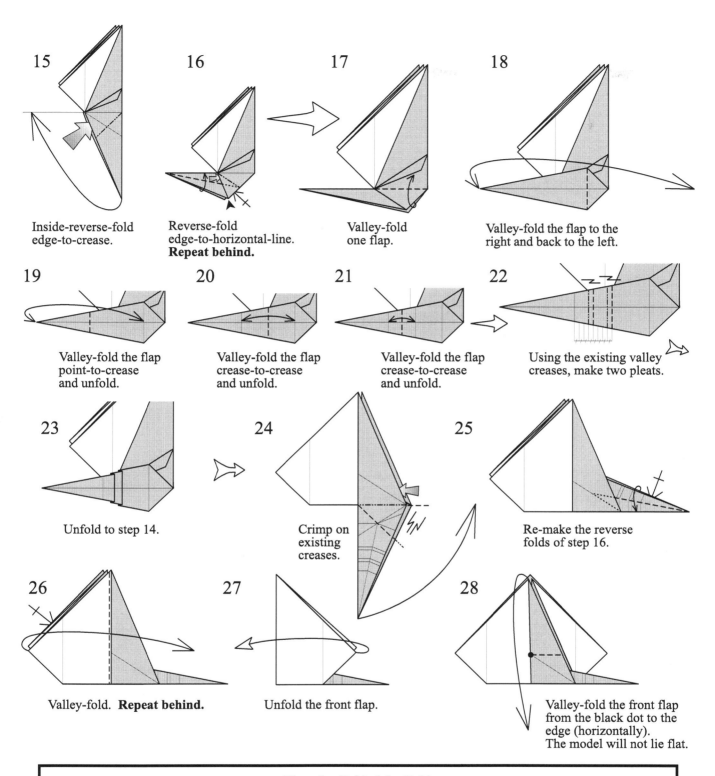

Thoughts Behind the Folds

For the last few years I've been on an origami pop-up card campaign, so the idea to design a Pop-up Dragon came very naturally. My first attempts were to use the same base as my Pegasus Pop-up, but found that the head just wasn't long enough. So then I decided to try to work directly from my Dragon (based on Robert Neale's Dragon). I unfolded the hind legs and tail and realized the model still looked like a dragon. So, with the unfolded paper I set out to make a card, which was not difficult. The flapping mechanism came later from experimenting. The process of replacing the rear end of an origami animal with a card really opens the door to a whole host of possible new animal pop-up cards. Anyone care to tackle John Montroll's Stegosaurus?

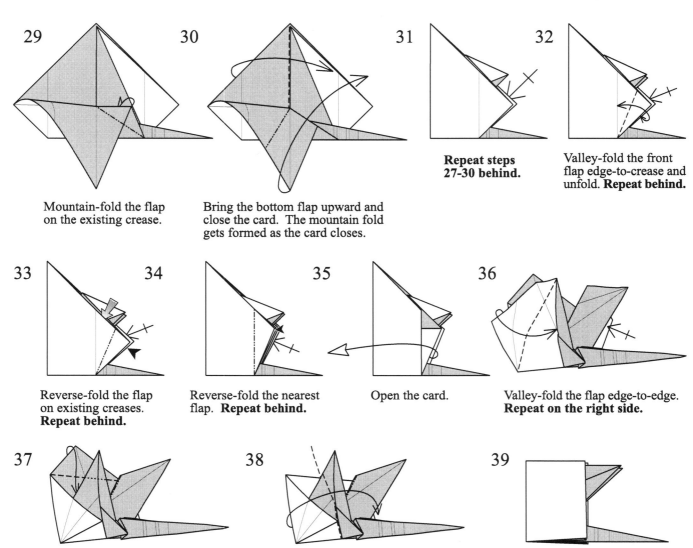

29. Mountain-fold the flap on the existing crease.

30. Bring the bottom flap upward and close the card. The mountain fold gets formed as the card closes.

31. Repeat steps 27-30 behind.

32. Valley-fold the front flap edge-to-crease and unfold. **Repeat behind.**

33. Reverse-fold the flap on existing creases. **Repeat behind.**

34. Reverse-fold the nearest flap. **Repeat behind.**

35. Open the card.

36. Valley-fold the flap edge-to-edge. **Repeat on the right side.**

37. Valley-fold the rear flap and insert the corner into the sink made in step 9.

38. Close the card. The folds on the wings happen naturally when the card is closed.

39. Like this. The next view is a cutaway.

PERFORM IT!

Hold up the closed card and say to the audience, **"I'm going to tell you what this one is. It's a dragon, that will pop-up, spread its wings, fly around, and it might even breathe FIRE! Ready, set, everyone say, 'Pop-up!'"** [Audience says, "Pop-up!"] Open the model and say, **"Here's the dragon... It spread its wings, it's flying over your heads, It's about to breathe fire! No, it's not going to breathe fire, do you know why?"** To whatever the audience says, reply, **"Because it's PAPER, and what would happen if it breathed fire?... It would burn! So, no, it's not going to breathe fire, at least not today!"**

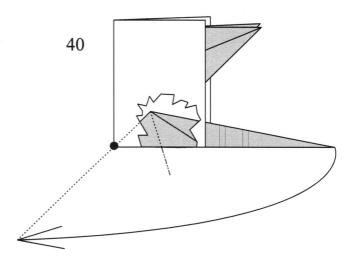

40. Cutaway View. Inside-reverse-fold the flap to the black dot **so that the flap becomes white**; there are two possible slots to choose from that will result in making the flap white. Either one is fine.

116 *Origami Pop-ups*

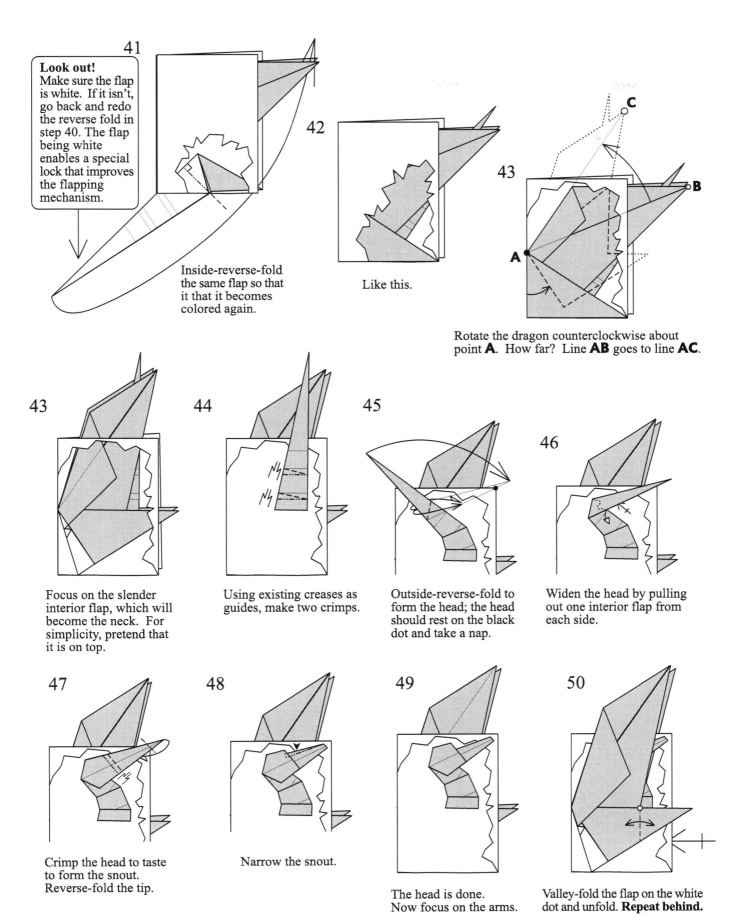

Flapping Dragon Pop-up Card 117

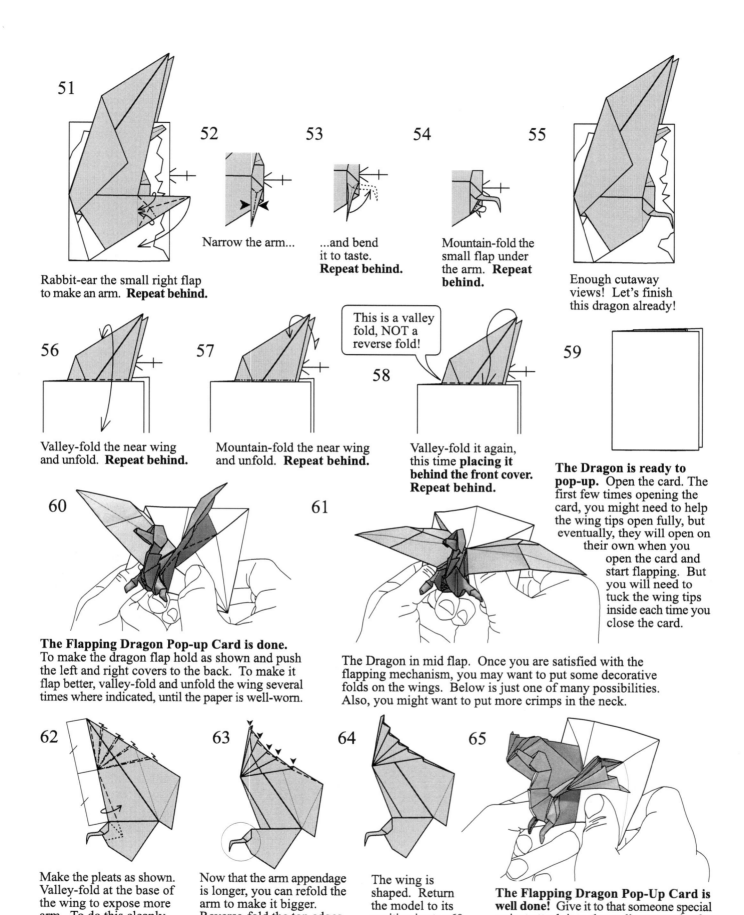

Rearing Pegasus Pop-up

By Jeremy Shafer ©2005

The sky is the limit. Open up and fly away!

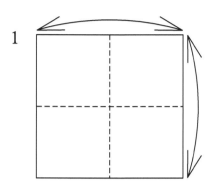

1. A 16-inch square will make a 4-inch square card (when closed). White side up, valley-fold and unfold.

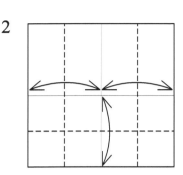

2. Valley-fold edge-to-crease and unfold on three sides.

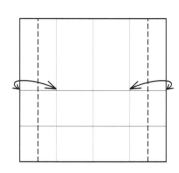

3. Valley-fold edge-to-crease and unfold.

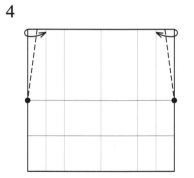

4. Valley-fold on the black dots corner-to-crease and don't unfold!

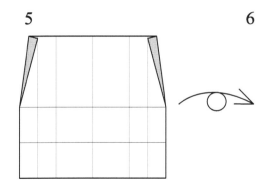

5. **Turn over.**

6. Valley-fold edge-to-crease.

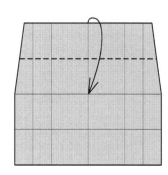

7. **Turn over.**

8. Valley-fold on existing creases.

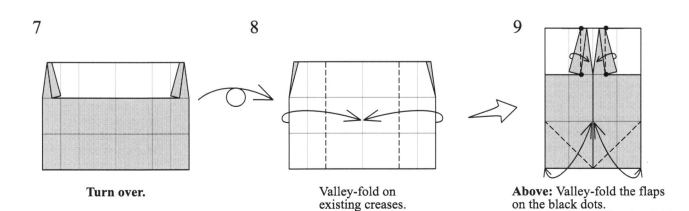

9. **Above:** Valley-fold the flaps on the black dots.
Below: Valley-fold and unfold corner-to-point.

Rearing Pegasus Pop-up Card

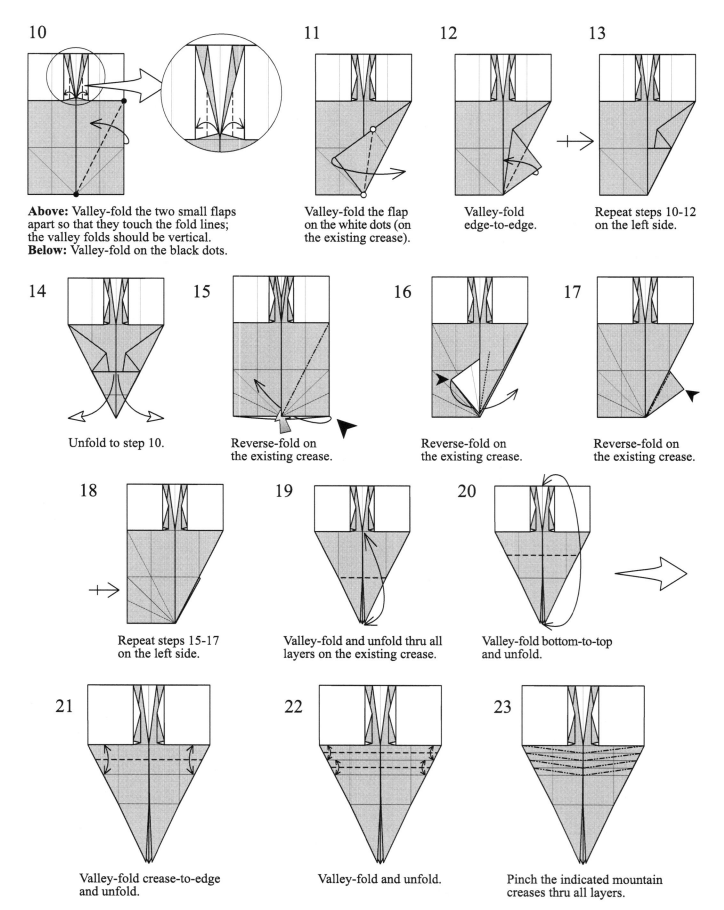

120 *Origami Pop-ups*

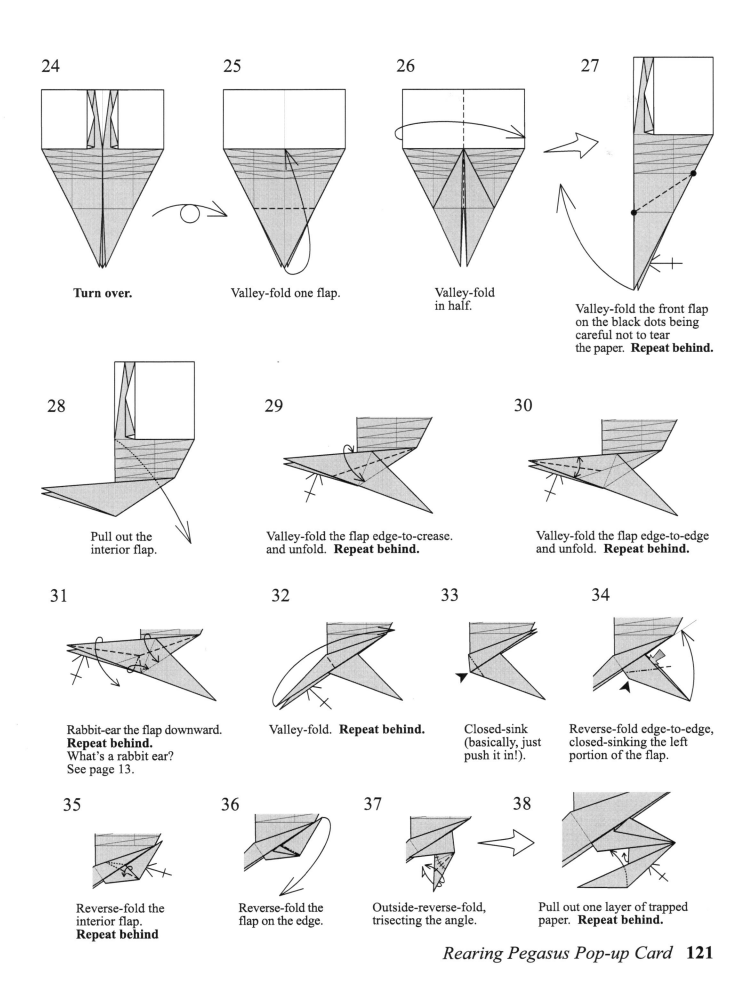

Rearing Pegasus Pop-up Card 121

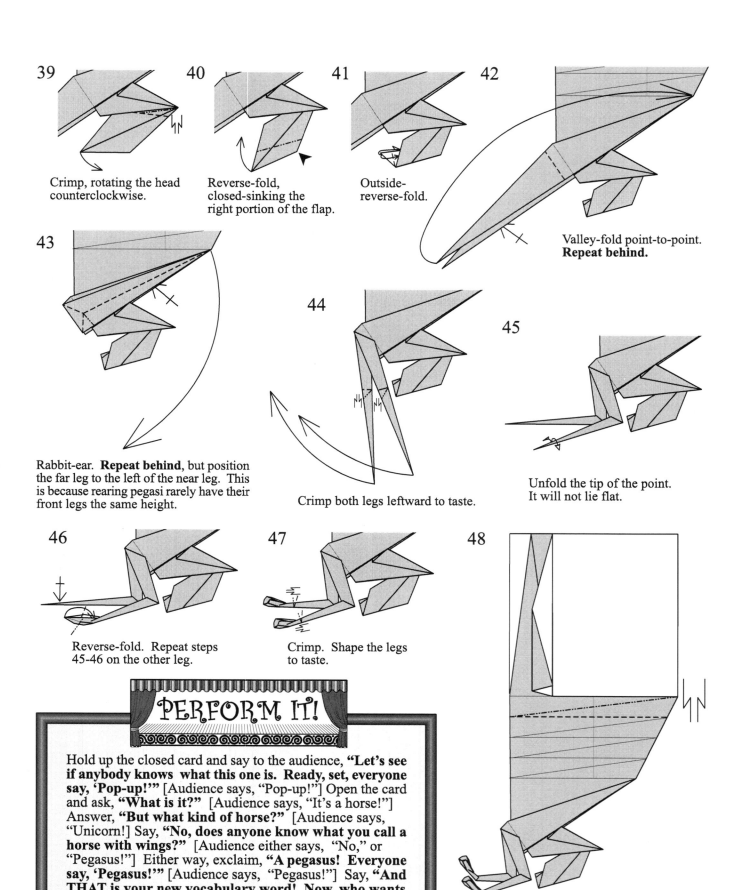

39 Crimp, rotating the head counterclockwise.

40 Reverse-fold, closed-sinking the right portion of the flap.

41 Outside-reverse-fold.

42 Valley-fold point-to-point. **Repeat behind.**

43 Rabbit-ear. **Repeat behind**, but position the far leg to the left of the near leg. This is because rearing pegasi rarely have their front legs the same height.

44 Crimp both legs leftward to taste.

45 Unfold the tip of the point. It will not lie flat.

46 Reverse-fold. Repeat steps 45-46 on the other leg.

47 Crimp. Shape the legs to taste.

48 Crimp on the exiting creases.

PERFORM IT!

Hold up the closed card and say to the audience, **"Let's see if anybody knows what this one is. Ready, set, everyone say, 'Pop-up!'"** [Audience says, "Pop-up!"] Open the card and ask, **"What is it?"** [Audience says, "It's a horse!"] Answer, **"But what kind of horse?"** [Audience says, "Unicorn!"] Say, **"No, does anyone know what you call a horse with wings?"** [Audience either says, "No," or "Pegasus!"] Either way, exclaim, **"A pegasus! Everyone say, 'Pegasus!'"** [Audience says, "Pegasus!"] Say, **"And THAT is your new vocabulary word! Now, who wants to get kicked in the head by a Pegasus?"** Make the Pegasus gently kick any willing volunteers. **"Isn't it so much fun?!"**

49

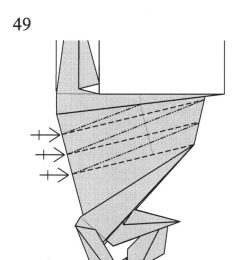

Repeat step 48 three more times.

50

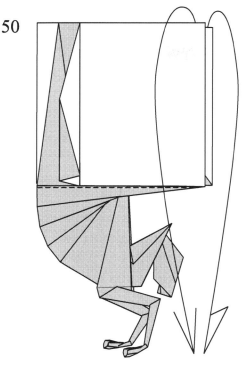

Outside-reverse-fold the card, covering up the pegasus.

51

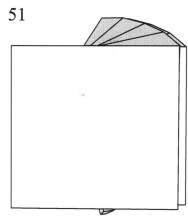

Like this. Try opening and closing the card. If you like the model as is, and if you don't mind the paper that's sticking out the top of the card, then you are welcome to stop here. Otherwise, continue to the next step, which is a cutaway view. Do not really tear the paper!

52

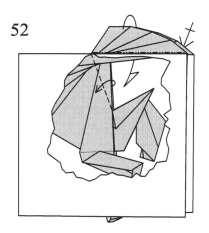

Reverse-fold the extruding flaps into the card. Inside the card the reverse fold extends to the pegasus' neck. **Repeat behind.**

53

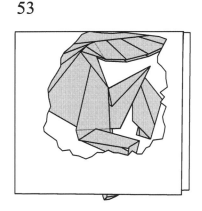

Like this. Shape the pegasus to taste and you're done.

54

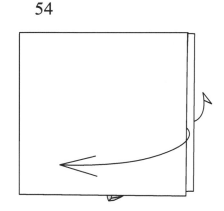

Done! Open Sesame!

55

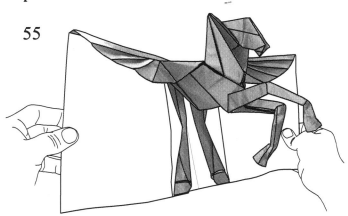

The completed Rearing Pegasus Pop-Up. Open the card as shown and pull the left and right sides apart, and the pegasus will rear up. If you rear up high enough, the pegasus will return to a position similar to step 50 and you can call it, "Pegasus in Flight."

Warning: During operation, keep face at safe distance from model or risk getting bloody nose. Wear safety glasses. Keep out of reach of children.

Rearing Pegasus Pop-up Card **123**

Pop-up People

The theme of this chapter is people pop-up cards, which make great greeting cards because people can relate to people, which include baby people, adult people, snow people, heads of people and quartets of heads of people! And if you think I used the word *people* too many times in the last sentence, then you people are nit-picky people.

Baby on a Bed (Intermediate)

By Jeremy Shafer ©2000

Why wait nine months? Now you can make a baby in about nine minutes and with a lot less labor! AND... no diaper changing, no screaming, no getting woken up 10 times a night, etc.

1.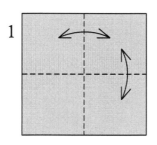
For a white baby on a colored bed, begin colored side up. Valley-fold in half in both directions and unfold.

2.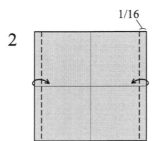
Valley-fold the left and right sides inward. The width of the resulting long slender flap is 1/16th of the side of the square. How can you make it exactly 1/16th? Fold steps 1-4 on page 157.

3.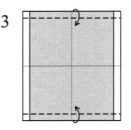
Valley-fold the top and bottom sides inward the same amount.

4.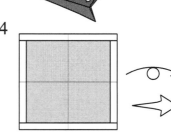
Turn over left to right.

5.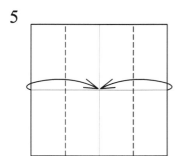
Valley-fold the left and right sides to the middle.

6.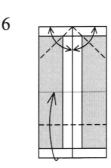
It's a big capital **I**!
Above: Valley-fold the top corners edge-to-edge and unfold.
Below: Valley-fold the bottom edge to the middle crease.

7.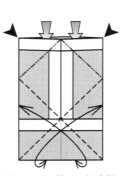
It's a small capital **I**!
Above: Reverse-fold the top corners.
Below: Valley-fold edge-to-edge and unfold on both sides.

8.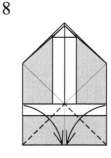
Valley-fold the flaps down if they are not already down.

9.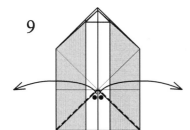
Pull the corners apart as far as they will go and flatten. Watch the black dots.

10.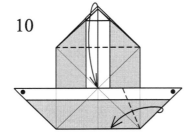
Above: Fold the top down (all layers).
Below: Valley fold the bottom right flap edge-to-edge.

11.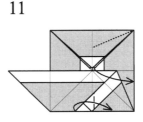
Above: Slide out an arm from behind the front layer and bring it to the right edge of the model and flatten.
Below: Valley-fold the foot to taste.

12.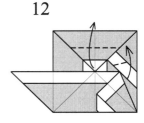
Above: Valley-fold the head as far up as possible.
Below: Valley-fold the arm to taste.

Baby on a Bed

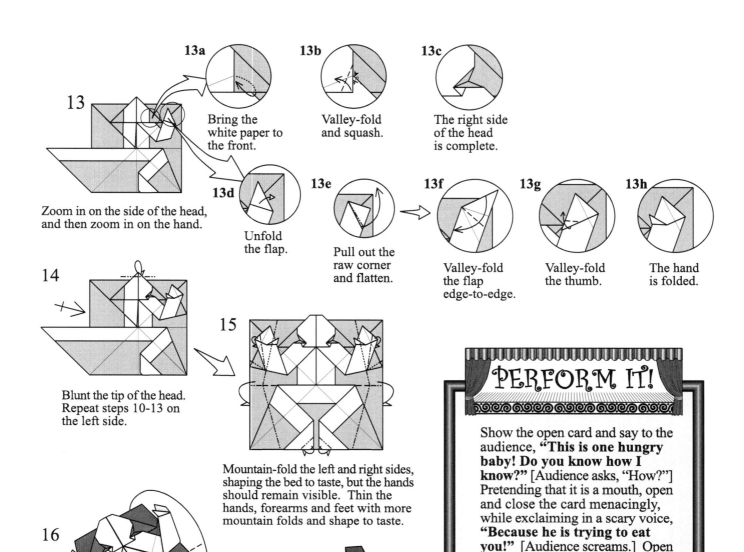

PERFORM IT!

Show the open card and say to the audience, **"This is one hungry baby! Do you know how I know?"** [Audience asks, "How?"] Pretending that it is a mouth, open and close the card menacingly, while exclaiming in a scary voice, **"Because he is trying to eat you!"** [Audience screams.] Open the card and scoldingly yell at the baby, **"Bad baby! Don't try to eat my audience! They're too tough for you to chew!"**

PERFORM IT!

Glance into your origami box and then suddenly turn to the audience and whisper loudly, **"Shhh! I forgot to tell you, I have a baby and (s)he's taking a nap in my origami box, so we have to be quiet."** [Audience raises their eyebrows] **"What, you don't believe me? Do you want me to show him (her) to you? Fine, I will! Ready, set, everyone yell, 'Wake up!'"** [Audience yells, "Wake up!"] Take your baby out of the box and show it off, exclaiming through tears of joy, **"Isn't (s)he so beautiful?! And look, (s)he's still sleeping! Everyone say, 'Aaaawe!'"** [Audience say, "Aaaawe!"] Carefully return the baby to the box and then look up and say admonishingly, **"And you didn't believe me!"**

126 *Origami Pop-ups*

Flapping Jester Head Pop-up Card

By Jeremy Shafer ©2012

Now, whenever you tell a bad joke and the king cries "Off with his head! (or her head)," you can offer him this model and say, "It's already off, your majesty... and it flaps too!"

 1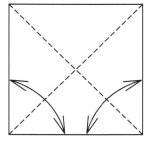

White side up, valley-fold in half diagonally and unfold in both directions.

2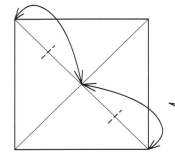

Valley-fold point-to-point and unfold, making two short crease marks.

 3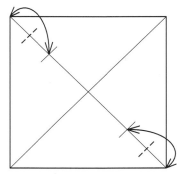

Valley-fold point-to-point and unfold making two more crease marks.

4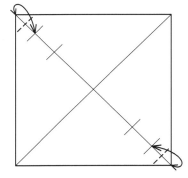

Valley-fold point-to-point and unfold making two more crease marks.

5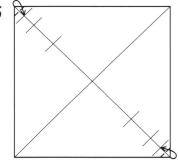

Valley-fold point-to-point and DON'T unfold!

 6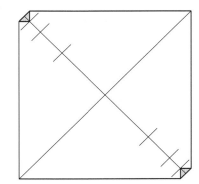

Turn over diagonally.

7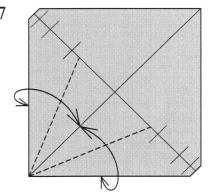

Valley-fold edge-to-crease and unfold; these creases extend to the existing crease.

Flapping Jester Head Pop-up Card **127**

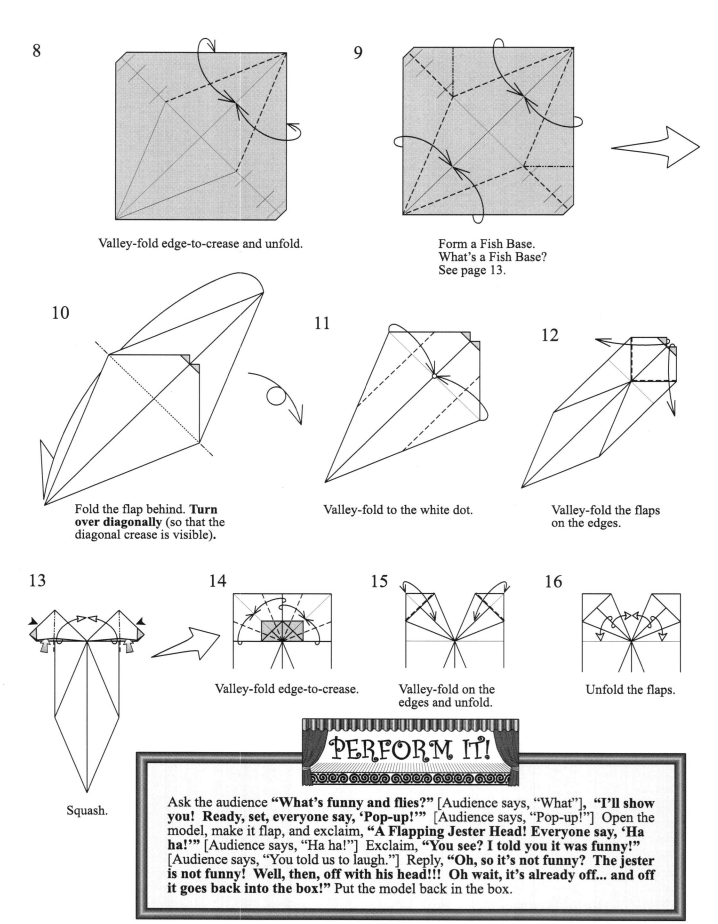

8. Valley-fold edge-to-crease and unfold.

9. Form a Fish Base. What's a Fish Base? See page 13.

10. Fold the flap behind. **Turn over diagonally** (so that the diagonal crease is visible).

11. Valley-fold to the white dot.

12. Valley-fold the flaps on the edges.

13. Squash.

14. Valley-fold edge-to-crease.

15. Valley-fold on the edges and unfold.

16. Unfold the flaps.

PERFORM IT!

Ask the audience **"What's funny and flies?"** [Audience says, "What"], **"I'll show you! Ready, set, everyone say, 'Pop-up!'"** [Audience says, "Pop-up!"] Open the model, make it flap, and exclaim, **"A Flapping Jester Head! Everyone say, 'Ha ha!'"** [Audience says, "Ha ha!"] Exclaim, **"You see? I told you it was funny!"** [Audience says, "You told us to laugh."] Reply, **"Oh, so it's not funny? The jester is not funny! Well, then, off with his head!!! Oh wait, it's already off... and off it goes back into the box!"** Put the model back in the box.

128 *Origami Pop-ups*

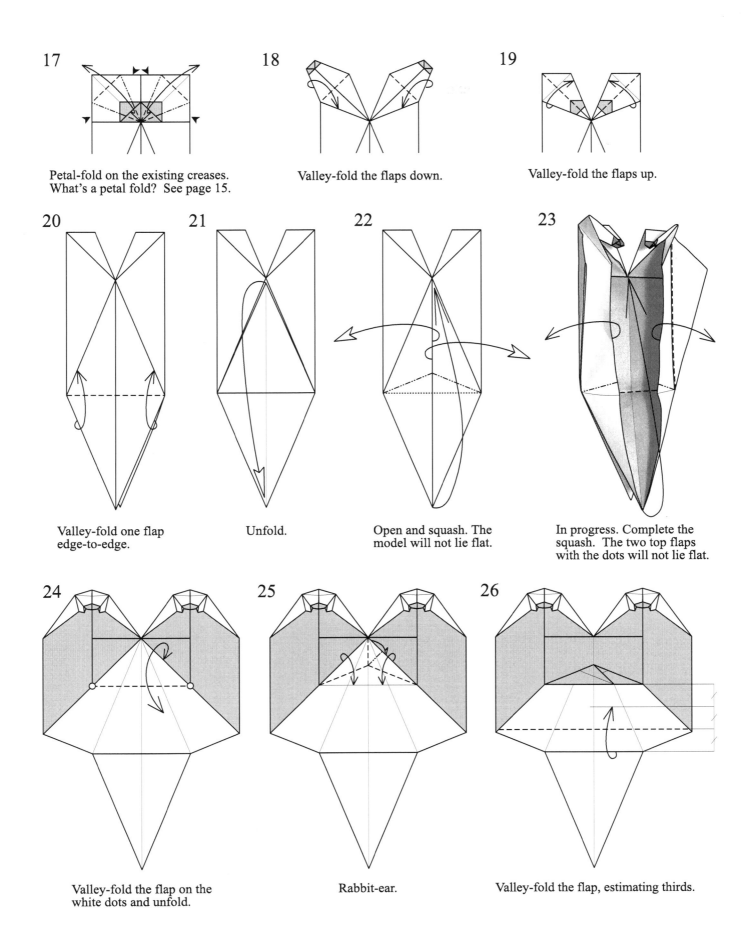

27

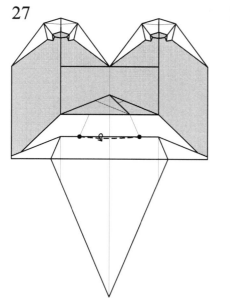

Valley-fold the edge down slightly to suggest a mouth.

28

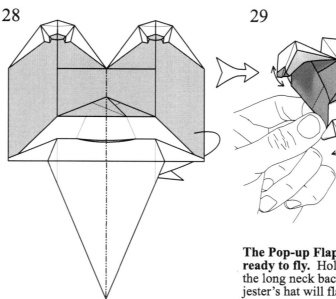

Mountain-fold the model in half.

29

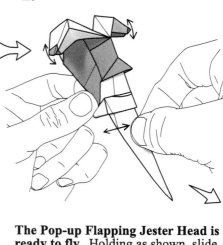

The Pop-up Flapping Jester Head is ready to fly. Holding as shown, slide the long neck back and forth and the jester's hat will flap. To close the Jester Head for storage, follow steps 30-34.

30

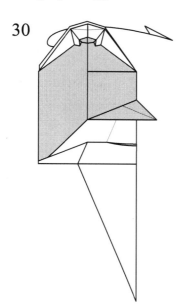

To make the model more compact for storage, first unfold to step 28.

31

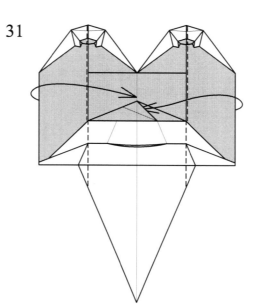

Valley-fold the left and right sides to the middle but keep the nose in front. The model will now lie flat.

32

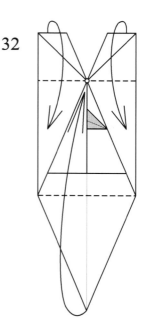

Above: Valley-fold the top flaps down on the white dot.
Below: Valley-fold the bottom flap up to the white dot.

33

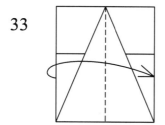

Valley-fold the model in half...

34

...and now you have your very own portable travel jester all set to accompany you on your next trip to Venice.

35

Now, practice returning the model to how it was in step 29 and making it flap. From my experience, audiences are entertained as much by the act of transforming the small rectangle into the large Jester Head as the actual act of making it flap.

Note: This model is based on my Biting Butt Bird (page 246).

Person Doing Sit-ups Card

By Jeremy Shafer ©2005

Sit-ups have never been so easy. Just fold this model and get your exercise done now!

1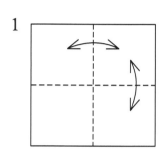

White side up, valley-fold in half and unfold in both directions.

2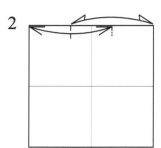

Divide the top edge of the model into thirds by folding the left side in front and the right side to the back.

3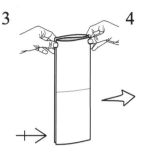

Fiddle with the folds until the thirds are exact. Repeat on the bottom. Unfold.

4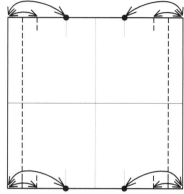

Fold the corners to the black dots and pinch. Unfold. Valley-fold the left and right sides to the new creasemarks and unfold.

5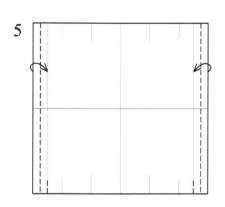

Valley-fold edge-to-crease.

6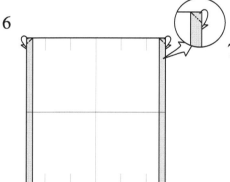

Make a tiny mountain folds on the corners edge-to-crease.

7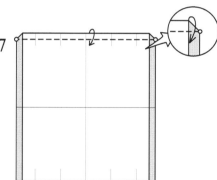

Valley-fold on the white dots.

8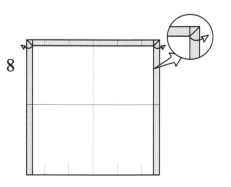

Pull the raw corner out and flatten.

9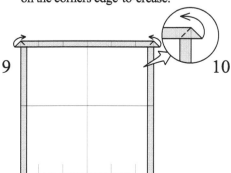

Valley-fold the tiny flaps upward.

10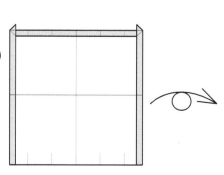

Turn over.

Person Doing Sit-ups Pop-up Card

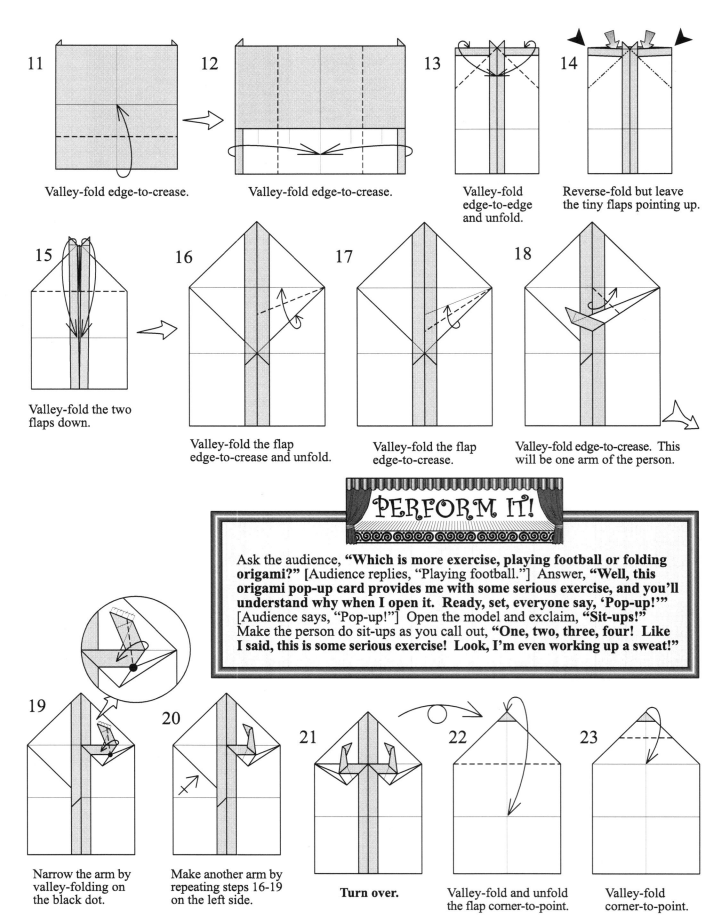

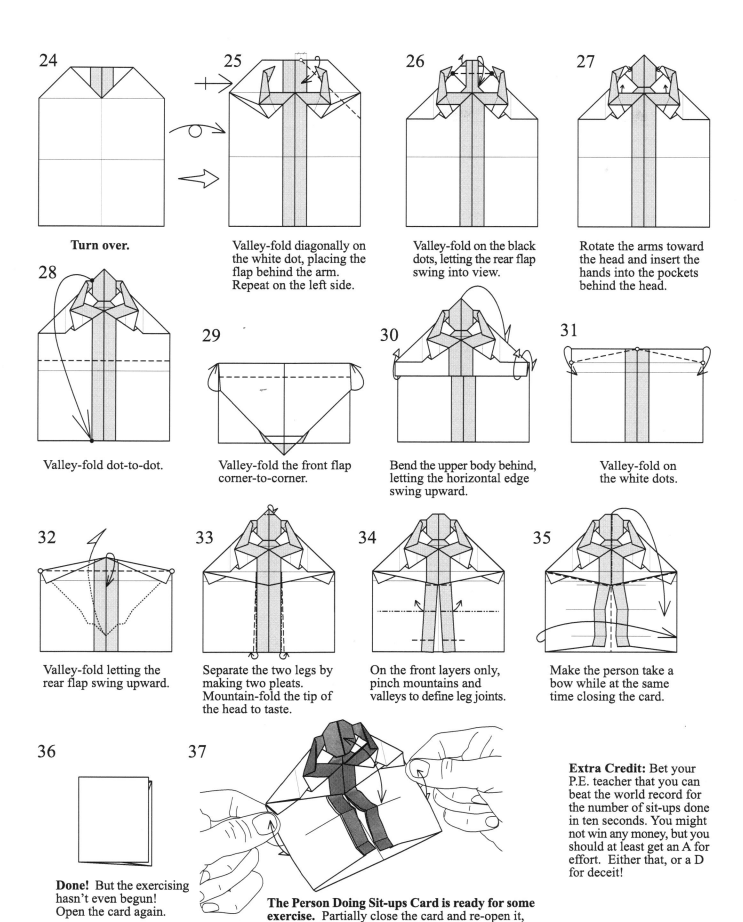

Person Doing Sit-ups Pop-up Card 133

Pop-up Housewife *(Intermediate)*

By Jeremy Shafer ©2009

This model could be dangerous to society, for men might choose not to marry, since now they can simply fold their very own pop-up housewife.

1

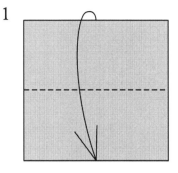

Colored side up, valley-fold in half top-to-bottom.

2

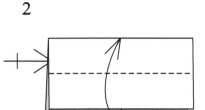

Valley-fold the top layer edge-to-edge. **Repeat behind.**

3

Valley-fold one flap edge-to-edge. **Repeat behind.**

4

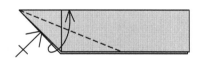

Valley-fold one flap edge-to-edge. **Repeat behind.**

5

Valley-fold edge-to-edge thru all layers.

6

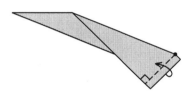

Valley-fold on the black dot.

7

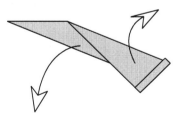

Completely unfold the model.

8

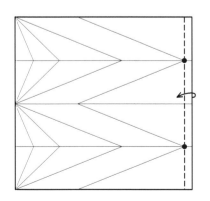

Valley-fold on the black dots.

9

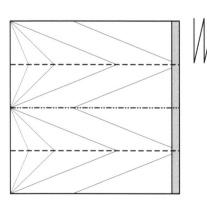

Pleat on existing creases.

Note: You might have noticed, the Housewife, Househusband and $ Cobra Pop-up were also published in my book, *Origami Ooh La La!* I've included them again in this book because these three models are major players in my origami act, and because this is a book of Pop-ups.

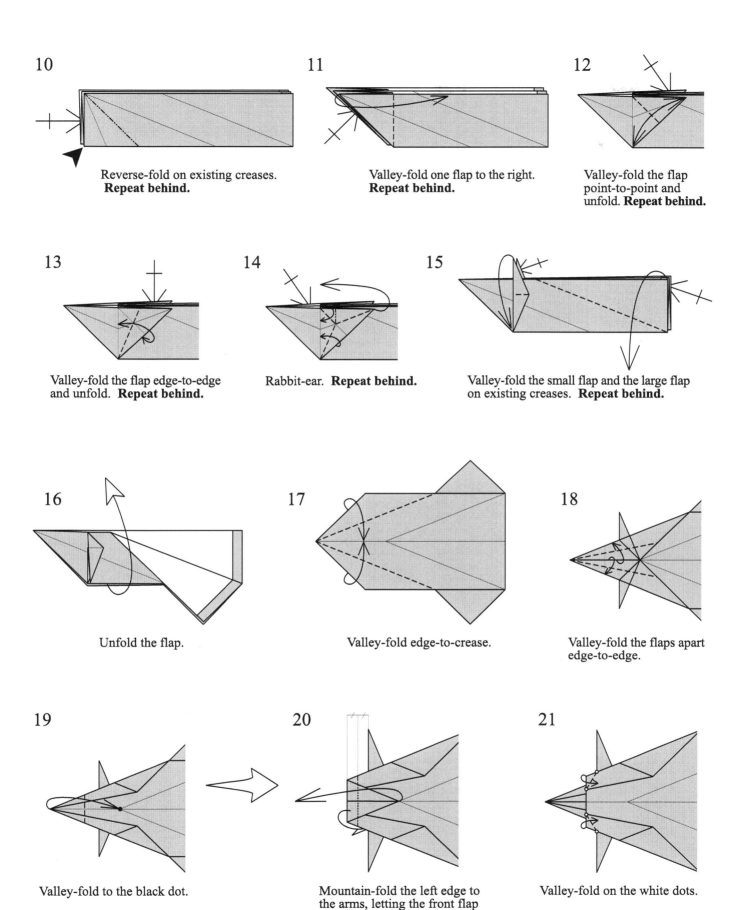

Pop-up Housewife 135

22

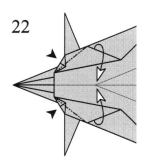

Unfold the two flaps and flatten.

23

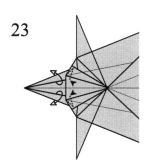

Unfold the two flaps and flatten.

24

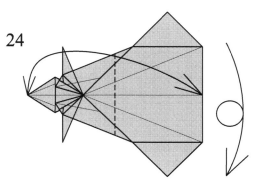

Valley-fold the model in half left-to-right and unfold. **Turn over top-to-bottom.**

25

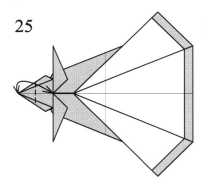

Valley-fold corner-to-point and unfold.

26

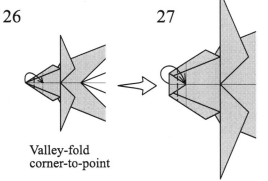

Valley-fold corner-to-point

27

Valley-fold point-to-point.

28

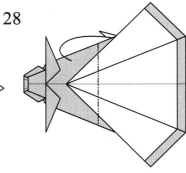

Mountain-fold on the existing crease.

29

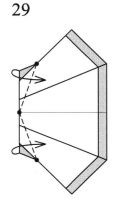

Valley-fold on the black dots.

30

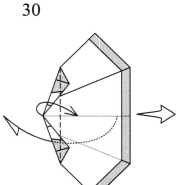

Valley-fold while letting the rear flap swing out to the left.

31

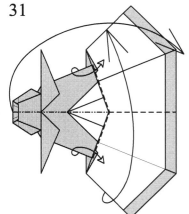

The housewife is recognizable! Following the arrows, fold the head and arms flap to the right while valley-folding the dress in half.

32

Cut-away View

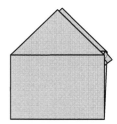

Normal View

The housewife is inside the house, so you could call the model complete, but there is one more tricky fold that will greatly improve its appearance. So, unfold to step 31.

136 *Origami Pop-ups*

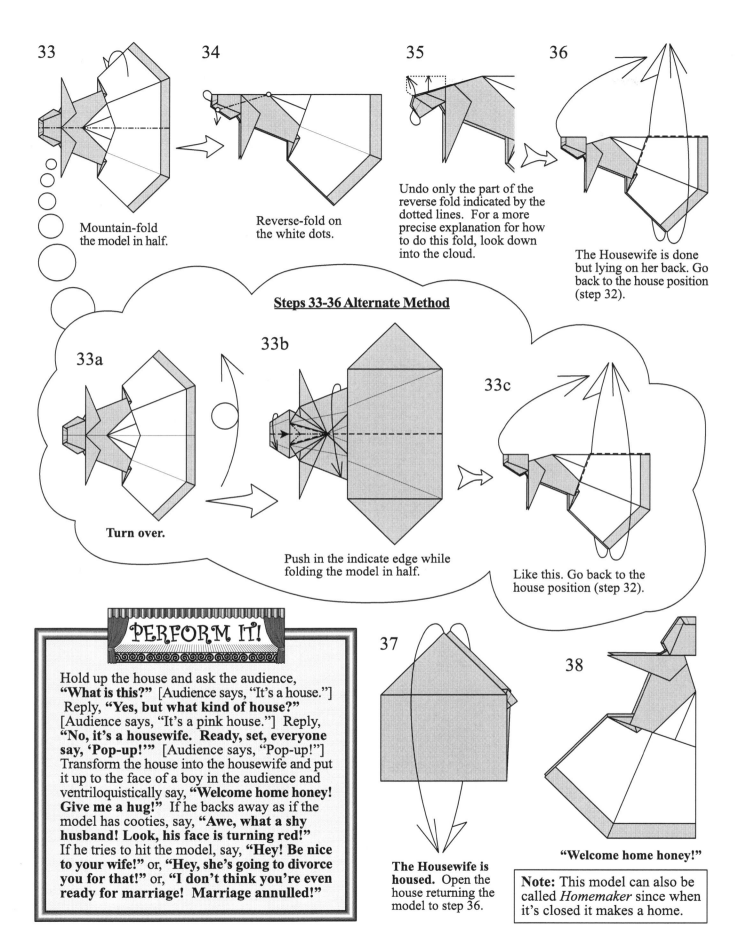

Pop-up Househusband (Intermediate)

By Jeremy Shafer ©2009

Watch out men, you too have competition! Like the Housewife, this model is dangerous too! Ironically, in most politically correct circles, it would be taboo to show the origami housewife unaccompanied by her manly counterpart, the Househusband.

"Welcome home honey... Dinner's in the microwave!"

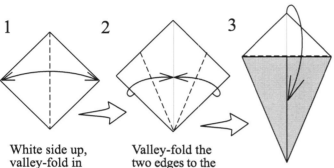

1. White side up, valley-fold in half diagonally and unfold.
2. Valley-fold the two edges to the crease.
3. Valley-fold on the edge. (Don't fall off!)

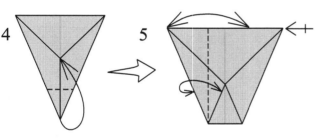 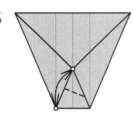 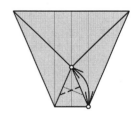

4. Valley-fold corner-to-corner.
5. Valley-fold edge-to-edge and unfold. **Repeat on the right side.**
6. Valley-fold the flap dot-to-dot and unfold.
7. Valley-fold the flap dot-to-dot and unfold.

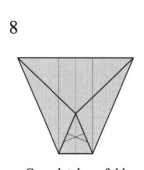 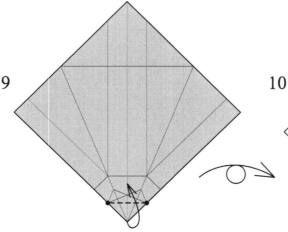 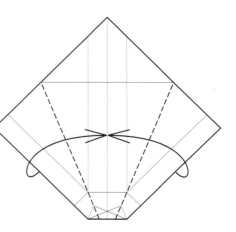

8. Completely unfold the model.
9. Colored side up, valley-fold on the black dots. **Turn over.**
10. Valley-fold on existing creases.

138 *Origami Pop-ups*

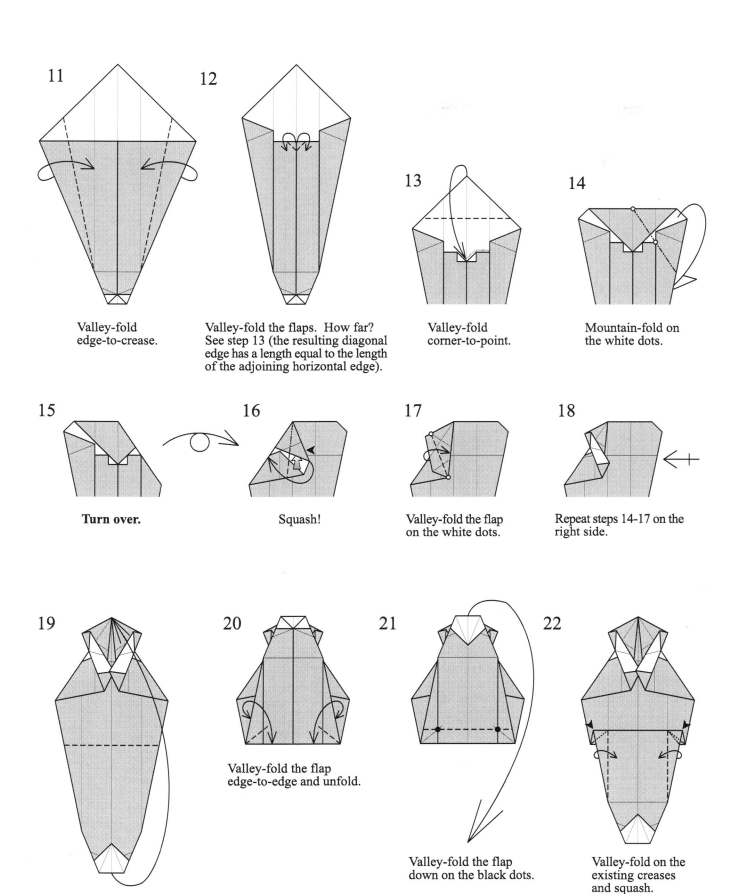

Pop-up Househusband 139

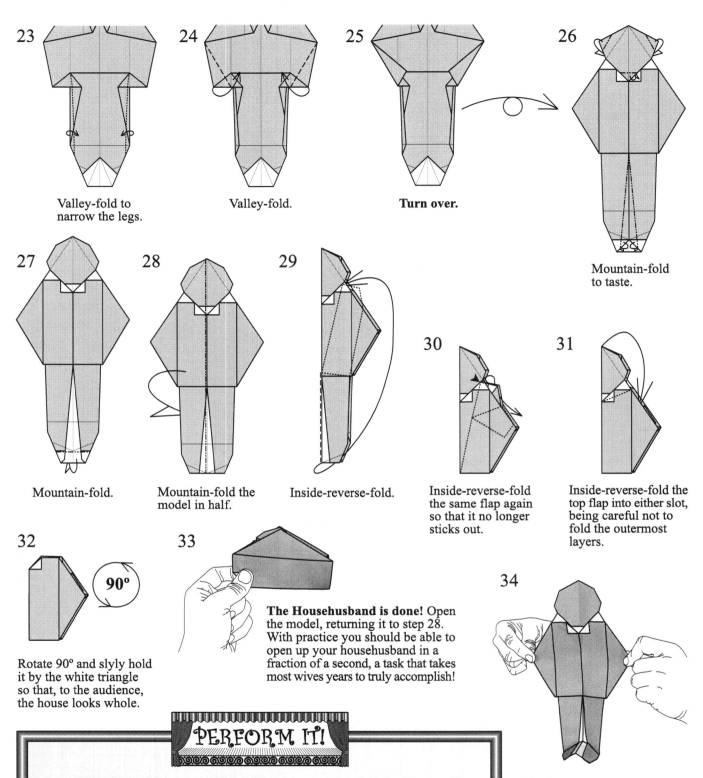

23 Valley-fold to narrow the legs.

24 Valley-fold.

25 **Turn over.**

26 Mountain-fold to taste.

27 Mountain-fold.

28 Mountain-fold the model in half.

29 Inside-reverse-fold.

30 Inside-reverse-fold the same flap again so that it no longer sticks out.

31 Inside-reverse-fold the top flap into either slot, being careful not to fold the outermost layers.

32 Rotate 90° and slyly hold it by the white triangle so that, to the audience, the house looks whole.

33 **The Househusband is done!** Open the model, returning it to step 28. With practice you should be able to open up your househusband in a fraction of a second, a task that takes most wives years to truly accomplish!

34 **The Househusband is complete.** If anyone asks why the husband has no hands, you can answer that his hands are in his pockets because it's winter and the house is cold.

PERFORM IT!

In an origami act, this model should be shown right after the Housewife (page 134). Say to your audience, **"And, just to be fair..."** Hold up the House (page 140, step 33), **"...what do you think this is?"** [Audience says, "A househusband!"] Say, **"Yes! A househusband! Here's the house, and ready, set, everyone say, 'Pop-up!'"** [Audience says, "Pop-up!"] Transform it into the househusband and put it up to the face of a girl in the audience and say, **"Welcome home honey! Dinner's in the microwave!"**

140 *Origami Pop-ups*

Snowman Pop-up Card

By Jeremy Shafer ©2009

Now you can make a snowman without freezing your hands off! Even better, this snowman will last through summer!

Intermediate

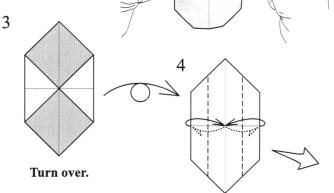

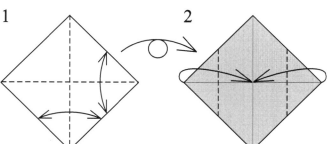

1. White side up, valley-fold in half diagonally and unfold in both directions. **Turn over.**

2. Valley-fold the left and right corners to the center.

3. **Turn over.**

4. Valley-fold the left and right sides to the middle, letting the two rear flaps swing back into view.

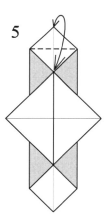
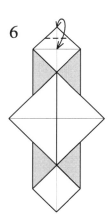
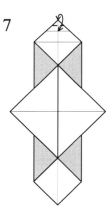
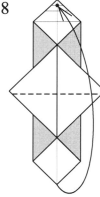
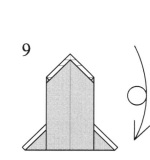

5. Valley-fold corner-to-point and unfold.

6. Valley-fold corner-to-point and unfold.

7. Valley-fold corner-to-point and unfold.

8. Valley-fold to the black dot.

9. **Turn over top-to-bottom.**

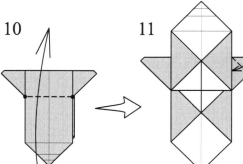
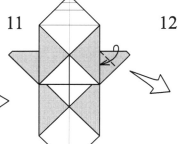
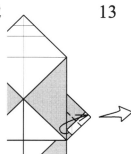
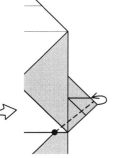
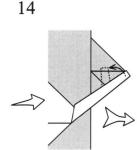

10. Valley-fold the flap on the black dots.

11. Valley-fold edge-to-edge.

12. Valley-fold the flap edge-to-edge.

13. Valley-fold the flap on the black dot.

14. Slide a thumb out from behind the front layer.

Snowman Pop-up Card **141**

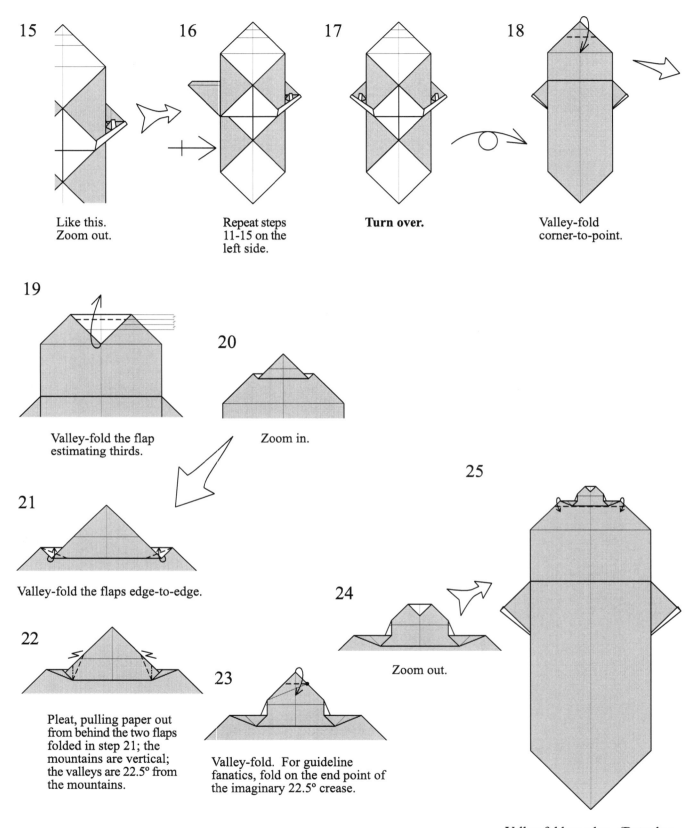

142 *Origami Pop-ups*

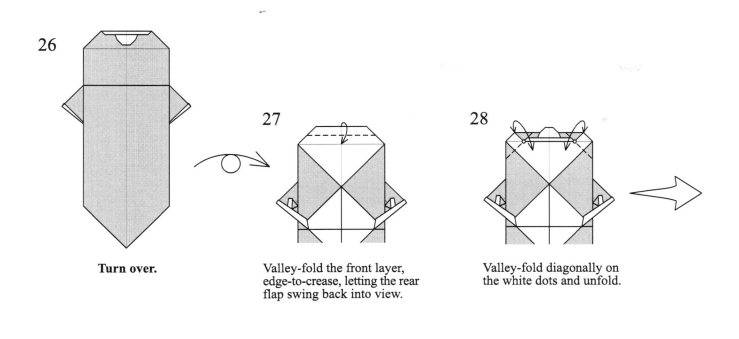

26 **Turn over.**

27 Valley-fold the front layer, edge-to-crease, letting the rear flap swing back into view.

28 Valley-fold diagonally on the white dots and unfold.

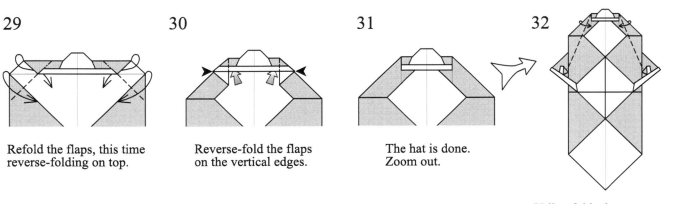

29 Refold the flaps, this time reverse-folding on top.

30 Reverse-fold the flaps on the vertical edges.

31 The hat is done. Zoom out.

32 Valley-fold edge-to-crease.

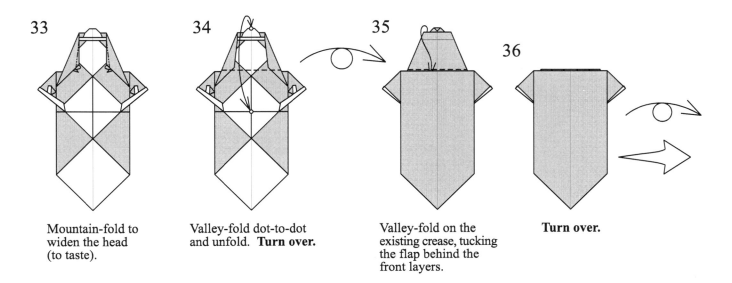

33 Mountain-fold to widen the head (to taste).

34 Valley-fold dot-to-dot and unfold. **Turn over.**

35 Valley-fold on the existing crease, tucking the flap behind the front layers.

36 **Turn over.**

Snowman Pop-up Card

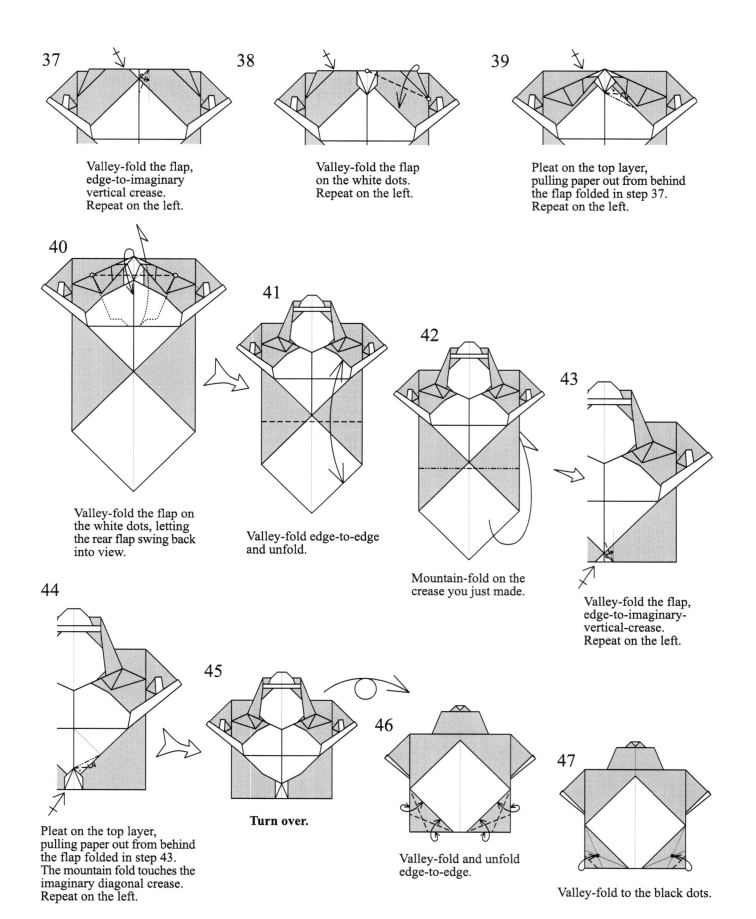

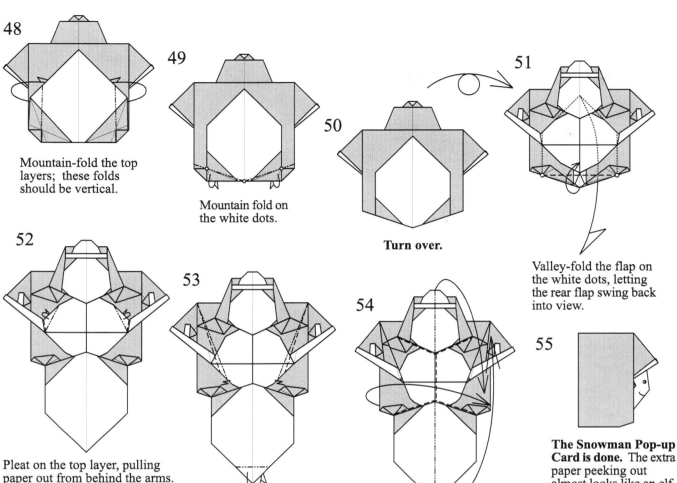

48 Mountain-fold the top layers; these folds should be vertical.

49 Mountain fold on the white dots.

50 Turn over.

51 Valley-fold the flap on the white dots, letting the rear flap swing back into view.

52 Pleat on the top layer, pulling paper out from behind the arms.

53 **Above:** Pleat the front layers. This helps shape the middle snowball and locks the layers together.
Below: Mountain-fold the bottom flap to taste.
Everywhere: Shape to taste unless your fingers are frostbitten from folding this origami snowman!

54 Close the card while lifting the top and bottom flaps and making them pass by each other as shown above (passing to the right).

55 **The Snowman Pop-up Card is done.** The extra paper peeking out almost looks like an elf. Or, if you rotate the model 90 degrees, it looks like a sun rising next to a mountain.

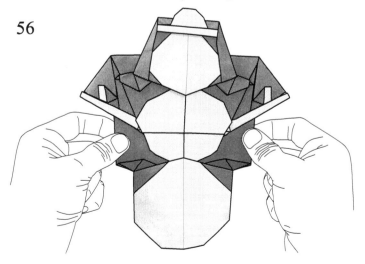

56

"I'm Frosty the Snowman; I don't mean to bug you,
But I'm icey cold and I'd sure like to hug you!"

PERFORM IT!

Hold up the closed card and say to the audience, **"Inside here is a little man who has lived in this card for years, but, out in the real world, men like him only live at most a few months! Can you guess what type of man he is?"** [Audience probably can't guess.] Say, **"Ready, set, everyone say, 'Pop-up!'"** [Audience says, "Pop-up!"] Open the card and ask, **"What is it?"** [Audience says, "It's a Snowman!"] Answer, **"Yes! Now, everyone freeze like a Snowman!"** [Audience strikes a pose.] **"Now, melt!"** [Audience melts.] Exclaim, **"My, what a short winter that was!"**

Snowman Pop-up Card

Barbershop Quartet

Sound sold separately. By Jeremy Shafer ©2002 *Rather Complex*

Or rather... "Quintet"

1

White side up. Begin dividing the square into 32 by folding in half, in fourths, in eighths and so on. It doesn't matter whether the creases are mountains or valleys. Put an additional valley crease between creases 0 and 1 and between creases 5 and 6 for later reference. Make the indicated mountains and valleys.

2

Close-up of the right side. Pleat through both layers.

3

Above: Pull the raw edge down to the reference crease and flatten; the top edge of the model will get adjusted.
Below: Pull the indicated edge up to the reference crease and flatten. The two lowermost folds will get adjusted.

4

Put the indicated horizontal edge behind the other horizontal edge.

5

Like this. Flatten the model to make the next step easier to diagram.

PERFORM IT!

Say to the audience, **"Inside here are four singers and an accordion! What song would you like them to sing?"** [Audience chooses a song.] Open the model and operate it while ventriloquistically singing the song. Finish by exclaiming, **"Bravo! Bravo!"**

146 *Origami Pop-ups*

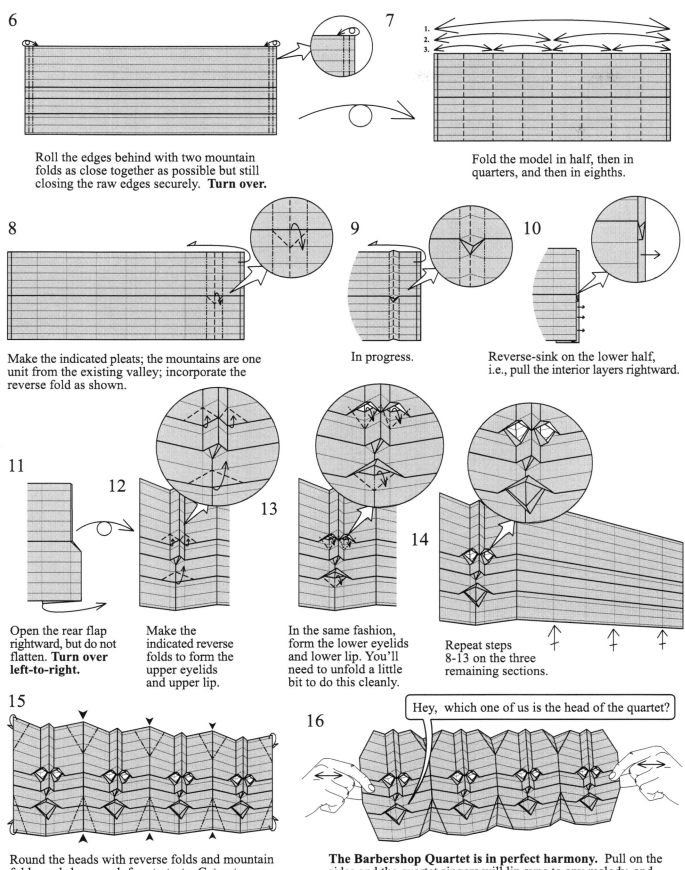

Hug Me! Envelope

By Jeremy Shafer ©2000

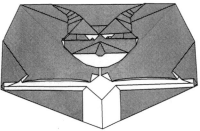

1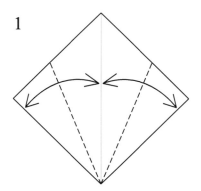

Begin white side up. Valley-fold the edges to the middle crease (see invisible step 0!). Unfold.

2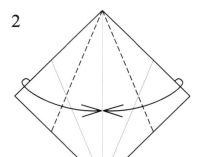

Valley-fold edge-to-crease.

3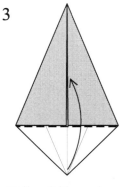

Valley-fold on edge. (Not on the cutting edge!)

4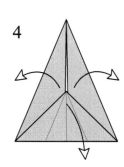

Completely unfold.

5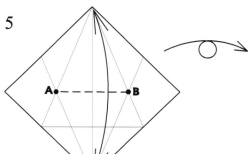

Valley-fold in half and unfold, creasing only between **A** and **B**. **Turn over left to right.**

6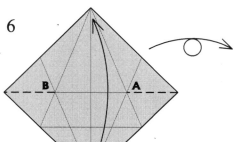

Valley-fold and unfold the paper again, this time creasing to the right of **A** and to the left of **B**. **Turn over left to right.**

7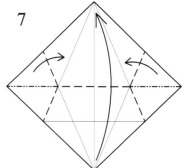

Using existing creases, fold the side corners in as you bring the bottom up.

8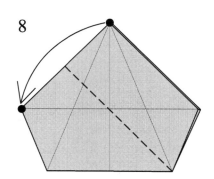

Valley-fold the top layer dot-to-dot...

9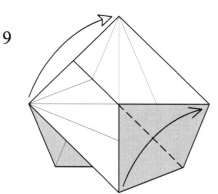

...and fold it back.

10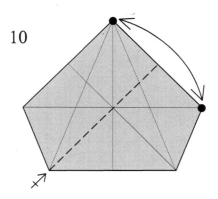

Repeat steps 8-9 on the other side.

148 *Origami Pop-ups*

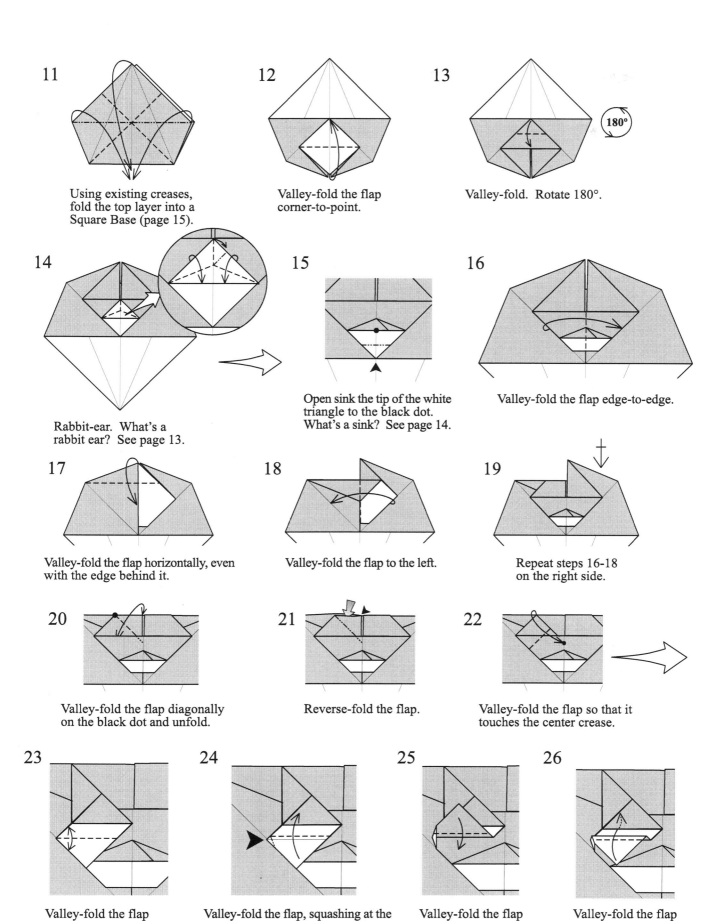

Hug Me! Envelope

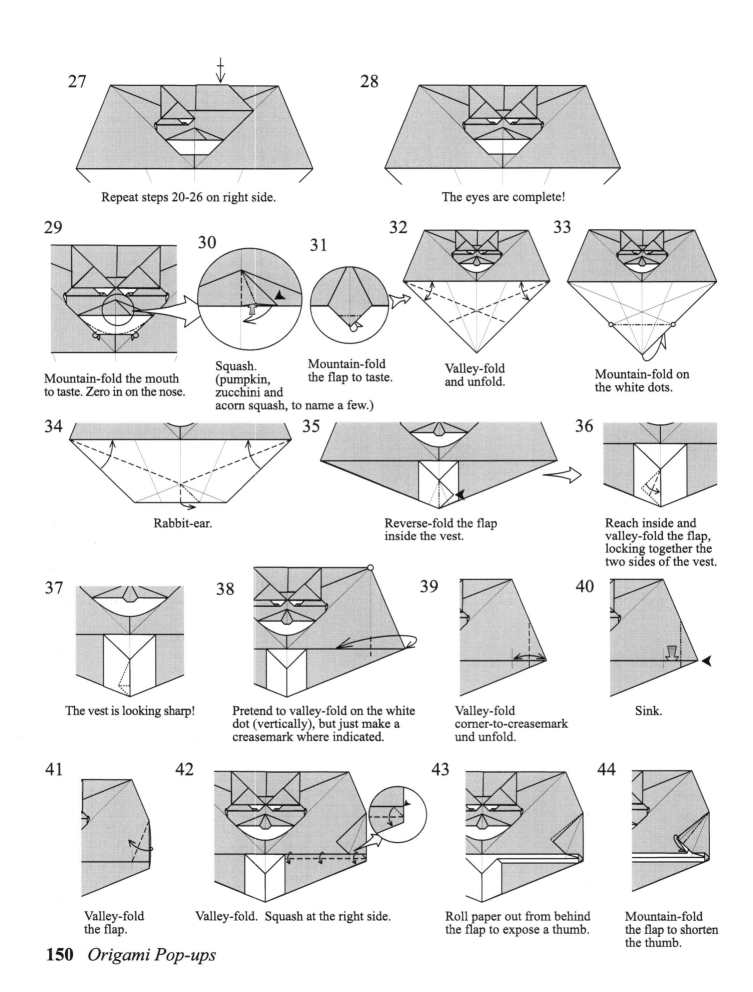

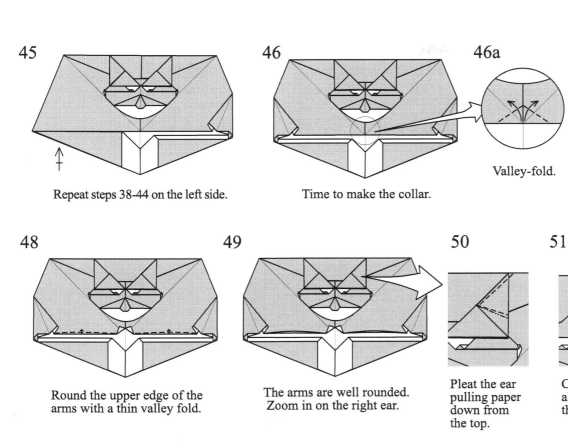

45. Repeat steps 38-44 on the left side.

46. Time to make the collar.

46a. Valley-fold.

47. The collar is sewn. That was easy!

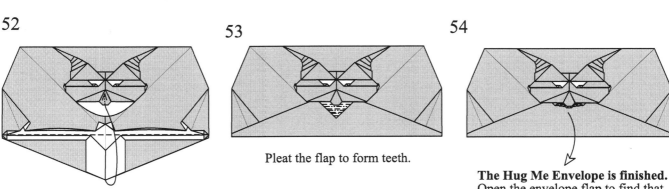

48. Round the upper edge of the arms with a thin valley fold.

49. The arms are well rounded. Zoom in on the right ear.

50. Pleat the ear pulling paper down from the top.

51. Continue pleating along the rest of the ear.

52. Valley-fold, inserting the flap into the pocket.

53. Pleat the flap to form teeth.

54. **The Hug Me Envelope is finished.** Open the envelope flap to find that our scary-looking creature isn't really so scary after all...

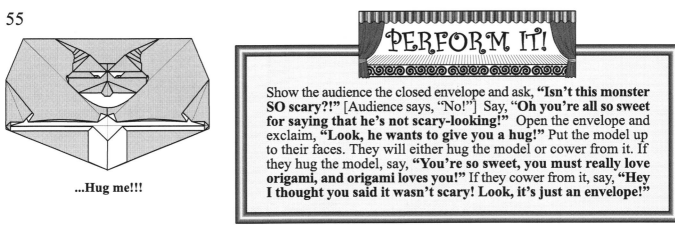

55. **...Hug me!!!**

PERFORM IT!

Show the audience the closed envelope and ask, **"Isn't this monster SO scary?!"** [Audience says, "No!"] Say, **"Oh you're all so sweet for saying that he's not scary-looking!"** Open the envelope and exclaim, **"Look, he wants to give you a hug!"** Put the model up to their faces. They will either hug the model or cower from it. If they hug the model, say, **"You're so sweet, you must really love origami, and origami loves you!"** If they cower from it, say, **"Hey I thought you said it wasn't scary! Look, it's just an envelope!"**

Pop-Up Numbers

The most logical application for origami numerical pop-up cards is to give as birthdays cards (double-digit birthdays require two cards), but they can also be used to commemorate other special events such as anniversaries, graduations, and even weddings (e.g., "Happy 3rd wedding! May THIS one last longer than the last two!").

To make the cards even more unique and special I recommend embellishing them with words and pictures. You might ask then, "What is the purpose of folding the numbers on there in the first place if we're just going to draw all over the card?" Good point! If you would rather draw the number instead of fold the number then skip to the Anything Pop-up Card (page 182), but for those who enjoy the concept of cards with actual folded numbers on them all from one square of paper, no cutting, gluing or drawing, then this chapter is for you!

Last One Standing

By Jeremy Shafer ©2005

Perfect for competitions of all kinds, this model demonstrates the true meaning of one-upmanship.

1

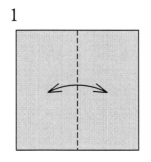

Colored side up, valley-fold in half and unfold.

2

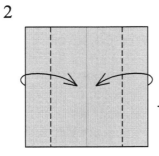

Valley-fold. This fold is to taste, but try to make it look at least somewhat like step three.

3

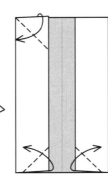

Valley-fold.

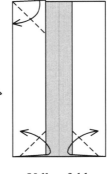

4

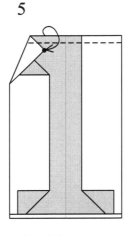

Valley-fold.

5

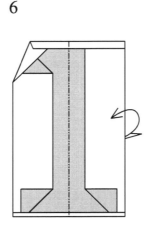

Valley-fold the top edge to the black dot.

6

I don't know about the others, but this one is complete! To make it stand, mountain-fold on the center vertical crease and unfold. Stand it up as shown in step 7.

7

The model is finished and standing tall, proud to be the number one!

8

Fold out of black paper and you will have a "One Night Stand!"

PERFORM IT!

Slowly say to the audience, **"I need some one to help me?"** [Audience raises their hands] Say, **"Oh, nevermind, I have some one!"** Pull out the model and, marveling at it, exclaim, **"This is SOME one!"** Balance the model on your hand and say, **"And, look, it can even do a hand stand!"** End by saying to the model, **"Thanks, One! You were ONE big help!"**

Last One Standing

Number One Pop-up Card

By Jeremy Shafer ©2005

No need to buy expensive birthday or anniversary cards, for this one will do fine, but, if you give it as birthday card, make sure to keep it out of the hands of the birthday child, lest it get the royal drool treatment, or worse, eaten as a one-course meal!

Intermediate

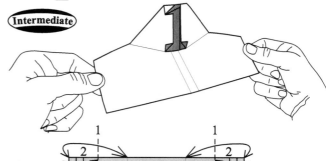

1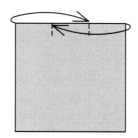

Colored side up, divide the top edge into thirds by making pinches.

2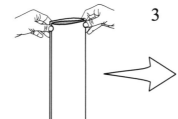

Here's one way to pinch thirds. Holding as shown, fiddle with the folds until they line up.

3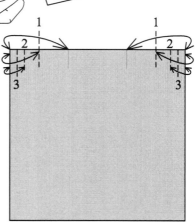

Make valley creasemarks in the order shown above.

4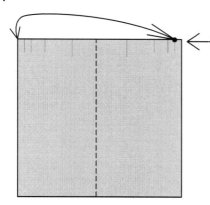

Valley-fold the left corner to the black dot and unfold. Repeat on the right corner.

5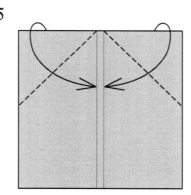

Valley-fold edge-to-crease.

6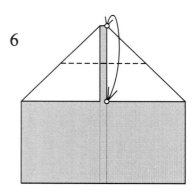

Valley-fold and unfold dot-to-dot.

7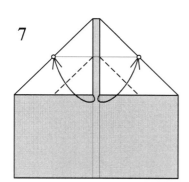

Valley-fold the corners to the white dots.

8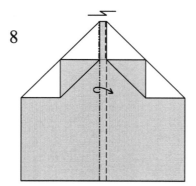

Pleat on the existing creases.

9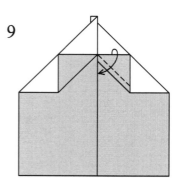

Valley-fold edge-to-edge.

154 *Origami Pop-ups*

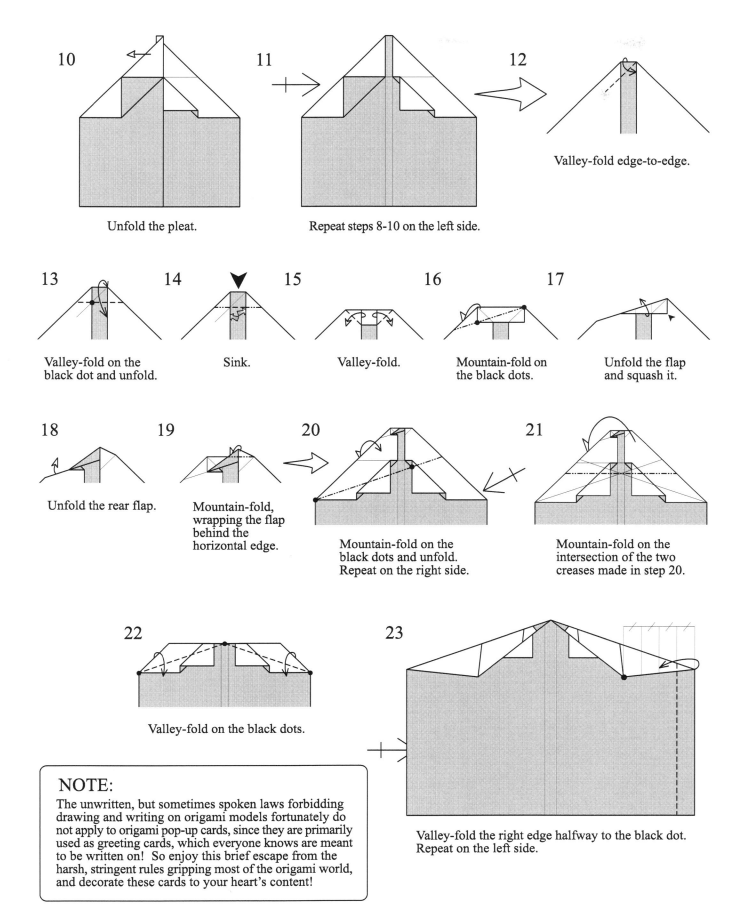

Number One Pop-up Card 155

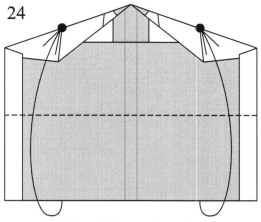

24

Valley-fold to the black dots.

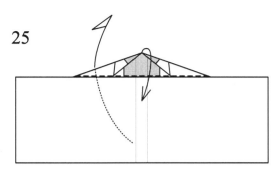

25

Valley-fold the flap down while letting the rear flap swing upward.

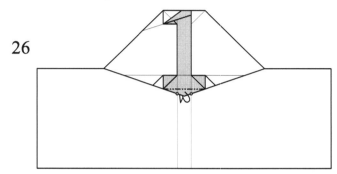

26

Mountain-fold sharply. The position of this fold will make the model want to spring open. If you would prefer a card that stays closed on its own, then make this fold instead on the white dots.

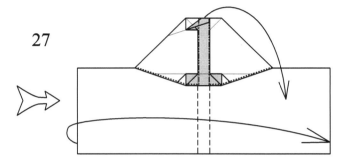

27

Close the card on existing creases, enclosing the "1" between the front and back covers of the card.

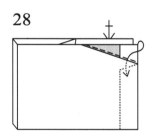

28

Valley-fold the corner tucking in the slot between the front layer and the interior dotted flap. **Repeat behind.**

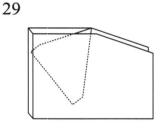

29

If folded correctly, the model should want to spring open on it's own. If you want to keep it closed, you could either tie string around the card or flatten it completely. Open the card.

30

The number one is done,
But your journey's just begun.
Seek anew what's next to do,
Befold the number TWO!

The Number One Pop-up Card is complete. In addition to writing a note on the card itself, a secret message can be written inside, under the flap that was folded up in step 24.

PERFORM IT!

Say to the audience, **"This is the NUMBER ONE pop-up card in my whole collection! Wanna see it?"** [Audience says, "Ya!"] **"Ready, set, everyone say, 'Pop-up!'"** [Audience says, "Pop-up!"] Open the card and say, **"See? I told you it was the number one!"**

156 *Origami Pop-ups*

Number Two Pop-up Card

By Jeremy Shafer ©2005

Whether it's a second birthday, a second anniversary, or even a second wedding, this pop-up card will be perfect for the occasion.

Intermediate

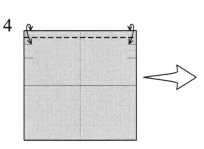

1 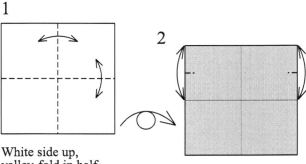 2 3

White side up, valley-fold in half and unfold in both directions. **Turn over.**

Valley-fold corner-to-crease and unfold but actually crease only where indicated.

Valley-fold to the crease marks and unfold, making two more crease marks.

4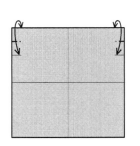

Valley-fold to the creasemarks and unfold.

5 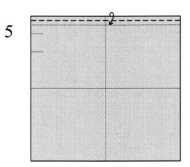 6 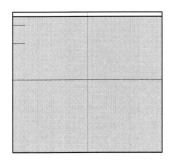 7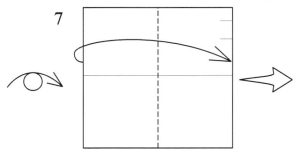

Valley-fold edge-to-crease.

Turn over left-to-right.

Valley-fold in half left-to-right.

8 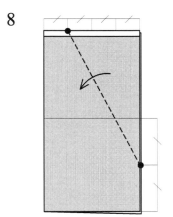 9 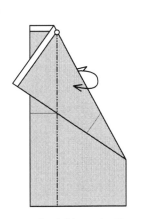 10 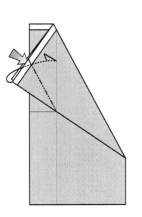 11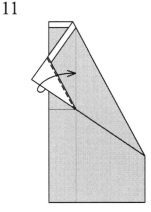

Valley-fold thru both layers on the black dots.

Mountain-fold vertically on the white dot **which is slightly below the top of the model!**

Mountain-fold the front flap edge-to-crease.

Valley-fold edge-to-crease.

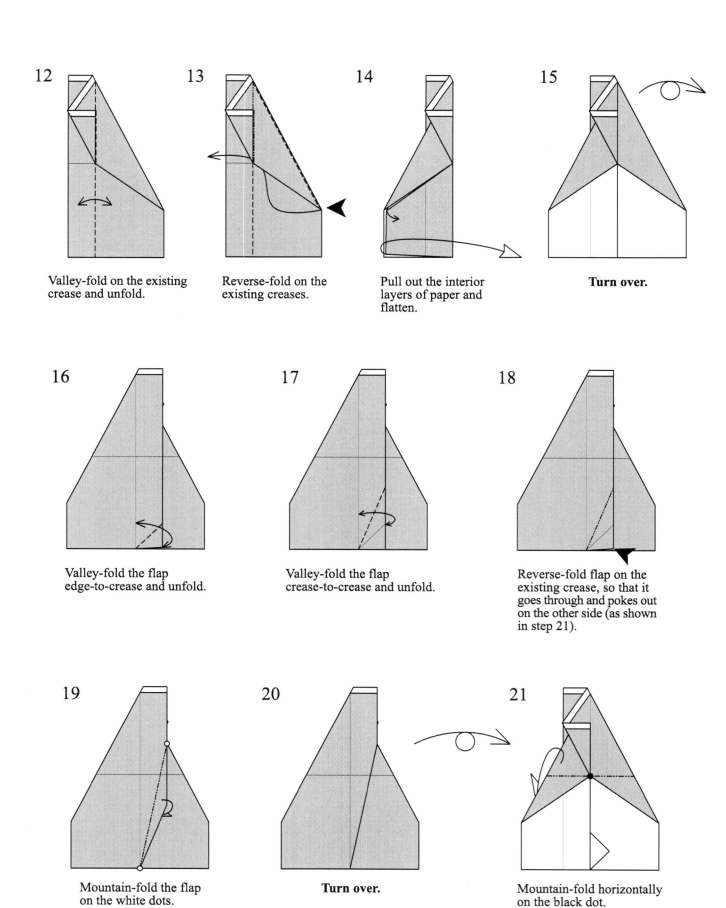

12. Valley-fold on the existing crease and unfold.
13. Reverse-fold on the existing creases.
14. Pull out the interior layers of paper and flatten.
15. **Turn over.**
16. Valley-fold the flap edge-to-crease and unfold.
17. Valley-fold the flap crease-to-crease and unfold.
18. Reverse-fold flap on the existing crease, so that it goes through and pokes out on the other side (as shown in step 21).
19. Mountain-fold the flap on the white dots.
20. **Turn over.**
21. Mountain-fold horizontally on the black dot.

158 *Origami Pop-ups*

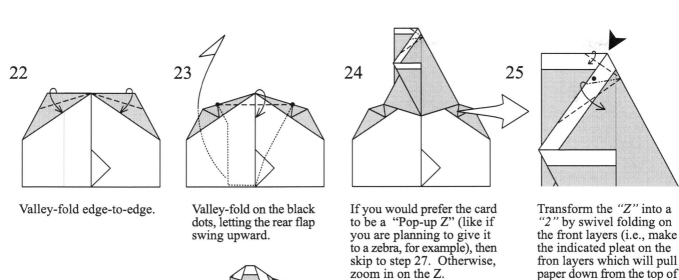

22 Valley-fold edge-to-edge.

23 Valley-fold on the black dots, letting the rear flap swing upward.

24 If you would prefer the card to be a "Pop-up Z" (like if you are planning to give it to a zebra, for example), then skip to step 27. Otherwise, zoom in on the Z.

25 Transform the *"Z"* into a *"2"* by swivel folding on the front layers (i.e., make the indicated pleat on the fron layers which will pull paper down from the top of the 2. Watch the black dot.)

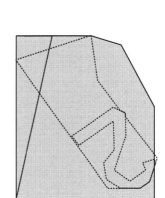

26 Valley-fold to finish the transformation.

27 Close the card on existing creases, enclosing the "*2*" between the front and back covers of the card.

28 **The Two is enclosed in the card and ready to pop out.**

29 **The Number Two Pop-up Card is ready to celebrate.** Draw a face on the card if you want. If you pull the bottom corners apart repeatedly, the nose will wiggle.

HAPPY BIRTHDAY!

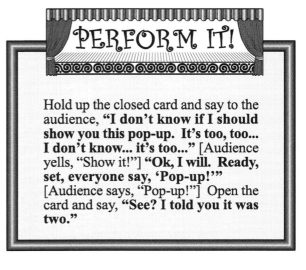

PERFORM IT!

Hold up the closed card and say to the audience, **"I don't know if I should show you this pop-up. It's too, too... I don't know... it's too..."** [Audience yells, "Show it!"] **"Ok, I will. Ready, set, everyone say, 'Pop-up!'"** [Audience says, "Pop-up!"] Open the card and say, **"See? I told you it was two."**

Number Two Pop-up Card

Number Three Pop-up Card

By Jeremy Shafer ©2005

Here's a good gift card for a three-year old or perhaps for a triplets' baby shower!

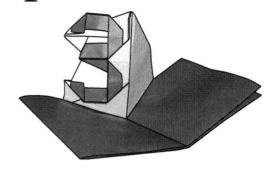

1

White side up, valley-fold the model in half and unfold. Valley-fold the top and bottom sides to the crease and unfold.

2

Make the valley creases in the order shown above. The third stays folded.

Say to the audience, **"This is a Pi pop-up card…"** Open the card and continue, **"…rounded down to the nearest integer."**

Colored Card Variation

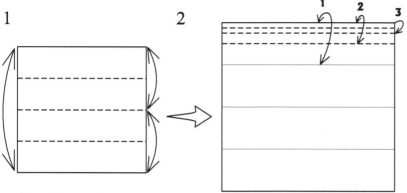

3

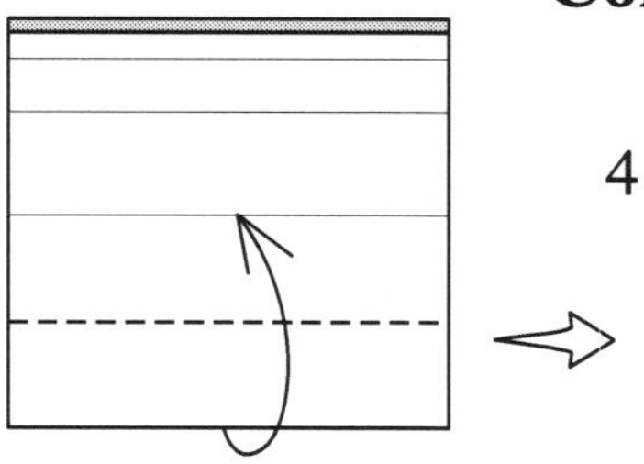

If you would prefer the card to be white so that you can write on it, skip to step 3 below. For a colored card, valley-fold the flap up as shown above.

4

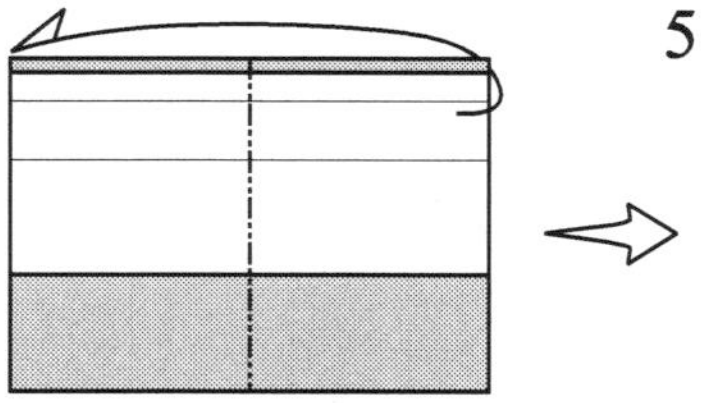

Mountain-fold the right edge to the left.

5

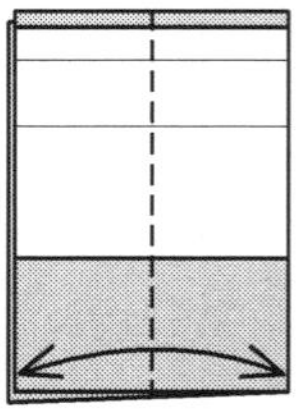

Valley-fold and unfold thru all layers. Continue to step 6 on the next page.

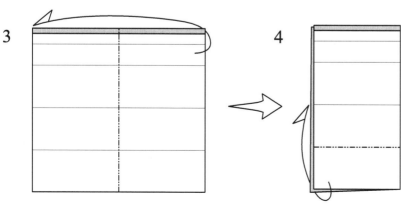

3

Mountain-fold in half.

4

Mountain-fold.

5

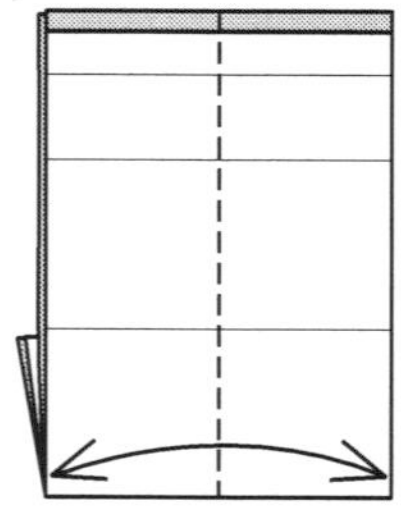

Valley-fold and unfold thru all layers.

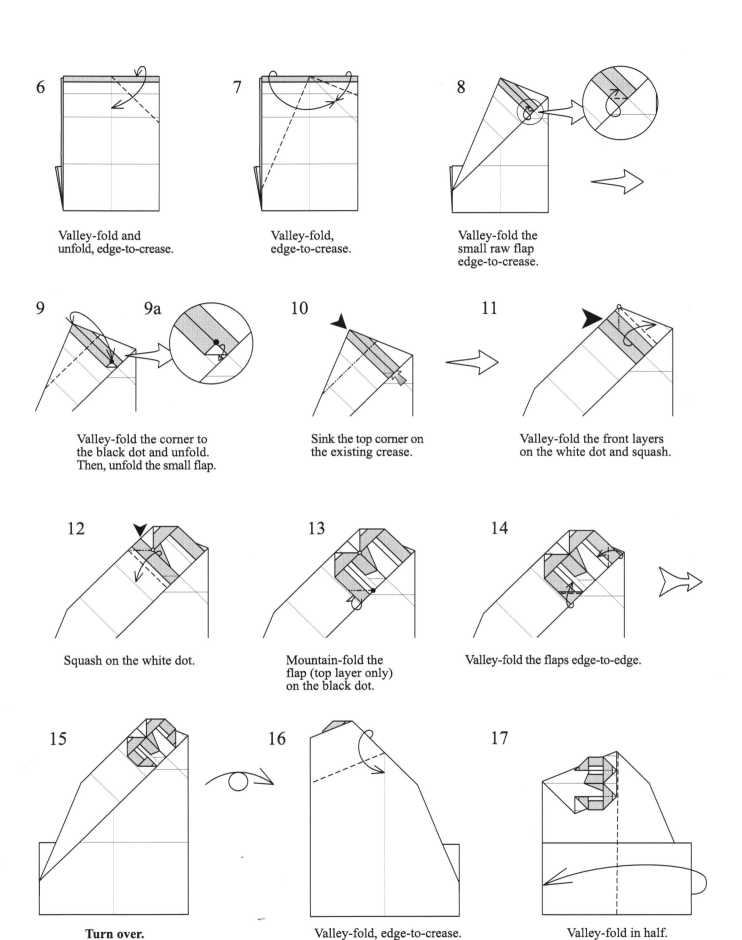

Number Three Pop-up Card 161

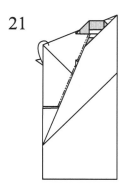

21 Mountain-fold the flap but keep the "3" intact.

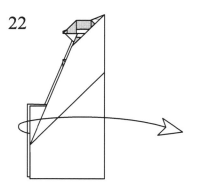

22 Open the card.

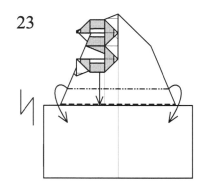

23 Pleat, bringing the "3" down to the top of the card.

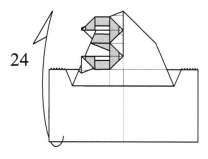

24 Swing the rear flap up.

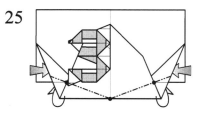

25 Mountain-fold the flaps on the black dots, inserting them in front of the rear layers.

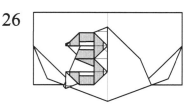

26 Turn over top-to-bottom.

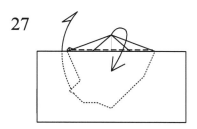

27 Valley-fold, letting the rear flap swing upward.

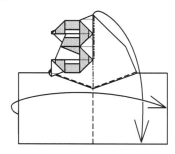

28 Close the card on existing creases, enclosing the "3" between the front and back covers of the card.

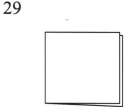

29 **The card is all ready for a one, two...**

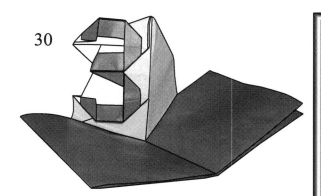

30 ...*THREE!*

PERFORM IT!

Hold up the closed card and say to the audience, **"Inside here is a three-faced iceberg monster! Wanna see it?"** [Audience says, "Ya!"] **"OK, ready, set, everyone say, 'Pop-up!'"** [Audience says, "Pop-up!"] Open the card and say, **"See? I told you it was a three-faced iceberg monster. There's the '3' and it's on one of the faces of the iceberg monster. Isn't it SCARY?!"** [Audience says, "No!"] **"Well, you should be very scared, because if I let this iceberg monster go, it might catch you, freeze you, and eat you later! You see, the danger is three-fold! But don't worry, I'll keep it safely locked up in this card."**

162 *Origami Pop-ups*

Number Four Pop-up Card

 Intermediate

By Jeremy Shafer
©2005

This card could be used as a birthday gift for a four-year-old or as the trophy for a four-square tournament.

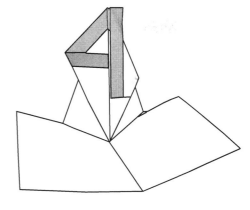

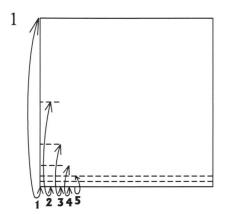

1. White side up, follow the above sequence of valley creasemarks. Numbers **4** and **5** are complete valley folds.

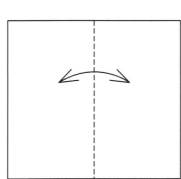

2. Valley-fold in half and unfold. **Turn over.**

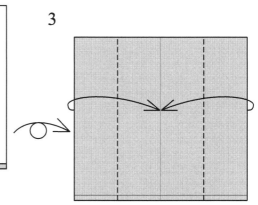

3. Valley-fold edge-to-crease.

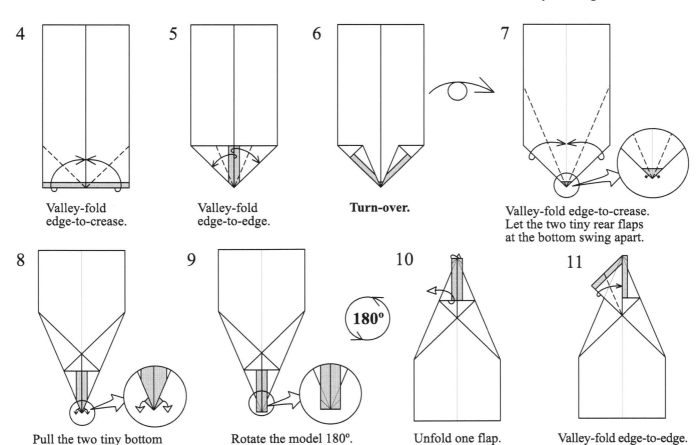

4. Valley-fold edge-to-crease.

5. Valley-fold edge-to-edge.

6. **Turn-over.**

7. Valley-fold edge-to-crease. Let the two tiny rear flaps at the bottom swing apart.

8. Pull the two tiny bottom flaps downward.

9. Rotate the model 180°.

10. Unfold one flap.

11. Valley-fold edge-to-edge.

Number Four Pop-up Card **163**

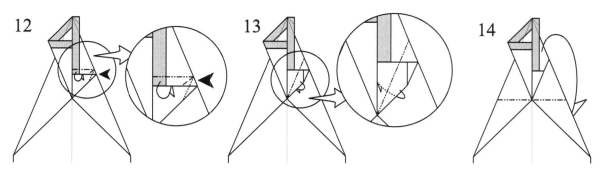

12. Shorten the bottom of the "4" by mountain-folding it and squashing the right side.

13. Mountain-fold the flap edge-to-edge.

14. Mountain-fold.

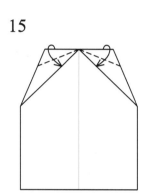

15. Valley-fold edge-to-edge.

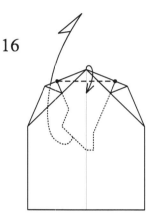

16. Valley-fold on the black dots, letting the rear flap swing upward.

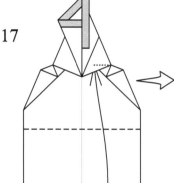

17. Valley-fold the bottom edge up to the dotted line, tucking it behind the top layers.

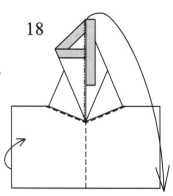

18. Close the card on existing creases, enclosing the "4" between the front and back covers of the card.

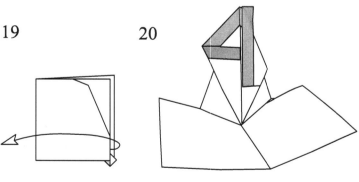

19. Ready, set, go for it, or, rather, go *four* it!

20. **The Number Four Pop-up is done!** Not only can you write your greeting on the inside of the card, but you can also open the fold made in step 17 and write a secret message!

PERFORM IT!

Say to the audience, **"Let's play the number game. You have to guess between 1 and 10, what number is in this card? I'll give you a hint: I have never shown you this model beFORE."** [Audience says, "Four!"] Open the card and exclaim, **"Wow, you're right! How did you know?"** [Audience says, "Because you said *before*!"] **"When? I hadn't even shown you this model beFORE."** [Audience says, "You said it again!!"]. **"I did not say, 'It again!' I said, 'I hadn't even shown you this model beFORE!' You guys are driving me CRAZY!"**

164 *Origami Pop-ups*

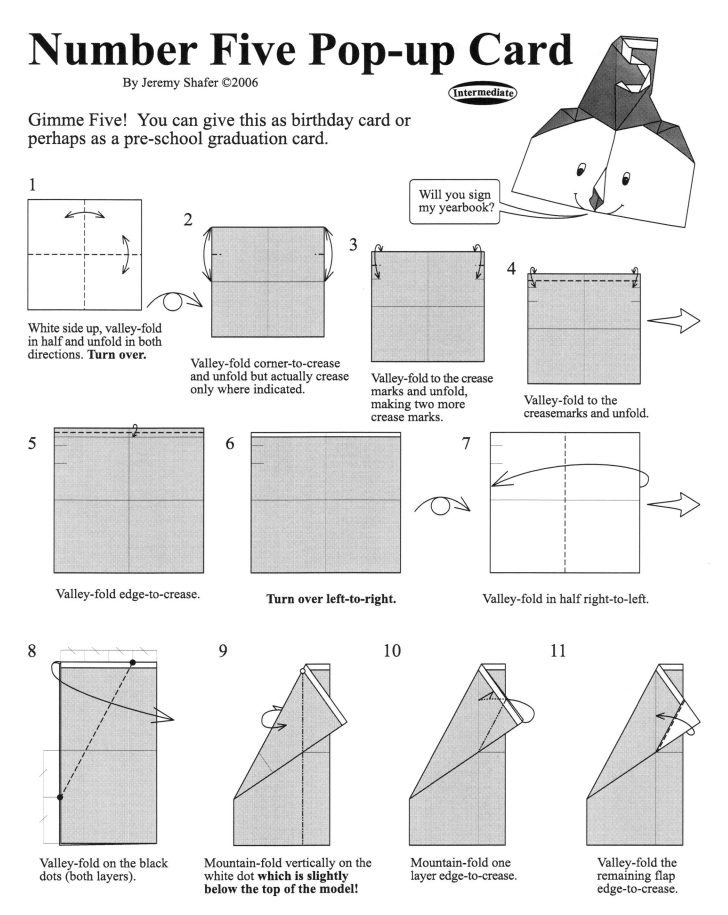

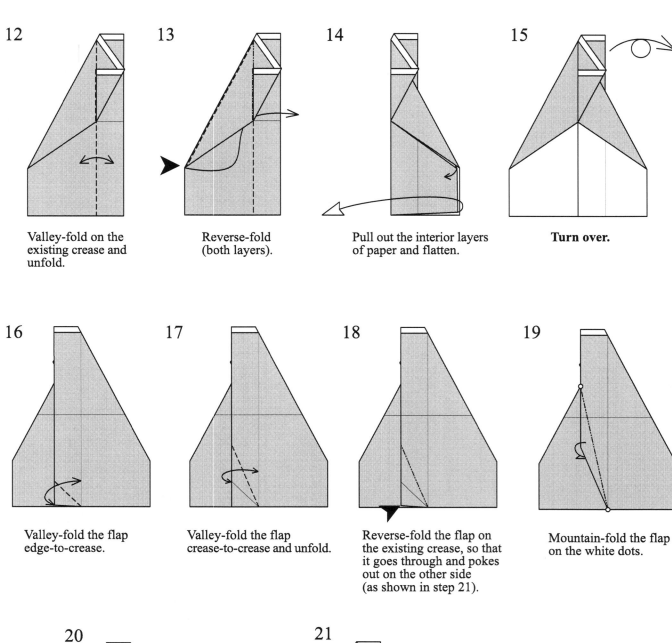

12 Valley-fold on the existing crease and unfold.

13 Reverse-fold (both layers).

14 Pull out the interior layers of paper and flatten.

15 Turn over.

16 Valley-fold the flap edge-to-crease.

17 Valley-fold the flap crease-to-crease and unfold.

18 Reverse-fold the flap on the existing crease, so that it goes through and pokes out on the other side (as shown in step 21).

19 Mountain-fold the flap on the white dots.

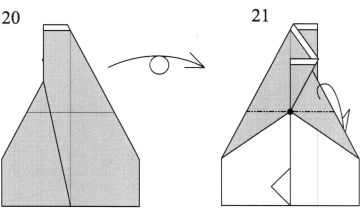

20 Turn over.

21 Mountain-fold horizontally on the black dot.

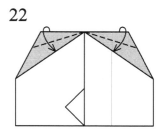

22 Valley-fold edge-to-edge.

166 *Origami Pop-ups*

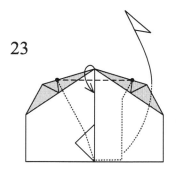

23 Valley-fold on the black dots, letting the rear flap swing upward.

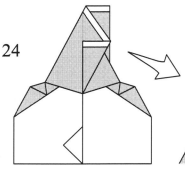

24 Zoom in on the backwards "Z."

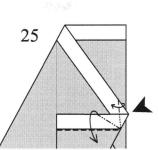

25 Now to form the "5"... Valley-fold the horizontal edge downward and squash on the right.

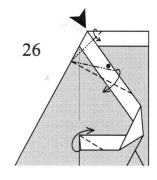

26 **Above:** Swivel fold (i.e., make the indicated pleat on the front layers which will pull paper down from the top of the 5. Watch the black dot.
Below: Valley-fold the flap to taste.

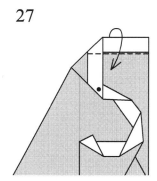

27 One last valley-fold and the "5" is done!

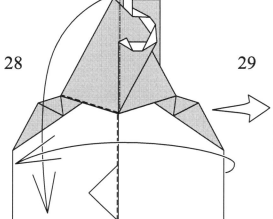

28 Close the card on existing creases, enclosing the "5" between the front and back covers of the card.

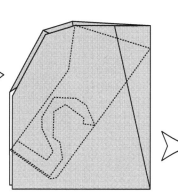

29 **The five is enclosed in the card and ready to pop out.**

30 **The Number Five Pop-up Card is ready to celebrate.** Draw a face on the card if you want. If you pull the bottom corners apart repeatedly, the nose will wiggle.

PERFORM IT!

Hold up the closed card and say to the audience, **"Everyone yell, 'High Five!'"** [Audience yells, "High Five!"] Open the card and say, **"And the Five says 'Hi' to you too!"**

Number Five Pop-up Card

Number Six Pop-up Card

Intermediate By Jeremy Shafer ©2006

Oddly enough, to fold this Number Six Pop-up Card you first have to precrease the paper into fourths and then into fifths.

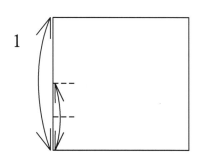

1. White side up, make two creasemarks on the left edge by folding first in half and then in fourths.

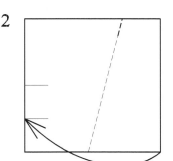

2. Bring the right corner to the fourths creasemark but only flatten at the top.

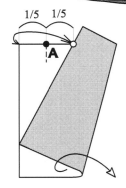

3. Make creasemark **A** by valley-folding the left corner to the white dot and unfolding.

Note: This clever method for constructing fifths was discovered by Koji Husimi and is based on Haga's Theorem.

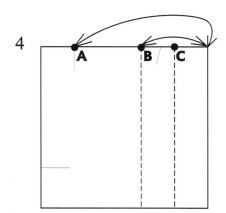

4. Valley-fold the right corner to point **A** and unfold, forming point **B**. Valley-fold the right corner to point **B** and unfold, forming point **C**.

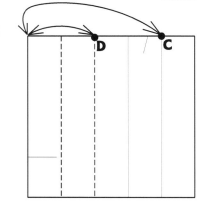

5. Valley-fold the left corner to point **C** and unfold. Valley-fold the left corner to point **D** and unfold.

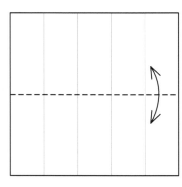

6. The square is divided into fifths! Valley-fold in half and unfold.

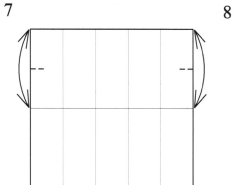

7. Valley-fold corner-to-crease and unfold but actually crease only where indicated.

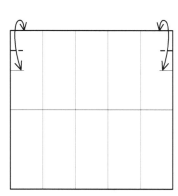

8. Valley-fold to the crease marks and unfold, making two more crease marks.

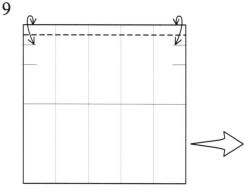

9. Valley-fold to the creasemarks and unfold.

168 *Origami Pop-ups*

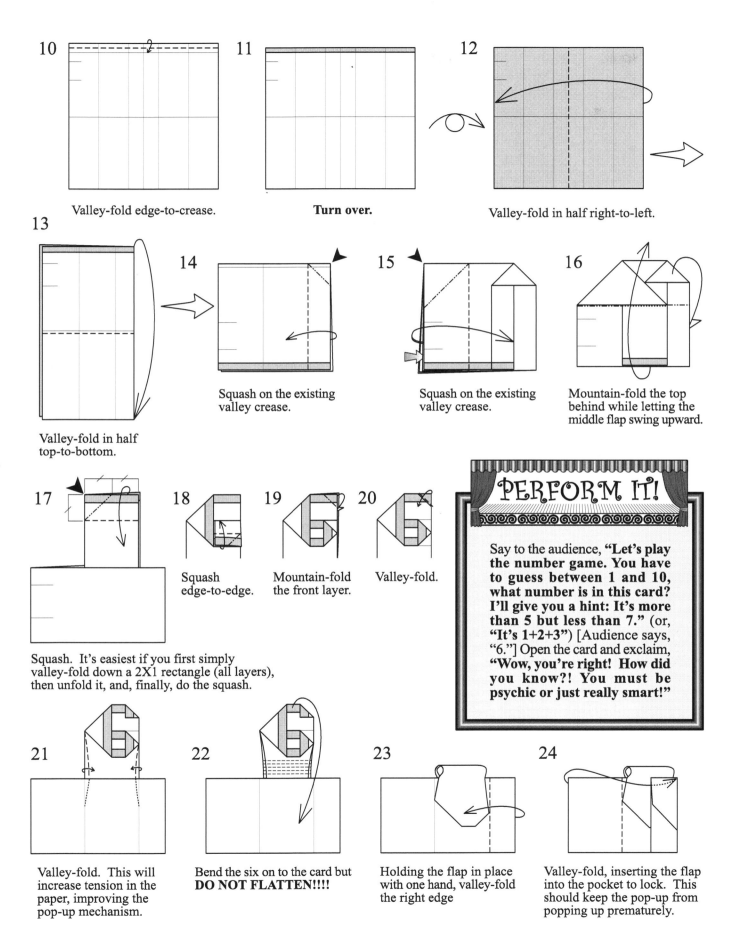

25

The number six is ready to pop up when the covers are opened.

26

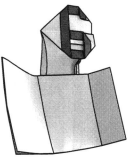

The Number Six Pop-up Card is done. Because of the tension in the paper, the six should pop-up on its own every time the card is opened. However, after continued use, the paper may lose its tension and the six may no longer pop up enough, in which case there's another way to expose the six...

27

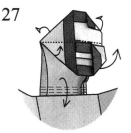

Following the arrows, pull the six down over the card but do not flatten. Close the card (steps 22-25).

28

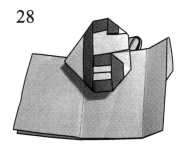

This way, the six will be visible no matter how much it pops up.

29

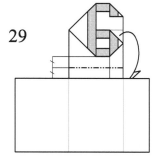

In case you would prefer a Pop-up Six Card that is in the style of the other number pop-up cards, go back to step 21 and mountain-fold the flap.

30

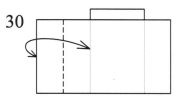

Valley-fold edge-to-crease (all layers) and unfold.

31

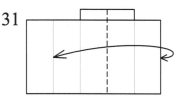

Valley-fold edge-to-crease (all layers) and unfold.

32

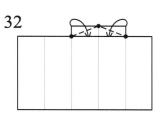

Valley-fold on the black dots, inserting the flaps behind the front layer.

33

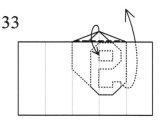

Valley-fold on the edge, letting the rear flap swing upward.

34

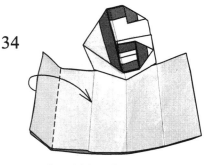

Valley-fold on the existing crease.

35

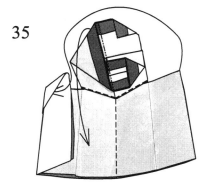

Close the card on existing creases, enclosing the "6" between the front and back covers of the card. Insert the corner into the pocket to lock.

36

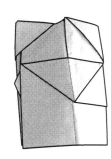

Like this. Open it up again and write your greeting.

37

All done! Now you just need to figure out if it's six of one or half dozen of the other.

170   *Origami Pop-ups*

Number Seven Pop-Up Card

Rather Simple

By Jeremy Shafer ©2006

This model works well as a card for a 7th birthday or 7th anniversary, or, for new relationships, it can be used as a "weekiversary" card, commemorating one whole week together, but, careful, that might be too soon to reveal your origami obsession to your new boyfriend or girlfriend, and, besides, if they didn't remember to get you a gift too, it could jeopardize the new relationship!

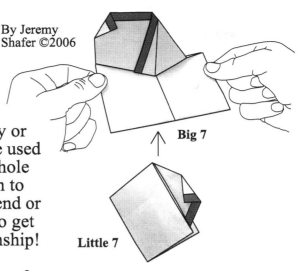

Big 7

Little 7

1

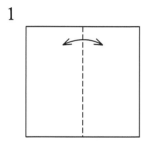

White side up, valley-fold in half and unfold. **Turn over.**

2

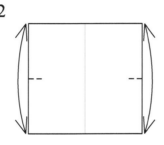

Valley-fold in half and unfold but actually crease only where indicated.

3

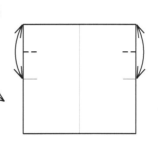

Valley-fold to the crease marks and unfold, making two more crease marks.

4

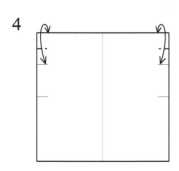

Valley-fold to the crease marks and unfold, making two more crease marks.

5

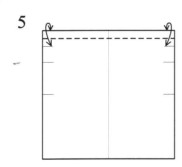

Valley-fold to the creasemarks and unfold.

6

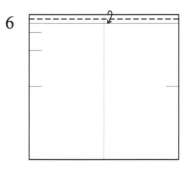

Valley-fold edge-to-crease.

7

Turn over left-to-right.

8

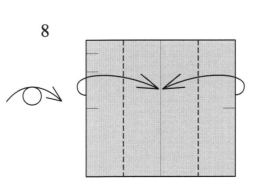

Valley-fold edge-to-crease.

Number Seven Pop-up Card **171**

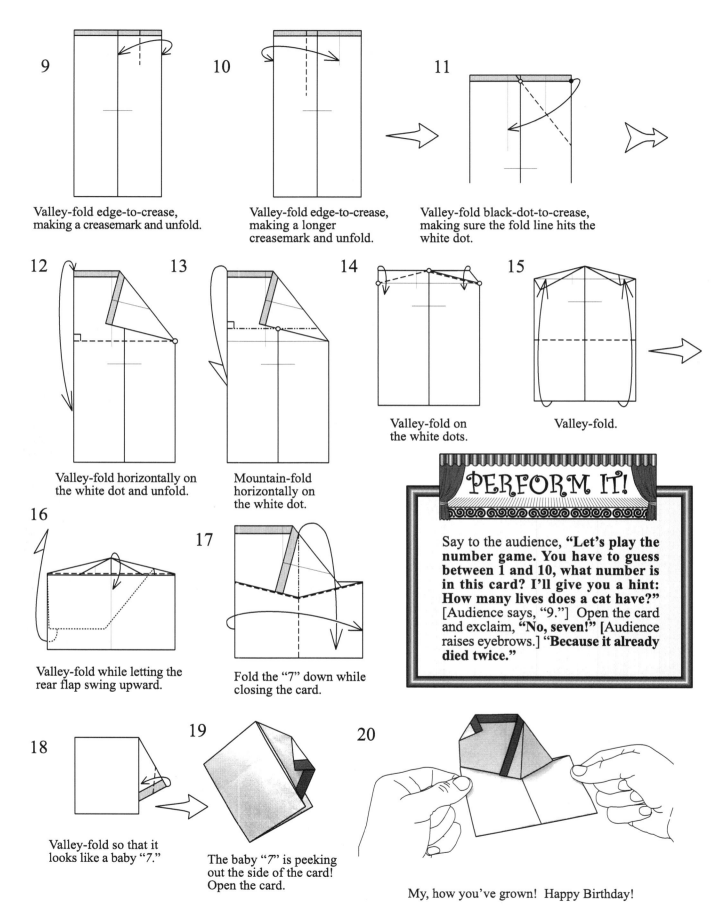

Number Seven Pop-Up Card Take Two!

By Jeremy Shafer
©2006

For a more classical, aesthetically pleasing Seven Pop-up Card, start by folding steps 1-17 of the Number Seven Pop-up Card.

18

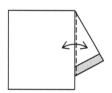

Valley-fold on the edge and unfold.

19

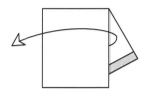

Open the card as before.

20

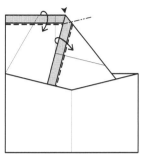

Valley-fold both edges at the same time and flatten.

21

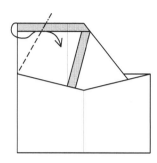

Reverse-fold on the existing crease.

22

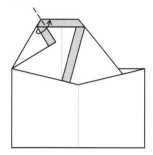

Valley-fold the flap.

23

Valley-fold edge-to-edge.

24

Valley-fold the tiny flap, like turning the page of a book.

PERFORM IT!

Say to the audience, "Let's play the number game. You have to guess between 1 and 10, what number is in this card. I'll give you a hint: How many months does it take before a baby is born?" [Audience says, "9"] "Let's see if you're right." Open the card, look at it, and exclaim, "Oh dear! This baby is very premature! We'd better close the card back up!"

25

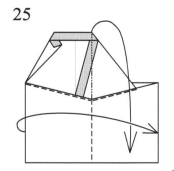

Fold the "7" down while closing the card.

26

Note that the seven is now completely contained within the card. Open it up.

27

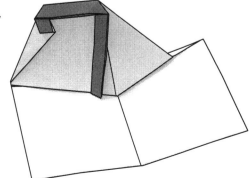

It's way more better than cola, it's 7 Up!

Number Eight Pop-Out Card

By Jeremy Shafer ©2006

Intermediate

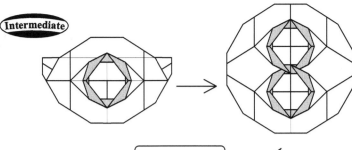

I'm an albino eight ball.

Here's a model that goes from 0 to 8 in a fraction of a second.

1

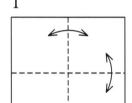

White side up, valley-fold in half and unfold in both directions.

2

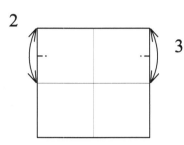

Valley-fold corner-to-crease and unfold but actually crease only where indicated.

3

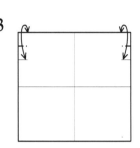

Valley-fold to the crease marks and unfold, making two more crease marks.

4

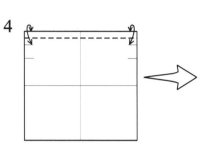

Valley-fold to the creasemarks and unfold.

5

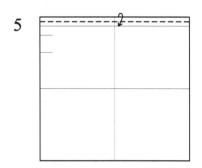

Valley-fold edge-to-crease.

6

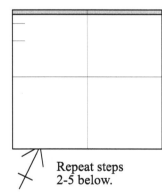

Repeat steps 2-5 below.

7

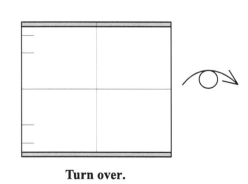

Turn over.

8

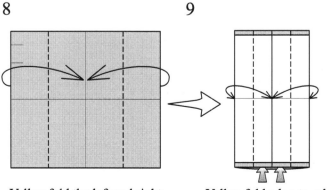

Valley-fold the left and right sides to the middle crease.

9

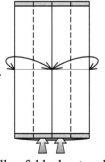

Valley-fold edge-to-edge on the front layer only and unfold.

10

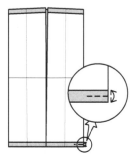

Valley-fold edge-to-edge and unfold, creasing only on the right side.

11

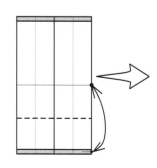

Valley-fold dot-to-dot and unfold.

174 *Origami Pop-ups*

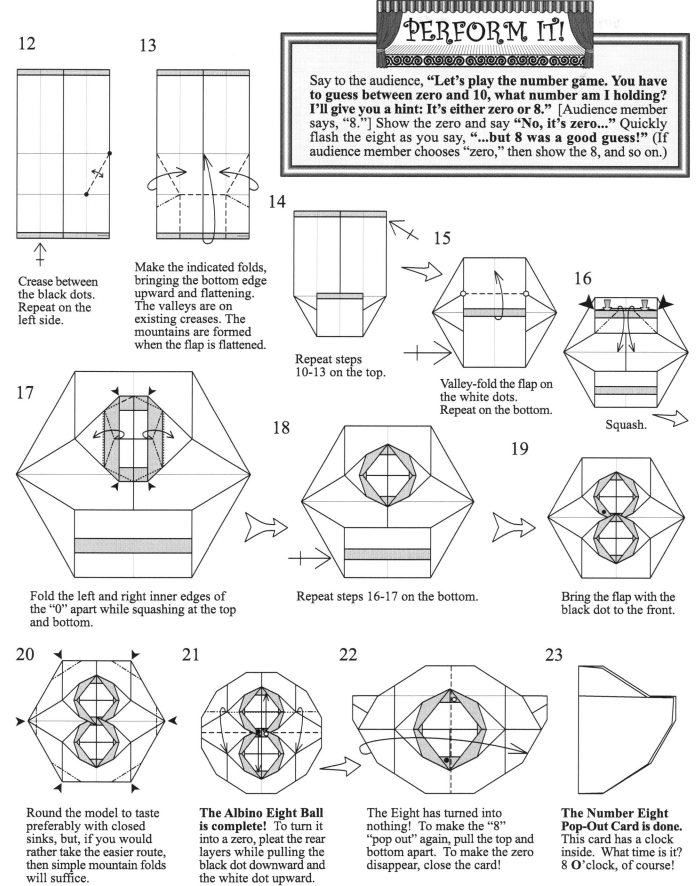

Number 9 Pop-up

By Jeremy Shafer ©2007

This makes a nice greeting card for a child's ninth birthday and also for a cat's ninth life.

(Intermediate)

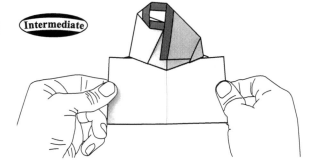

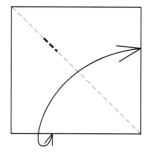

1. White side up, valley-fold diagonally in half and unfold, but actually crease only where indicated (in bold).

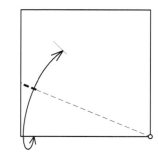

2. Valley-fold on the white dot edge-to-creasemark, but actually crease only on the left edge.

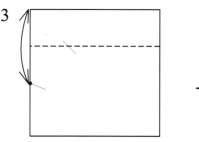

3. Valley-fold the top edge to the black dot and unfold.

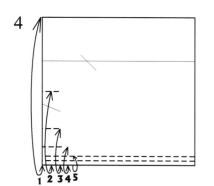

4. Follow the above sequence of valley creasemarks (i.e., fold in half, fourths, eighths and so on). Numbers 4 and 5 are complete valley folds.

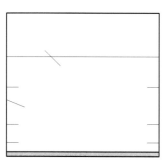

5. Turn over.

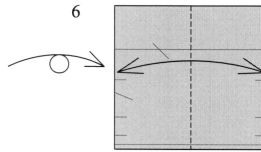

6. Valley-fold in half and unfold.

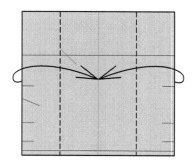

7. Valley-fold edge-to-crease.

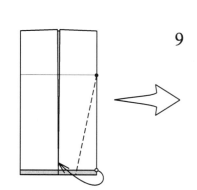

8. Valley-fold on the black dot so that the white dot touches the middle; CAREFUL, the white dot is not exactly on the corner!

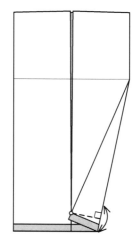

9. Valley-fold on the white dot and unfold; this crease is perpendicular to the right edge.

176 *Origami Pop-ups*

10

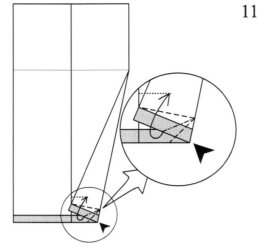

Squash on the existing valley crease resulting in a horizontal top colored edge and a vertical right colored edge.

11

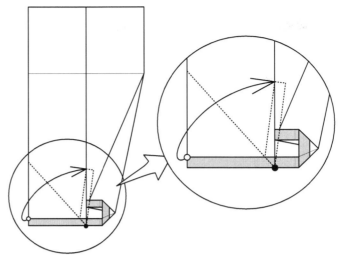

Valley-fold on the the black dot, so that the white dot touches the middle line.

12

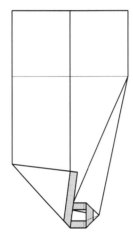

Rotate the model 180°.

13

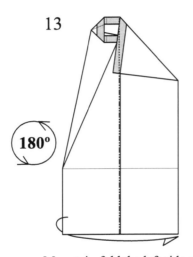

Mountain-fold the left side of the model behind, but don't fold the stem of the "9."

14

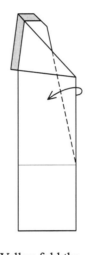

Valley-fold the flap lining up with the folded edge behind it.

15

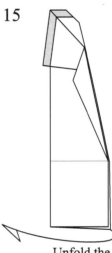

Unfold the rear flap.

16

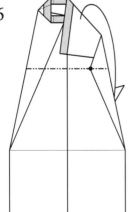

Mountain-fold horizontally on the black dot.

17

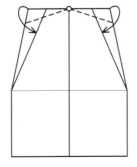

Valley-fold on the white dot so that the top corners touch the indicated edges.

18

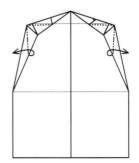

Pull the two edges as far apart as possible pulling paper out from underneath the top flaps, and flatten.

Number Nine Pop-up Card **177**

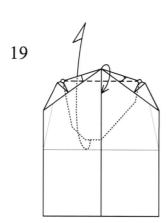

19. Valley-fold on the white dots, letting the rear flap swing upward.

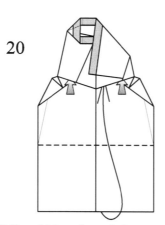

20. Valley-fold on the existing crease, inserting the flap behind the front layers.

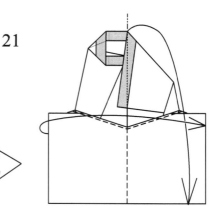

21. Fold the "9" down while closing the card.

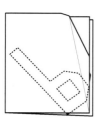

22. **The number 9 is contained in the card.** Open it up and let it go "pop!"

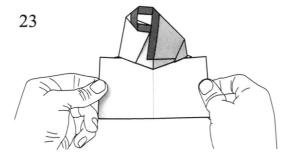

23. **The Number 9 Pop-up Card is open for viewing!** Remember, if while writing a message in the card, you run out of space, there is more space under the front flap (see step 20). Just make sure that wherever you run out of space you note, "pull flap out," so the recipient will be sure to see the complete message.

PERFORM IT!

Say to the audience, **"Let's play the number game. You have to guess between 1 and 10, what number is in this card? I'll give you a hint: How many sides does a heptagon have?"** [Audience says, "7"] Open the card and exclaim, **"No, nine!"** [Audience raises eyebrows.] Say, **"You forgot to count the front side and the back side!"**

Surprise Random Bonus Heart Model (Space Filler)...

Kangaroo Heart

Why wasn't this mentioned in the contents? Because then it wouldn't have been a surprise!

By Jeremy Shafer ©2007

This model is so cheesy that even some vegans will abstain from folding it! Nevertheless, it is simpler than most origami heart models, and it has a cool name too! So have a heart and fold this model today, or vice versa.

I recommend decorating your finished heart with markers. That way, when you show it to people, you can say to them, "I'm an aspiring *Heartist*."

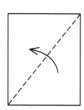  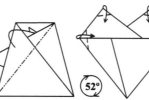 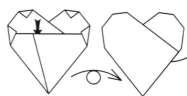

Begin with an 8 1/2-inch by 11-inch rectangle of printer paper. Valley-fold.

Valley-fold corner-to-corner, overlapping the flaps.

Mountain-fold both flaps into the pocket.

Valley-fold to taste.

The Kangaroo Heart Card is done. Now you just need to decide what to put in the pocket. A baby heart, perhaps?

Look, the back side even looks better!

Zero Pop-up

Intermediate By Jeremy Shafer ©2007

This Pop-up card can be given to newborn babies. Alternatively, you could give newborns the Number 9 Pop-up, to celebrate the completion of 9 months of increasingly cramped confinement in the womb.

1.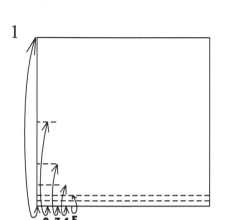
White side up, follow the above sequence of valley creasemarks. Numbers **4** and **5** are complete valley folds.

2.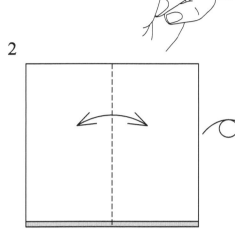
Valley-fold in half and unfold. **Turn over.**

3.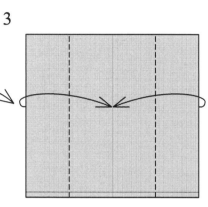
Valley-fold the left and right sides to the middle.

4.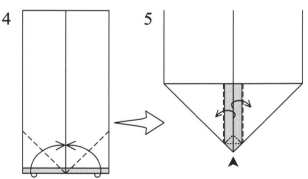
Valley-fold edge-to-edge.

5.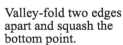
Valley-fold two edges apart and squash the bottom point.

6.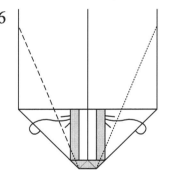
Valley-fold edge-to-edge tucking the flaps behind the "U."

7.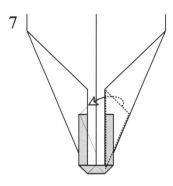
Reach in and pull out the trapped flap.

8.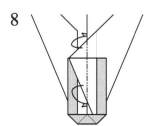
Mountain-fold the flap on the middle line, wrapping it behind the vertical raw edge.

9.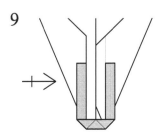
Repeat steps 7-8 on the left side.

PERFORM IT!

Say to the audience, "Let's play the number game. You have to guess what number is in this card? I'll give you a hint: How many eggs can a rooster lay in one day?" [Audience says, "One."] Open the card and exclaim, **"Zero, because roosters don't lay eggs; only hens do!"**

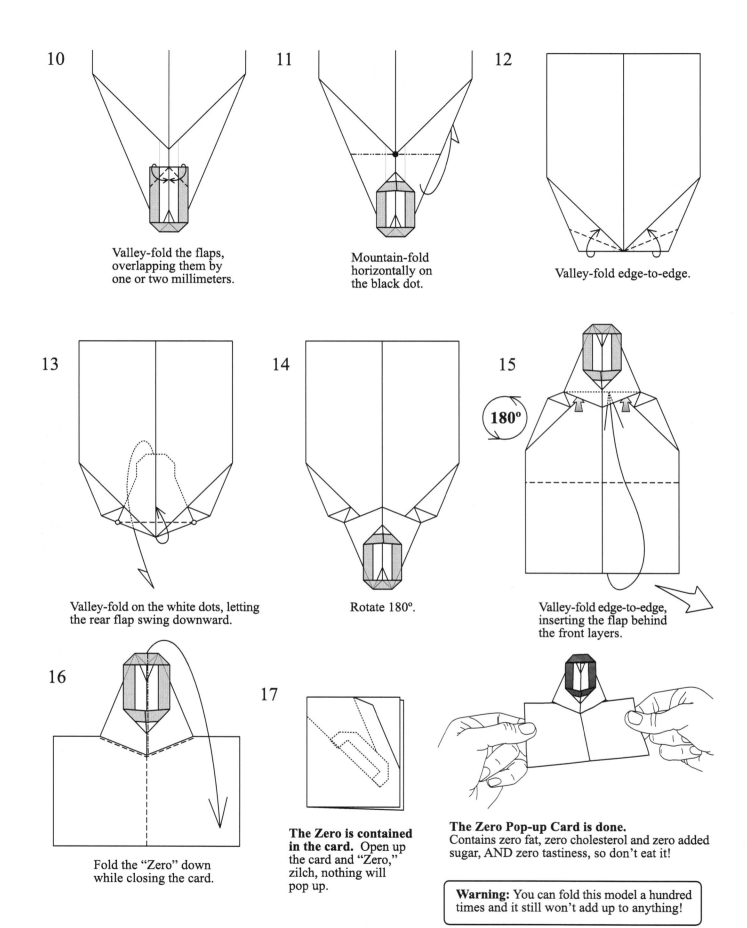

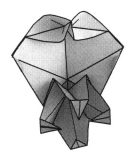 

Pop-Up Things

This chapter is primarily pop-ups that don't fall into the category of animals, people, or numbers... so, basically, everything else! For variety, I've thrown in a few non-pop-up designs too.

Now, time for a little origami design Q&A!

Question: How do you decide what thing to try to fold next?

Answer: Usually, when I set out to try to design something new in origami, the first step is deciding on a subject – deciding what new thing would be interesting and unique to design. Since most basic objects such as hearts, stars and flowers have been designed over and over by many origamists, in order to come up with something new and interesting, I try to mix subjects together. For example, let's say I'm in the mood to fold stars. Instead of just folding a star I will try to fold a star hat, star ring or star ship, preferably the latter since it's also a pun on Star Trek! Recently, I've been getting a lot of new ideas from design requests people make in the comments sections under my YouTube videos.

Question: What led you to start designing origami Pop-ups?

Answer: The desire to discover new yet-to-be-folded subjects is what led me to start designing origami pop-up cards, because while pop-up cards in general are popular and mainstream, I hadn't seen many other one-piece no-cuts origami pop-up cards out there, which means that most subjects I manage to make into pop-up cards are bound to be new. The other reason I started designing pop-up cards is because I realized they would work well in my origami show for kids.

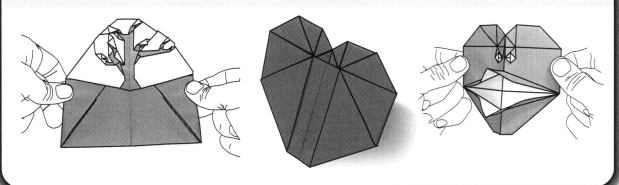

Anything Pop-up Card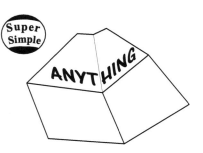

By Jeremy Shafer ©2013

This is your all-encompassing, Anything Pop-up Card. It can be anything you want as long as you are willing to draw it, and if you are opposed to drawing on origami then this model can still be anything; you'll just have to rely instead on your endless imagination!

1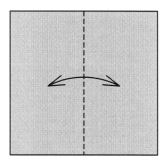

To end up with a completely white card, begin colored side up. For a colored card, begin white side up. Valley-fold in half and unfold.

2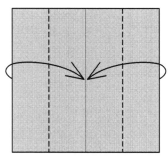

Valley-fold to the middle.

3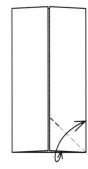

Bring edge to edge, but just make a tiny creasemark where the fold hits the raw edge.

4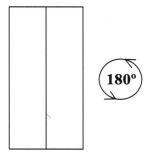

Rotate 180°.

5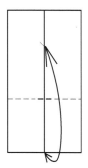

Bring the bottom edge to the creasemark and make a tiny creasemark in the middle, and unfold.

6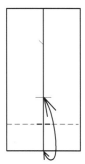

Valley-fold the bottom edge to the creasemark, creasing lightly, and unfold.

7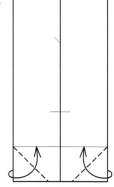

Valley-fold edge-to-crease.

8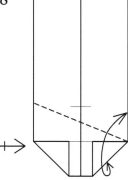

Valley-fold edge-to-edge and unfold. Repeat on the left side.

9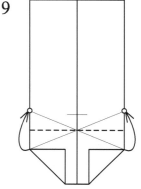

Valley-fold the corners to the white dots.

182 *Origami Pop-ups*

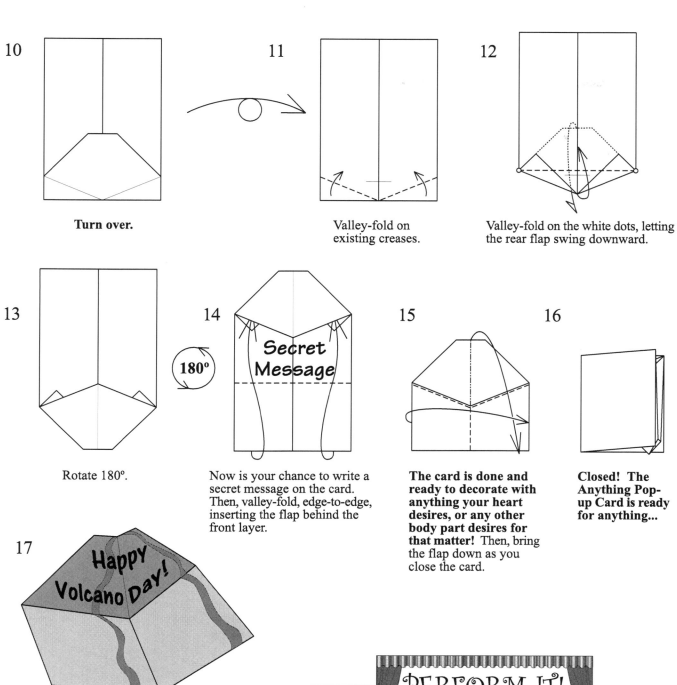

10 Turn over.

11 Valley-fold on existing creases.

12 Valley-fold on the white dots, letting the rear flap swing downward.

13 Rotate 180°.

14 Now is your chance to write a secret message on the card. Then, valley-fold, edge-to-edge, inserting the flap behind the front layer.

15 The card is done and ready to decorate with anything your heart desires, or any other body part desires for that matter! Then, bring the flap down as you close the card.

16 Closed! The Anything Pop-up Card is ready for anything...

17 ... even a volcano!...

18 ...or a million dollars!

PERFORM IT!

Write "$1,000,000" onto the card as shown to the left. Hold up the closed card and say to the audience, **"This card contains literally a million dollars! Wanna see?"** [Audience says, "Ya!"] **"Ready, set, everyone say, 'Pop-up!'"** [Audience says, "Pop-up!"] Open the card and say, **"See? One million dollars! That means I'm a millionaire! If you want it, I'll sell it to you for just $1000!"**

Anything Pop-up Card

Pop Star

By Jeremy Shafer ©2005

You've seen little twinkling stars and big shooting stars. Now, on the frontier of astronogami comes a newly discovered phenomenon...**Pop Stars!** Check out the findings!

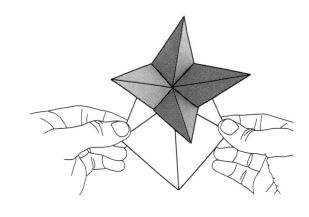

1

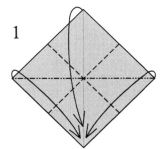

Begin by folding a white Square Base. What's a Square Base? See page 15.

2

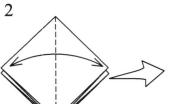

Valley-fold and unfold through all layers.

3

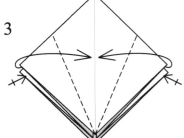

Valley-fold. **Repeat behind.**

4

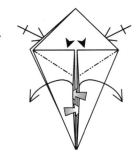

Squash. **Repeat behind.**

5

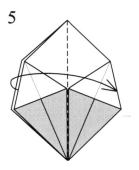

Valley-fold the left front flap rightward.

6

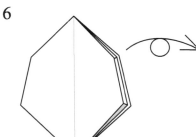

Turn over.

7

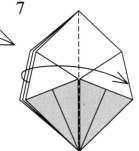

Valley-fold the left front flap rightward.

8

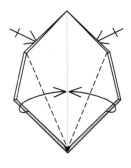

Valley-fold the front flaps to the middle crease. **Repeat behind.**

9

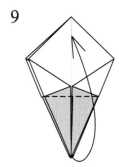

Valley-fold all layers.

10

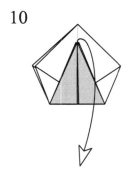

Bring one flap down.

11

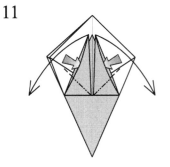

Squash the two flaps.

12

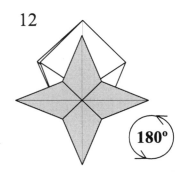

Rotate the model 180°.

184 *Origami Pop-ups*

13

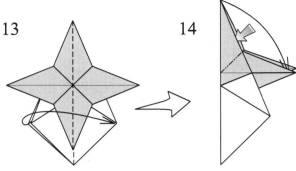

Valley-fold.

14

Reverse-fold into the middle slot.

15

Reverse-fold the interior flap in the same manner as the same way as in step 14.

16

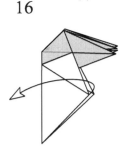

Open the card...

17

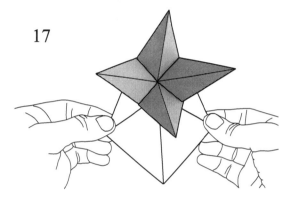

...and a Pop Star is born.

PERFORM IT!

Say to the audience, **"This next pop-up is the STAR of the show! Ready, set, everyone say pop-up!"** [Audience says, "Pop-up!"] Open the card and wait for the groans. Defend yourself by saying, **"But wait, it's not just a star, it's a shooting star. Do you want to see it shoot?"** Pretend that it's a ray gun {step 16} and fire it up in the air making sound effects. You see, it's a shooting star, and I can see you're all completely star struck!"

Alien Predator Pop-up Card

By Jeremy Shafer ©2005

Super Simple

Warning: This model is so scary, it will give you nightmares even during the day!*

1

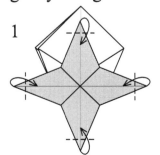

Begin by folding the Pop Star (page 184). Valley-fold the tips of the four flaps to taste.

*Unless you are a zombie fact-checker.

2

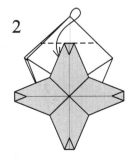

Valley-fold the top flap, inserting it behind the star.

3

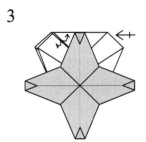

Above: Open the pocket to form an eye. Repeat on the right side.
Below: Perform steps 13-16 at the top of this page. Shape to taste.

4

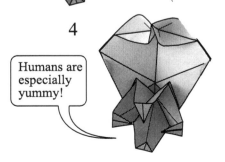

Humans are especially yummy!

The Alien Predator has landed and is hungry. Close the card and the jaws will gobble up unsuspecting prey. Hold the card near the jaws for best gobbling.

Pop Star 185

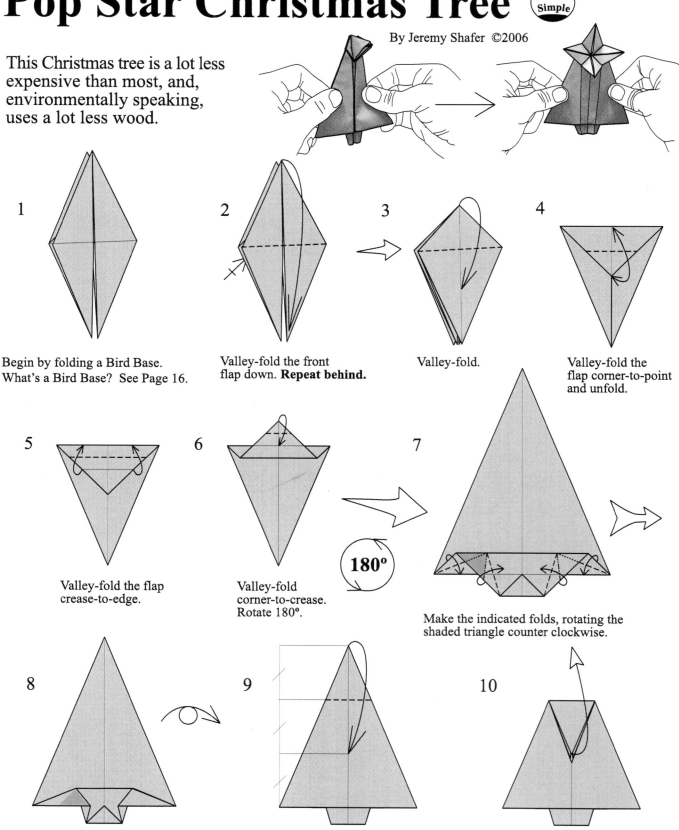

11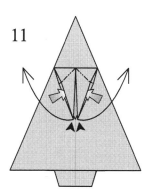
Squash two flaps.

12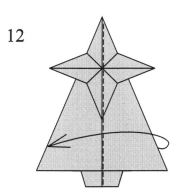
Valley-fold in half.

13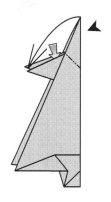
Reverse-fold into the middle slot.

14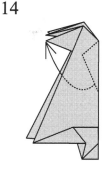
Reverse-fold the interior flap in the same manner as in step 13.

15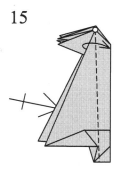
Valley-fold on the white dot. **Repeat Behind.**

16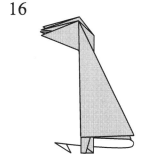
Swing the rear flap to the left and hold as shown.

17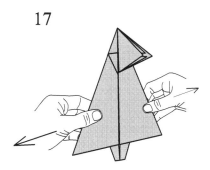
The Pop Star Christmas Tree is done. To make the star pop open, pull the sides apart.

18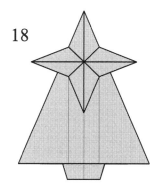
'Pop' goes the Christmas Tree!

PERFORM IT!

Hold the model up as shown in step 16 and say to the audience, **"This is a Christmas duck. Why? Because it's really a.... Ready, set, everyone say, "Pop-up!"** [Audience says, "Pop-up!"] Open the card as shown in step 17 and say, **"Because it's really a Christmas Tree! And it's even decorated. Wanna see? Ready, set, everyone say pop-up!"** [Audience says, "Pop-up!"] Pull the sides apart so that the star pops open and start singing your favorite Christmas carol while making the tree do a dance.

Pop Star Christmas Tree

Star Pop-up Card

By Jeremy Shafer ©2005

Rather Simple

Who needs a trophy? Present this greeting card as an award, and make the winner feel like a star!

1

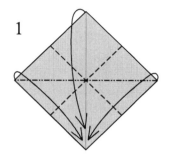

A 6-inch square will make a greeting card slightly bigger than one-inch square (when closed). Begin by folding a white Square Base. What's a Square Base? See page 15.

2

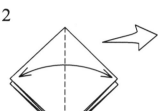

Valley-fold in half through all layers and unfold.

3

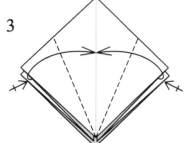

Valley-fold the front flaps edge-to-crease. **Repeat behind.**

4

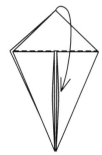

Valley-fold on edge.

5

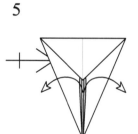

Unfold the left and right flaps. **Repeat behind.** Leave the top flap folded.

6

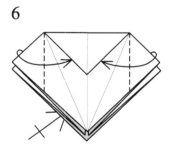

Valley-fold the front flaps edge-to-edge. **Repeat behind.**

7

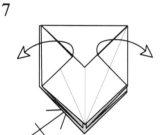

Unfold the left and right flaps. **Repeat behind.**

8

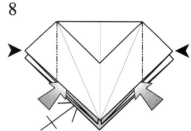

Reverse-fold on existing creases. **Repeat behind.**

9

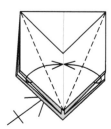

Valley-fold the front flaps edge-to-crease. **Repeat behind.**

10

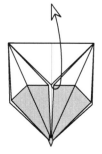

Unfold the top flap.

11

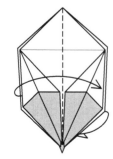

Minor Miracle Fold: Fold one flap from left to right and, to compensate, fold one rear flap from right to left.

12

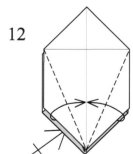

Valley-fold the front flaps edge-to-crease. **Repeat behind.**

188 *Origami Pop-ups*

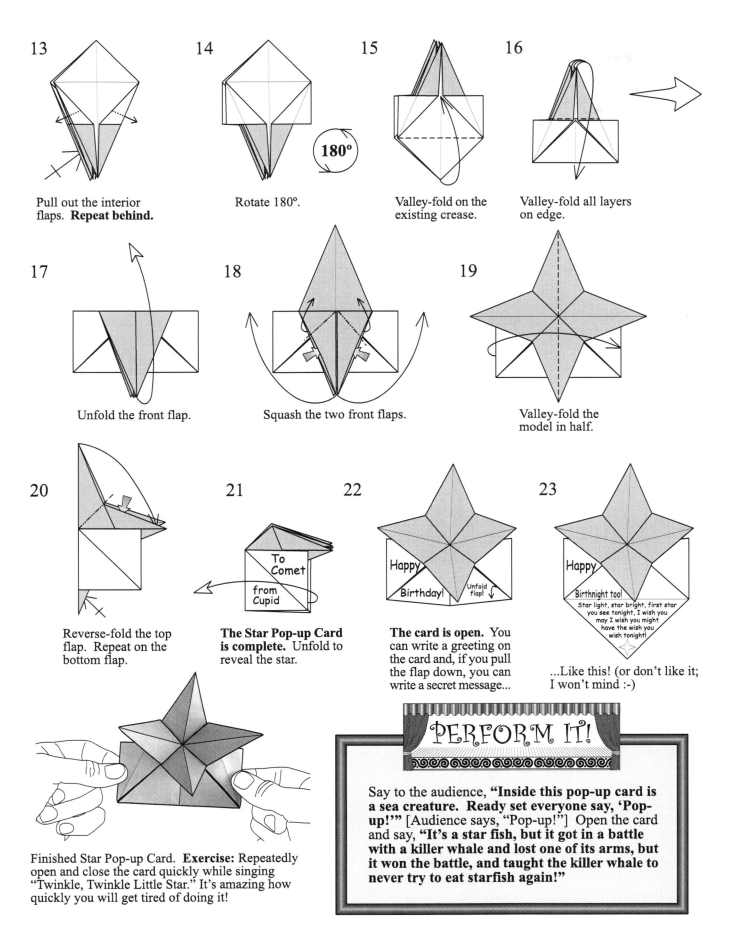

Winter Tree Pop-up Card

 By Jeremy Shafer ©2005

Perfect for Halloween... When kids come to the door and say, "Trick or Tree," open this card up and exclaim, "Tree!" They'll think it's funny so long as you still give them candy.

Here is a simple and inexpensive method of reforestation. Well, OK, just folding it won't really slow down the clear cutting of trees, but if you write a letter in it to your local senator pleading that more resources be allocated to reforestation and get one million people to sign it (You need to use big paper!) then it really might have an impact.

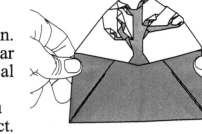

1

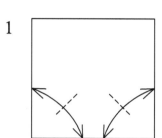

White side up, valley-fold and unfold edge-to-edge, marking the diagonals where indicated.

2

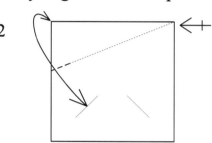

Lightly valley-fold one corner to the existing crease mark, creasing firmly only on the edge of the paper. Unfold and repeat on the other corner.

3

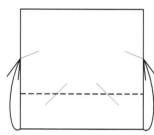

Valley-fold to the crease marks.

4

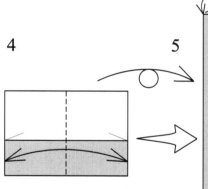

Valley-fold and unfold. **Turn over.**

5

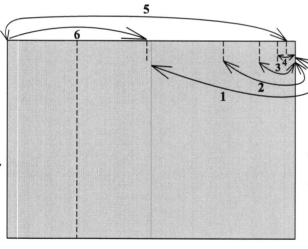

Above describes a sequence of folds to arrive at step 6 in a guidelined manner. If you so wish, you may skip the sequence and eyeball it instead.

6

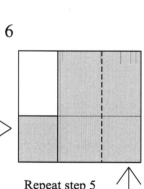

Repeat step 5 on the right side.

7

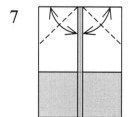

Valley-fold edge-to-edge and unfold.

8

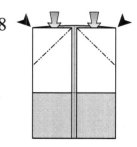

Reverse-fold on existing creases.

9

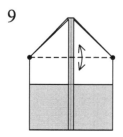

Valley-fold all layers on the black dots and unfold.

10

Valley-fold all layers to the crease and unfold.

190 *Origami Pop-ups*

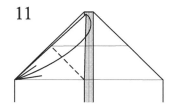

11 Valley-fold the left flap corner-to-corner.

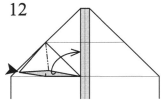

12 Squash.

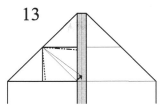

13 Slide the raw corner upward and to the right so that it touches the middle crease and flatten, adjusting the creases as needed.

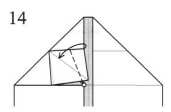

14 Valley-fold corner-to-crease; the fold line originates at the white dot.

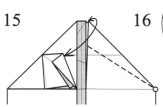

15 Valley fold corner-to-edge and unfold; the fold line originates at the white dot.

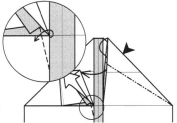

16 Left: Make a tiny valley fold where circled.
Right: Reverse-fold the flap on the existing crease.

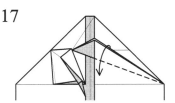

17 Valley-fold the front flap down.

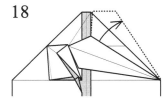

18 Pull the edge upward and to the right as far as it goes and flatten.

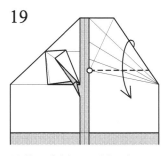

19 Valley-fold on white dot. (The non-existent creases are edges behind the front layer)

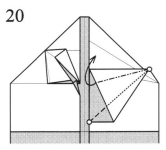

20 Squash; the valley fold is between the white dots and goes underneath the front layer; the mountain fold is formed when you flatten.

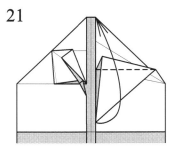

21 Valley-fold the flap.

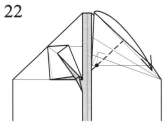

22 Valley-fold the flap diagonally as far as it will go (i.e., fold it on the black dot).

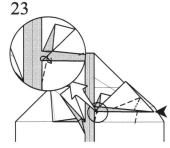

23 Left: Make a tiny valley fold
Right: Squash to further define the branches.

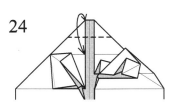

24 Valley-fold to the crease and unfold.

PERFORM IT!

Say to the audience, **"Trick or Treat!... Well, do you want a Trick, or a Treat?"** [Audience says, "Treat!"]
"Ready, set, everyone say, 'Pop-up!'" [Audience says, "Pop-up!"] Open the card and ask, **"You did say you wanted a tree, right?"** [Audience says, "No, a TREAT!"] Respond, **"Oh, well then I tricked you, because it's just a tree! Ha ha!"**

Thoughts Behind the Folds

My interest in trees was sparked even before my interest in origami. When I was as young as 7 years old, a few years before getting into origami, I would spend hours drawing mazes and trees. Many years later, I experimented with folding the outline of a tree using the edge of origami paper. Then when I got into designing origami pop-ups, designing a pop-up tree was a natural next step. **Challenge:** What other outline drawings can you adapt into pop-ups? **Ideas:** Star, heart, peace sign, yin yang, hand, flower, waterfall, Chinese or Japanese characters.

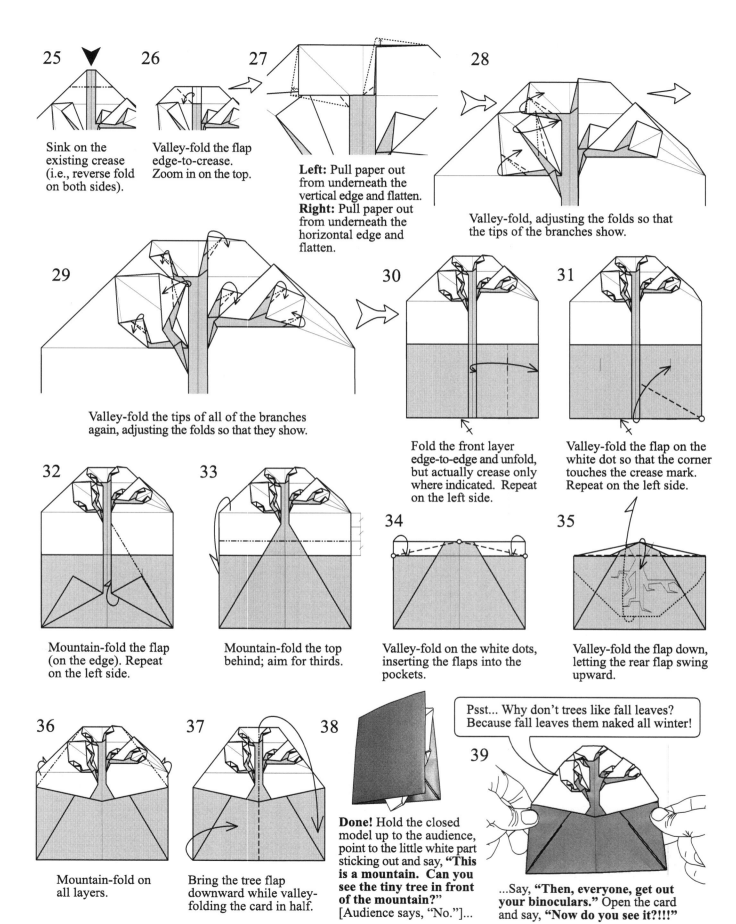

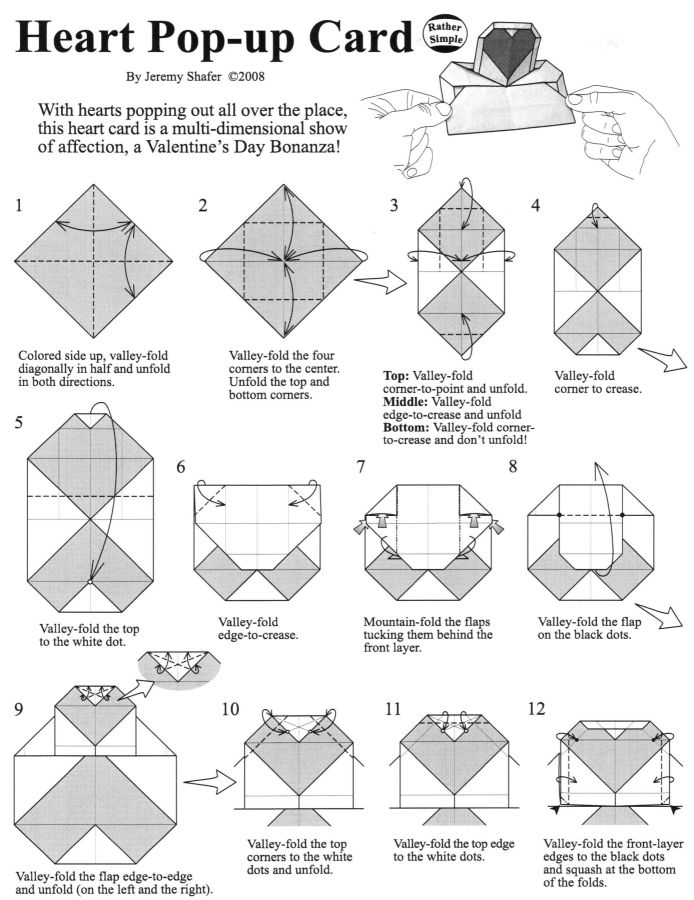

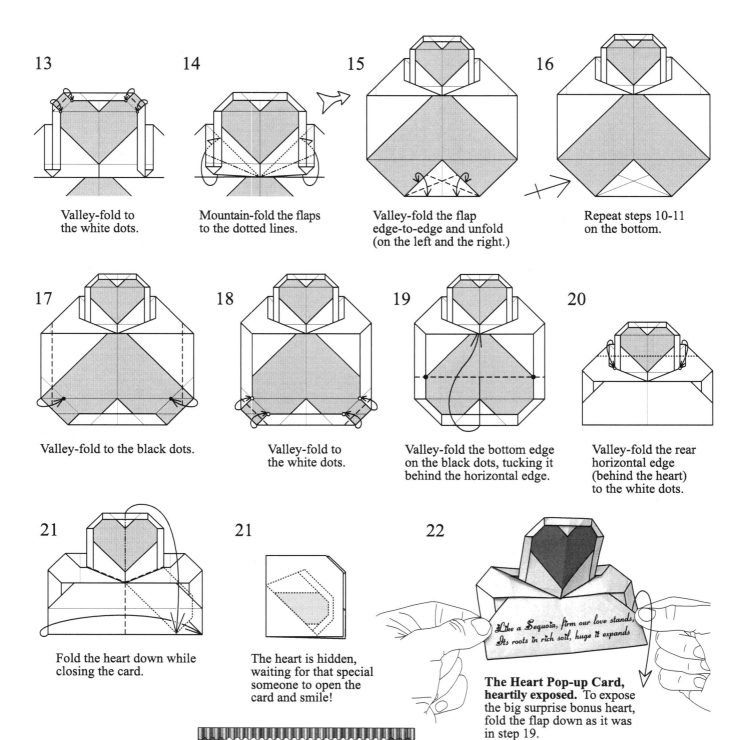

PERFORM IT!

Say to the audience, **"This pop-up card is so lovely it brings tears to my eyes."** Pretend to cry. **"Ready, set, everyone say, 'Pop-up!'"** [Audience says, "Pop-up!"] Open the card, and cry, **"Isn't it so lovely?! But it's even lovelier than you think!"** Expose the big surprise bonus heart, show it to the audience and cry loudly, **"Waaaaaaaaaaaaaaaaaaa!"**

Sacred Heart

From the Pure Land of Mountains and Valleys! By Jeremy Shafer ©2009

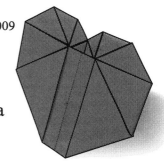

Two triangular geometric spiraling progressions converge to form a heart, which giftwise, if you are plotting to win the heart of a math brainiac, will factor nicely into your calculations.

1

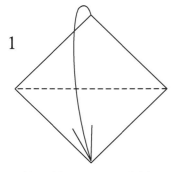

White side up, valley-fold in half diagonally. This model requires making precise folds.

2

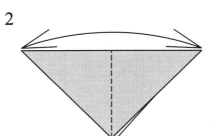

Valley-fold in half and unfold.

3

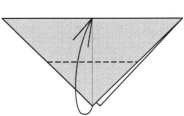

Valley-fold the front flap point-to-point.

4

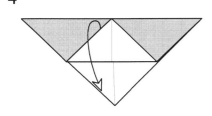

Unfold the flap.

5

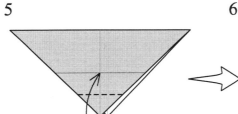

Valley-fold the front flap point-to-point and unfold.

6

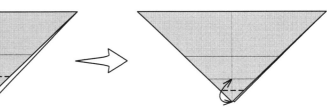

Valley-fold the front flap point-to-point and unfold.

7

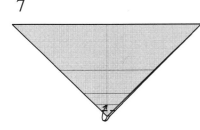

Valley-fold point-to-point on BOTH layers.

8

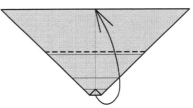

Valley-fold bottom-to-top.

9

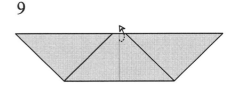

Unfold the tips of the flaps.

10

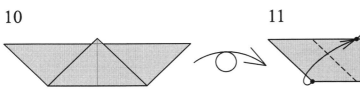

Turn over.

11

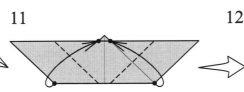

Valley-fold dot-to-dot.

12

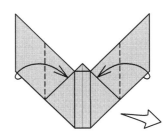

Valley-fold edge-to-edge.

Sacred Heart **195**

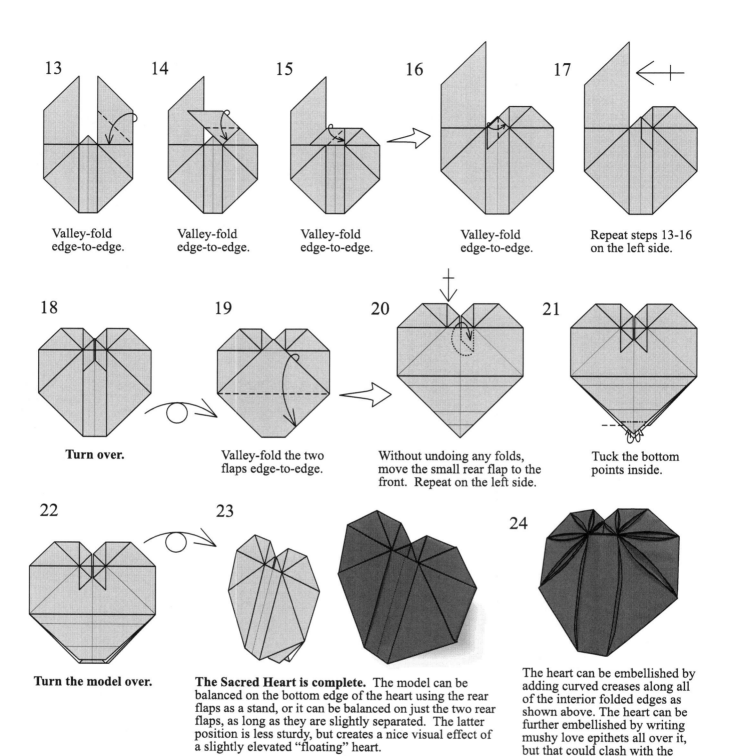

13 Valley-fold edge-to-edge.

14 Valley-fold edge-to-edge.

15 Valley-fold edge-to-edge.

16 Valley-fold edge-to-edge.

17 Repeat steps 13-16 on the left side.

18 Turn over.

19 Valley-fold the two flaps edge-to-edge.

20 Without undoing any folds, move the small rear flap to the front. Repeat on the left side.

21 Tuck the bottom points inside.

22 Turn the model over.

23 **The Sacred Heart is complete.** The model can be balanced on the bottom edge of the heart using the rear flaps as a stand, or it can be balanced on just the two rear flaps, as long as they are slightly separated. The latter position is less sturdy, but creates a nice visual effect of a slightly elevated "floating" heart.

24 The heart can be embellished by adding curved creases along all of the interior folded edges as shown above. The heart can be further embellished by writing mushy love epithets all over it, but that could clash with the pureland mountains and valleys of which the model is comprised.

PERFORM IT!

Hold up the model and say to the audience, **"This is a sacred heart. It has magical powers. It can actually speak! Do you want to hear it?"** [Audience says, "Yes!"]. **"Shh, it just spoke! Did you hear it?"** [Audience says, "No!"]. **"It said 'I love you!,' but you didn't hear it because it was speaking in sign language."** Audience protests. Either end there, or do the Perform It routine on the next page.

196 *Origami Pop-ups*

Speaking One's Heart

Here's one way to bring the Sacred Heart to life, or at least make it more animated.

 By Jeremy Shafer ©2009

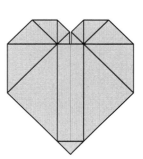

1
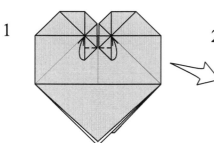

Fold steps 1-20 of the Sacred Heart. Valley-fold the two corners. Zoom in.

2
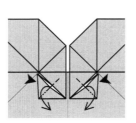

Squash.

3
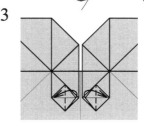

Valley-fold.

4
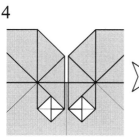

Zoom out.

5
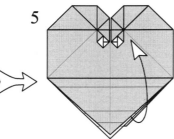

Unfold a single-layer flap.

6
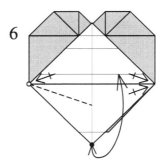

Fold the black dot to the horizontal crease and unfold, forming a crease between the white dot and the vertical middle crease. Repeat three times, forming three more such creases.

7
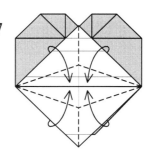

Form the mouth by folding on the existing creases.

8
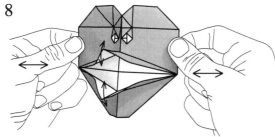

Speaking One's heart is ready to speak. Push in and out on the sides and the heart will speak... or at least mouth the words! To store the model, unfold to step 7.

9
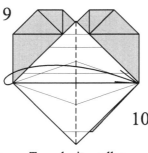

To make it smaller, fold it in half.

10
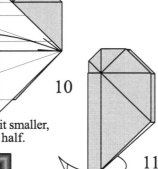

Here is a half-hearted model. Unfold the back flap.

11

Here's the back side, whole-heartedly.

PERFORM IT!

Show the back side of the model and say to the audience, **"This is a magical talking heart. What would you like it to say?"** [Audience makes requests.] Turn the model over and, operating the puppet, ventriloquistically repeat whatever the audience says. Finish by saying, **"So, as you can see, this heart is almost as smart as a talking parrot... not bad for a silly piece of paper! I think it deserves a round of hearty applause!"**

Speaking One's Heart 197

Harlequin Heart By Jeremy Shafer ©2009

If a Harlequin Jester had an origami heart, it would no doubt look something like this!

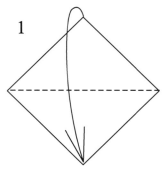

1. White side up, valley-fold in half diagonally. This model requires making precise folds.

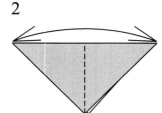

2. Valley-fold in half and unfold.

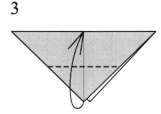

3. Valley-fold the front flap point-to-point.

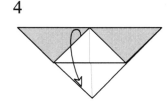

4. Unfold the flap.

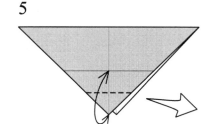

5. Valley-fold the front flap point-to-point and unfold.

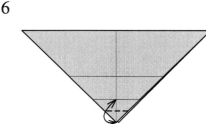

6. Valley-fold the front flap point-to-point and unfold.

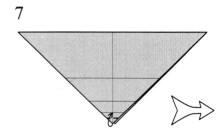

7. Valley-fold the front flap point-to-point and DON'T unfold!

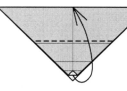

8. Valley-fold front flap so that the tiny white triangle touches the top edge.

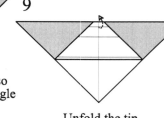

9. Unfold the tip of the flap.

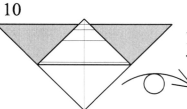

10. Turn over.

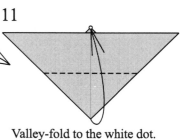

11. Valley-fold to the white dot.

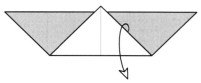

12. Unfold the front flap.

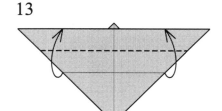

13. Valley-fold the front flap crease-to-edge.

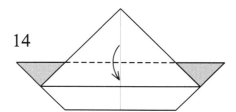

14. Valley-fold the flap on the existing crease.

198 *Origami Pop-ups*

15

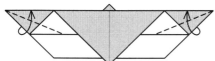

Valley-fold the front layer edge-to-edge.

16

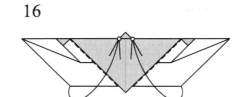

Valley-fold to the white dots.

17

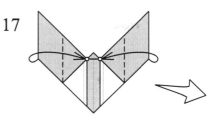

Valley-fold to the white dots.

18

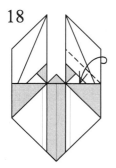

Valley-fold edge-to-edge.

19

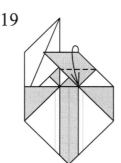

Valley-fold edge-to-edge.

20

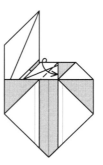

Valley-fold edge-to-edge.

21

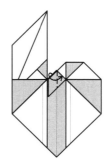

Valley-fold edge-to-edge.

22

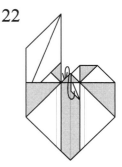

Without undoing any folds, move the small white flap to the rear.

23

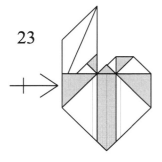

Repeat steps 18-22 on the left side.

24

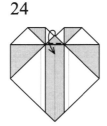

Valley-fold.

25

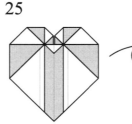

The Harlequin Heart is ready to seek the hand of a beautiful princess or perhaps a handsome prince! Turn over.

26

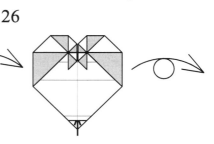

As you can see, the Harlequin Heart is pretty on both sides! For a decorative writing utensil, insert a pen into the hole indicated by the arrow and turn the model over, as shown in step 27. Or, if you would like to make a Harlequin Heart Wand, insert a large rolled up piece of paper – like the Flying Candy Cane (See page 245) – into the hole. Or, if you would like to make it into a heart card, simply valley-fold it in half as pictured in step 28.

PERFORM IT!

Put the model on the end of a straw and say to the audience, **"This is the most amazing origami model. It's a rocket heart! Three, two, one, everyone say, 'Blast off!'"** [Audience says, "Blast off!"] Blow the model off of the straw up into the air and exclaim, **"Wasn't that the most amazing thing you've ever seen?!"** [Audience says, "No."] Mutter, **"Well then, I guess I blew it."**

27

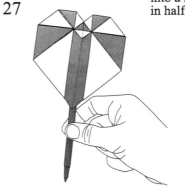

Harlequin Heart Pen

28

Harlequin Heart Card

Harlequin Heart **199**

Book of Love By Jeremy Shafer ©2010

Romance a loved one by giving them this origami Book of Love. For extra points, adorn the book with a handwritten love poem, story, or romance novel!

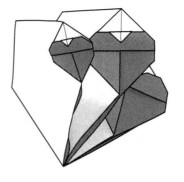

1

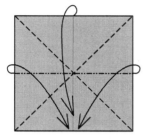

Begin by folding a white Waterbomb Base. What's a Waterbomb Base? See page 14.

2

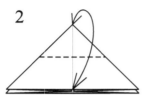

Valley-fold top-to-bottom and unfold.

3

Sink. What's a sink? See page 14.

4

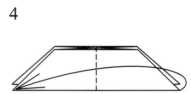

Valley-fold one flap.

5   6   7   8

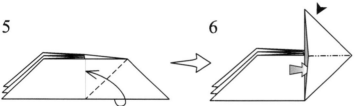

Valley-fold edge-to-crease.

Squash.

Valley-fold the flap point-to-point.

Valley-fold the flap edge-to-edge and unfold, creasing only on the top.

9

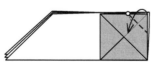

Valley-fold the flap on the white dot, corner-to-crease.

10

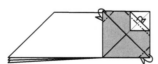

Mountain-fold the flaps to taste, forming the shape of a heart.

11

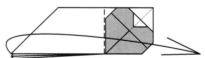

Valley-fold one flap to the right.

Thoughts Behind the Folds

This model was designed as an anniversary present to my wife and, yes, I really did embellish it with a poem! **Challenge:** What else can you fold from this base other than four hearts? **Ideas:** a blooming flower in various stages, a variety of faces (call it "Facebook!"), letters of the alphabet (L-O-V-E comes to mind), stages of the moon.

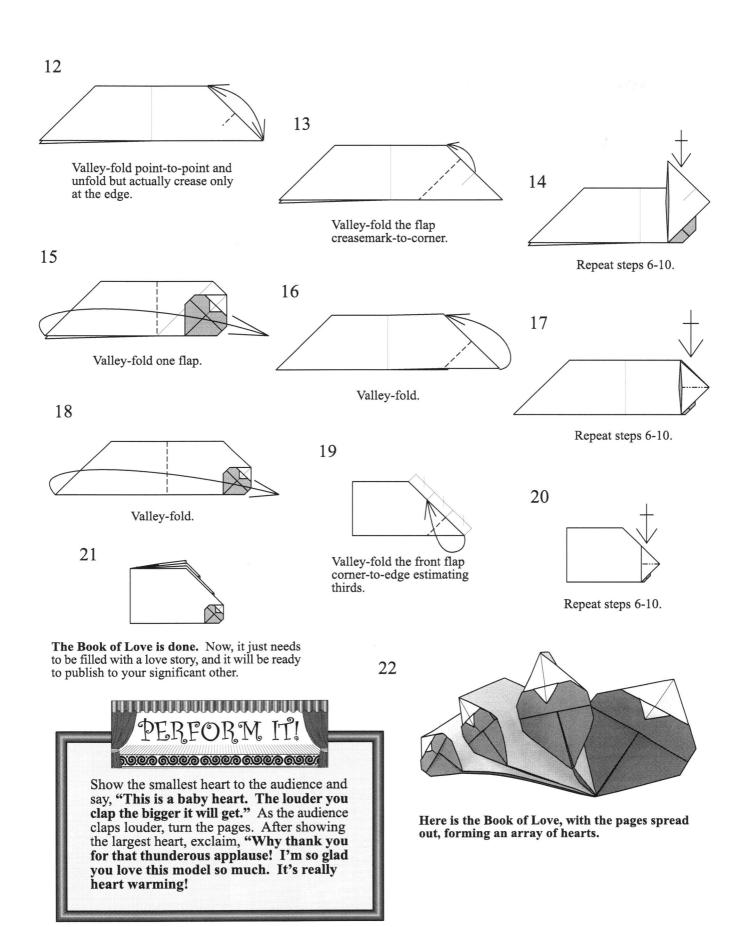

Book of Love

Flip Book of Love By Jeremy Shafer ©2010

An origami motion picture! The movie industry has never seen anything like it! At just four frames, it's still a rather primitive medium, but, if you apply the same method to more complex origami bases, it has the potential for much longer films – up to eight or perhaps even sixteen frames!

1

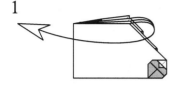

Begin by folding the Book of Love. Unfold three flaps.

2

Valley-fold one flap to the right edge.

3

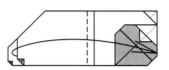

Valley-fold another flap to the right edge.

4

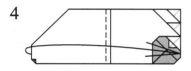

Valley-fold the final flap to the right edge.

5

The Flip Book of Love is ready for it's first screening.

Author's Advice: Filling the Flip Book with love poetry or prose will greatly enhance its audience reception, but that is beyond the scope of this origami diagram.

6

Holding as shown flip the pages. It's the Growing Heart feature film – complete with just four frames! One of the shortest films ever, but also one of the longest one-piece origami flip books, since, as far as I know, there are no others!

Note: If you would like a flip book that has more pages, fold steps 1-13 of the Clematis Pop-up (page 224) and fold the resulting square into a Waterbomb Base. This will give you eight triangular flaps, which can be folded into hearts of increasing size, like in this model. Even more pages can be achieved in the realm of box pleating, but we'll leave that for the sequel!

Book of Love with Foldouts

By Jeremy Shafer ©2010

7

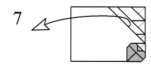

The Flip Book of Love has a nice rectangular appearance, but what can we do with those awkward pleats inside the book? Well, there is a way to lock them by making several tiny triangular internal valley folds, but why bother with the hassle when you can...

8

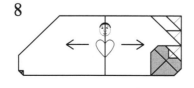

...make them into foldouts. Make a drawing on the pleat such as the one shown above. When you pull the pleat apart...

9

...the drawing changes. The pleat on the next page is narrower, but you can still make it into a foldout, perhaps a rosebud that transforms into a rose.

TV Heart

By Jeremy Shafer ©2009

Love TV? Well, now you too can be on your very own heart-shaped TV. Just fold this simple model, step behind it and PRESTO! You're a star! But there's more... This TV even comes with its own self-promoting commercial! So, don't hesitate! Pick up the piece of paper and fold this model today!

1

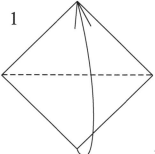

White side up, valley-fold in half.

2

Valley-fold in half and unfold.

3

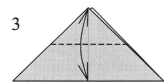

Valley-fold on both layers top-to-bottom and unfold.

4

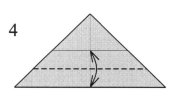

Valley-fold the bottom edge to the crease and unfold.

5

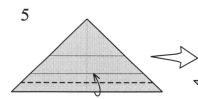

Valley-fold to the crease.

6

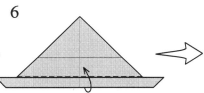

Valley-fold on the crease.

7

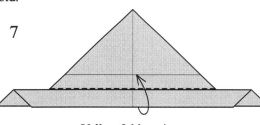

Valley-fold again...

8

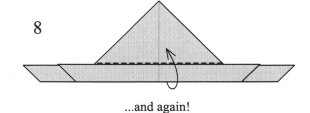

...and again!

9

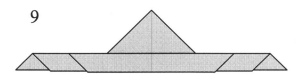

Rotate the model 180°.

PERFORM IT!

Hold up the finished model and say, **"This is a TV heart. Whoever wants to be on TV raise your hand?"** [Everyone raises their hand.] Look through the hole with one eye and say, **"You're all on TV! And so am EYE!"** Repeat, **"So am EYE!,"** and wink your eye until they get the pun. And for extra PUN, you can call it..........................

TV Heart 203

10

Valley-fold the bottom corner on to the right edge so that the black dot touches the top edge.

11

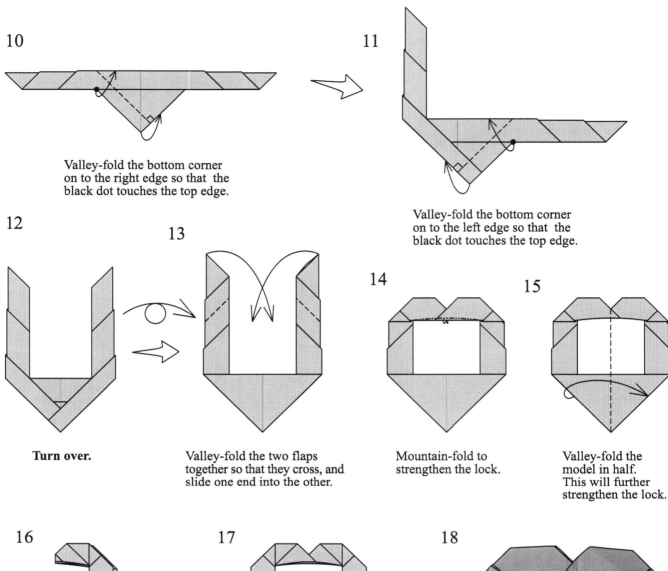

Valley-fold the bottom corner on to the left edge so that the black dot touches the top edge.

12

Turn over.

13

Valley-fold the two flaps together so that they cross, and slide one end into the other.

14

Mountain-fold to strengthen the lock.

15

Valley-fold the model in half. This will further strengthen the lock.

16

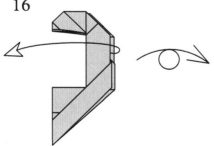

The TV Heart is ready go live. Ask your audience to try to guess what it is. When they give up, open it, look through the hole and say, "It's a TV Heart! Live from New York, it's Saturday Night!" or something to that effect.

This model can also be used as a greeting card. Actually, any flat model folded in half can be called a greeting card, but hearts work especially well. Open the greeting card and **turn it over.**

17

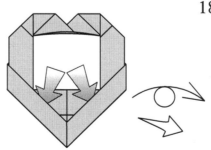

Back Side. To use this model as a heart picture frame, insert a picture into the pockets indicated by the arrows. **Turn the model over again.**

18

The TV Heart is broadcasting the next Pixar film, a romance comedy about an origamist who doesn't know how to draw.

204 *Origami Pop-ups*

Lovey-Dovey Heart Card (Super Simple)

By Jeremy Shafer ©2010

Two Doves in love! You can't get much more lovey-dovey than that! But, adorning the model with love poems will certainly earn you bonus points!

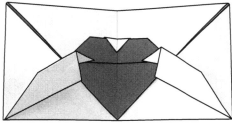

1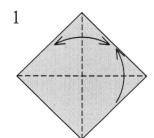

Colored side up, valley-fold in half vertically and unfold. Valley-fold in half horizontally.

2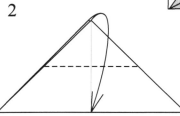

Valley-fold both layers top-to-bottom.

3

Valley-fold the front flap to the top.

4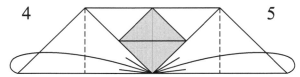

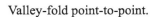

Valley-fold point-to-point.

5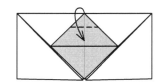

Valley-fold the flap to taste.

6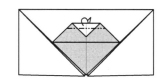

Mountain-fold the flap to taste.

7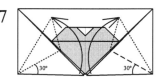

Valley-fold the flaps; aim for 30°, but to taste is alright too.

8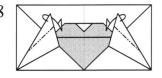

Mountain-fold the flaps to taste.

9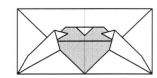

Tastefully done. If the model seems too abstract for your tastes, then use markers to color the doves... to taste! This model can also be used as an envelope. Close the card.

10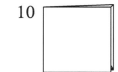

Do not disturb! The doves are nesting in the privacy of their very own flat.

PERFORM IT!

Say to the audience **"This model is too lovey dovey. I don't think I should show it to you, or should I?** [Audiences says, "Show it!"]. **"OK!"** Open the card, and explain, **"There's the two doves, there's the heart, and, and... I can't continue! It's just too lovey-dovey!"** Pretend to start to cry. **"And there's more... Look whats inside!"** Pull out a Kangaroo Heart (page 178) from inside the envelope and burst into tears, **"Waaaaaah! It's so sweet!"**

PERFORM IT!

This Perform It box is for the Star Greeting Card on the next page. Insert a picture or a drawing of an eye in both sides of the card. Hold up the closed card and say, **"This is an eight-pointed star but it's really only half of the star. Do you want to see the whole star?"** [Audiences says, "Yes!"]. Open the card so that the audience sees the outside covers and say, **"Isn't it super-cool-looking?"** [Audience raises their eyebrows] Turn it over and, showing the eyes, say, **"Come on, you know it's cool-looking!"**

Lovey Dovey Heart Card **205**

Star Greeting Card

(Rather Simple)

By Jeremy Shafer ©2004

1
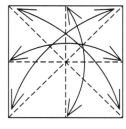

White side up, valley-fold in half and unfold in all directions.

2
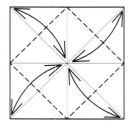

Valley-fold all four corners to the center and unfold.

3
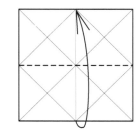

Valley-fold in half.

4
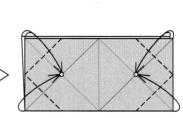

Valley-fold all corners to the white dots.

5
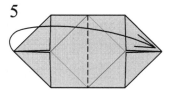

Valley-fold in half.

6
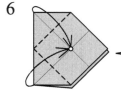

Valley-fold to the white dot.

7
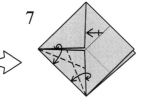

Valley-fold the flap edge-to-edge and unfold (on both edges of the flap). Repeat on the top flap.

8
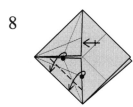

Valley-fold the flap so that the black dots touch the lower left edge of the model. Repeat on the top flap.

9
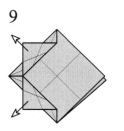

Unfold to step 6.

10
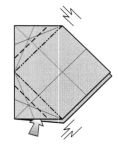

Crimp on existing creases.

11
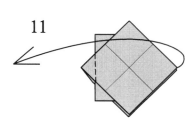

Open the card and flatten.

12
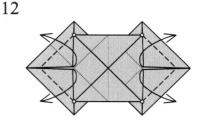

Valley-fold the flaps on the white dots parallel to the outer edges.

13
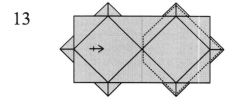

The Star Card is finished and open. Before closing it, a message can be written on the two squares. Or, to use this model as a picture frame, cut out a picture to the shape of the dotted lines and insert it into the right frame. Insert another picture into the left frame if desired.

14

Close the card.

15

Done!

206 *Origami Pop-ups*

Miracle of Life Greeting Card

Rather Simple

By Jeremy Shafer ©2006

This is a perfect greeting card for wannabe grandparents to give to their recently married daughters or sons.

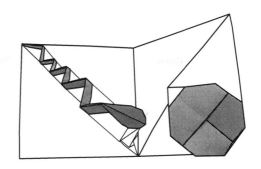

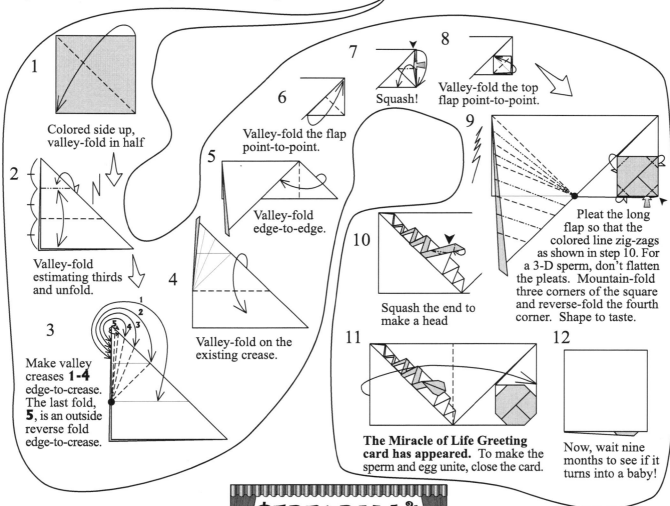

PERFORM IT!

Hold up the closed card and say to the audience, **"This is the story of how we came to be, but first, I have a question: What came first, the chicken or the..."** [Audience says, "Egg!"] Quickly open the card, but cover the sperm with your hand, and say, **"Yes. Egg! But in our case, it wasn't a chicken, and it wasn't rooster either! It was a tiny squiggly snake with a seed-like head that rhymes with *worm*."** [Audience says, "Sperm!"] Uncover the sperm and say, **"Yes, sperm!"** Say as you slowly close the card, **"And the sperm and the egg came together, and POOF! That's how we came to be! Everyone say, 'AMAZING!'"** [Audience says, "AMAZING!"]. As you put the model away, say, **"We'll save the rest of the details for when you get older."**

Go Fish Greeting Card

By Jeremy Shafer
©2006

This card was used as an invitation for the North American Go Fish Federation Pro Tournament. Not really, but if there were a NAGFFPT they would surely bite and get hooked on this card, and reel-ly bait in line to learn how to fold it!

Rather Simple

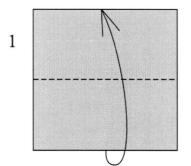

1. Colored side up, valley-fold in half.

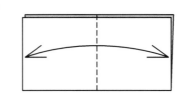

2. Valley-fold in half and unfold.

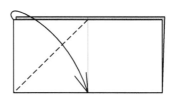

3. Valley-fold one layer point-to-point.

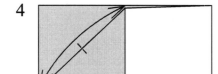

4. Valley-fold point-to-point and unfold, making a tiny creasemark.

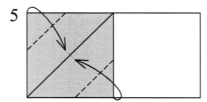

5. Valley-fold the flaps almost to crease mark (to taste).

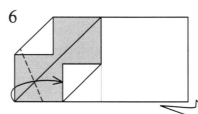

6. Valley-fold the corner to the edge to form the back of the tail should be diagonal (45°).

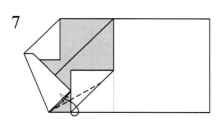

7. Valley-fold the front flap, tucking it into the pocket.

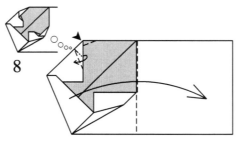

8. The fish is done, but it can be shaped further with a swivel fold or two, if desired. When you're happy with your fish, close the card.

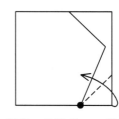

9. Valley-fold diagonally (45°) on the black dot.

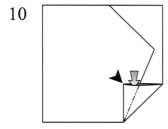

10. Squash.

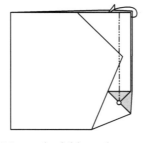

11. Mountain-fold one layer vertically on the white dot.

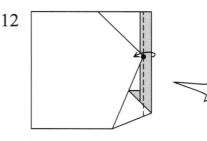

12. Valley-fold on the black dot.

208 *Origami Pop-ups*

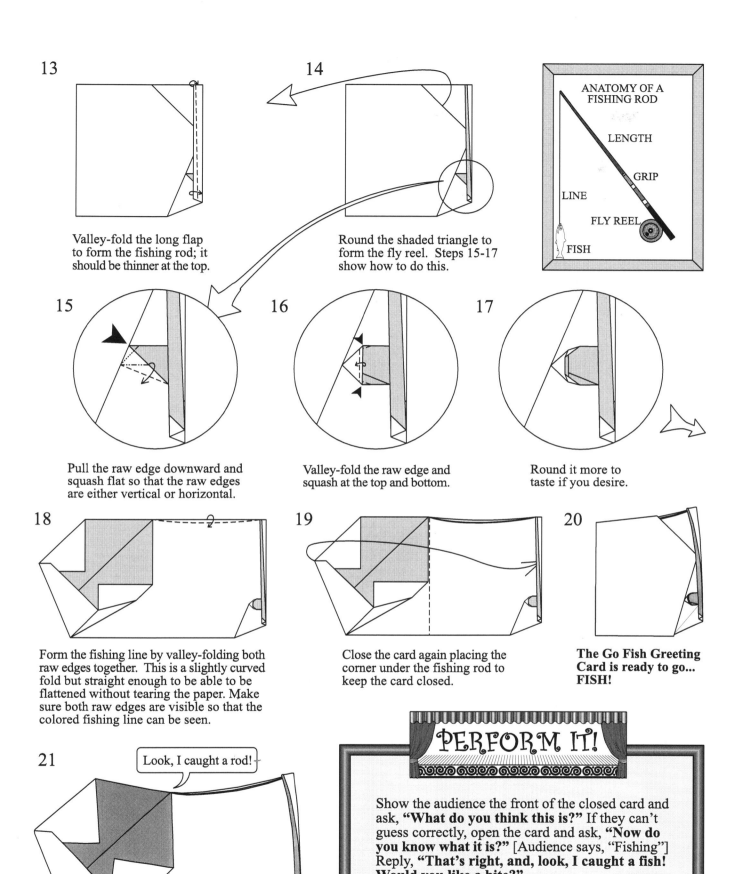

Double Heart Bookmark

By Jeremy Shafer ©2005

If you love reading, you'll love using this model as a bookmark! And if you don't love reading, you can still use it as a Valentine's Day card. And if you don't celebrate Valentine's day, you can at least use it to complete a deck of playing cards that happens to be missing the Two of Hearts. And if you don't play cards then, for crying out loud, use it as a wall decoration and stop being so difficult!

1
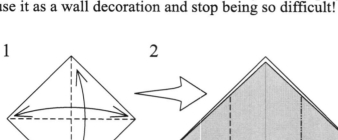

White side up, valley-fold in half diagonally left-to-right and unfold. Valley-fold in half bottom-to-top.

2

Divide the base of the model into thirds by valley-folding the left side in front and mountain-folding the right side behind, but don't flatten yet!

3
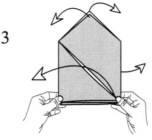

Fiddle with the folds until the thirds are exact and then flatten. Completely unfold.

4
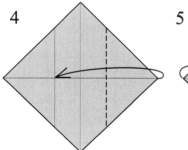

Valley-fold on the existing crease.

5
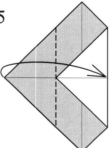

Valley-fold on the existing crease.

6
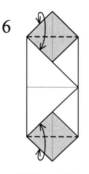

Valley-fold edge-to-edge and unfold.

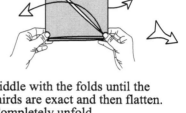

PERFORM IT!

Show the back of the card and say to the audience, **"This is an albino hot dog."** Make a disgusted face and say, **"You don't want to know what's in it! Or do you?"** [Audience says, "Yes."] Make another disgusted face and say, **"Ingredients? Two bloody-red hearts! You don't believe me! I'll show you!"** Turn the model over and, showing the hearts, say, **"I told you it was two hearts! I guess it's not as disgusting as I thought. Would you like a bite?"**

7 / 8
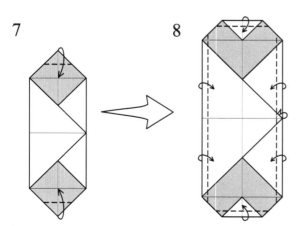

Valley-fold point-to-point.

Valley-fold. These folds are to taste, but try to make it look like step 9.

9
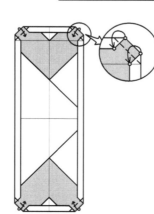

Valley-fold dot-to-dot.

10
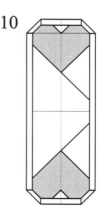

The Double Heart Bookmark is all made, ready to save the page of your favorite romance novel.

210   *Origami Pop-ups*

Airplane Silhouette

Someday we may be able to fold origami solar-powered airplanes, but in the meantime, here is an origami solar-powered airplane silhouette!

Rather Simple

By Jeremy Shafer
©2008

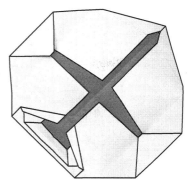

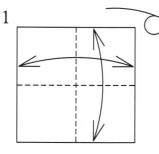

1. White side up, valley-fold in half and unfold in both directions.

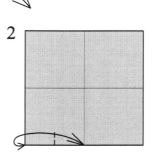

2. Valley-fold point-to-point and unfold, making a crease mark.

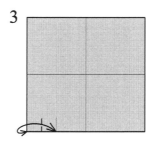

3. Valley-fold point-to-point, and unfold, making another crease mark.

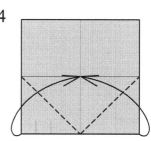

4. Valley-fold two corners to the center.

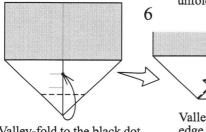

5. Valley-fold to the black dot.

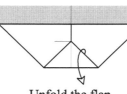

6. Valley-fold on edge and unfold (on both sides).

7. Unfold the flap.

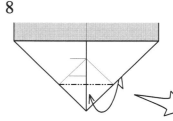

8. Mountain-fold on the existing crease and unfold.

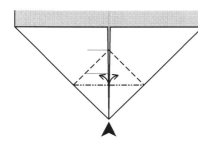

9. Open and squash the bottom on the existing creases.

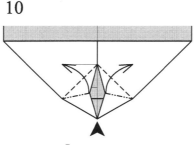

10. In progress.

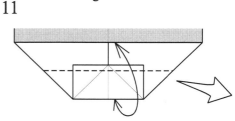

11. The squash is done and ready to serve. Valley-fold edge-to-edge and unfold.

PERFORM IT!

Show the back of the card and say to the audience, **"This is a cloud. Do you want to see the rain?"** [Audience says, "Yes."] **Well, it's a sunny day, so you can't see the rain, but you can see the plane!"** If the audience is young show the plane and say, **"Everyone spread your wings and fly like a plane!"** If the audience is older, say as you slide your hand across the model, **"This is a plane on a plane! Get it? The whole plane lies on a single plane! And it can fly too!"** Throw it. **"Ten-point landing!"**

Airplane Silhouette 211

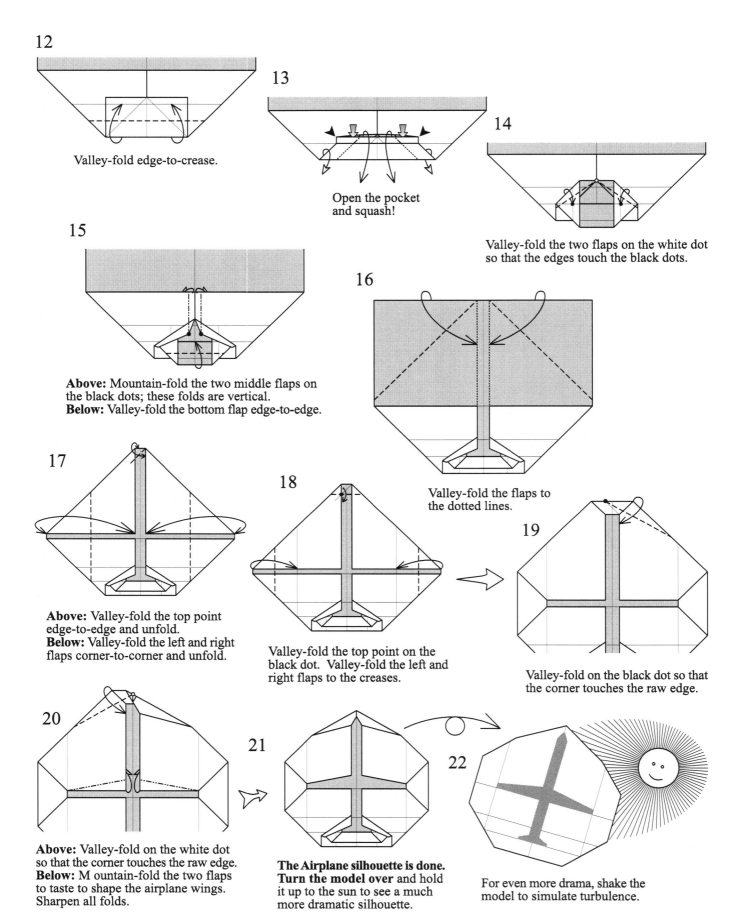

Peace Sign Pop-up Card

Intermediate

By Jeremy Shafer
©2007

Here's a model that can make amends, and help to turn foes into friends.

1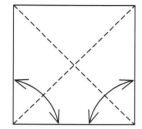

White side up, valley-fold and unfold diagonally in half in both directions.

2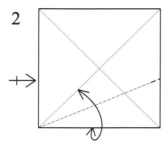

Line up the bottom edge with the diagonal crease, but flatten the paper only where the crease meets the right edge, and unfold. Repeat on the left side.

3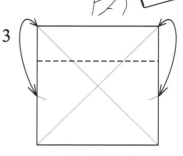

Valley-fold to the creasemarks made in step 2.

4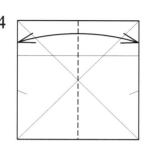

Valley-fold in half and unfold.

5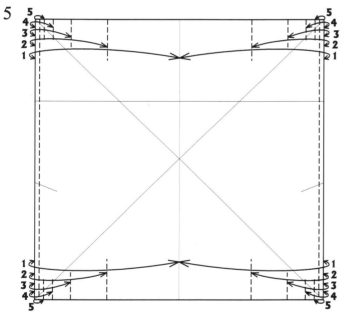

Bring the left and right edges to the vertical crease but flatten only at the top and bottom (**1**). Continue the sequence of valley creasemarks (**2-4**) and then make a complete valley fold (**5**) on each side.

6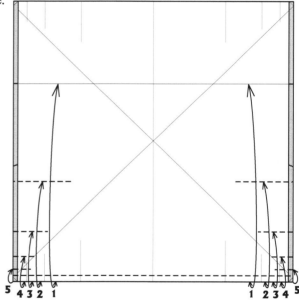

Bring the bottom edge to the horizontal crease, but flatten only at the left and right sides and unfold (**1**). Continue the sequence of valley creasemarks (**2-4**) and then make a complete valley fold (**5**) on the bottom.

7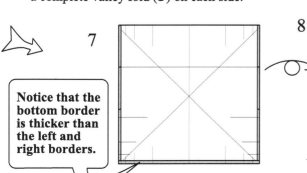

Notice that the bottom border is thicker than the left and right borders.

Turn over left-to-right.

8

Valley-fold the left and right edges of the model to center crease.

9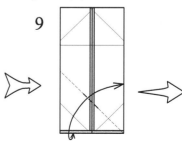

Line up the bottom edge with the right edge and flatten in the middle only, making a valley creasemark.

Peace Sign Pop-up Card 213

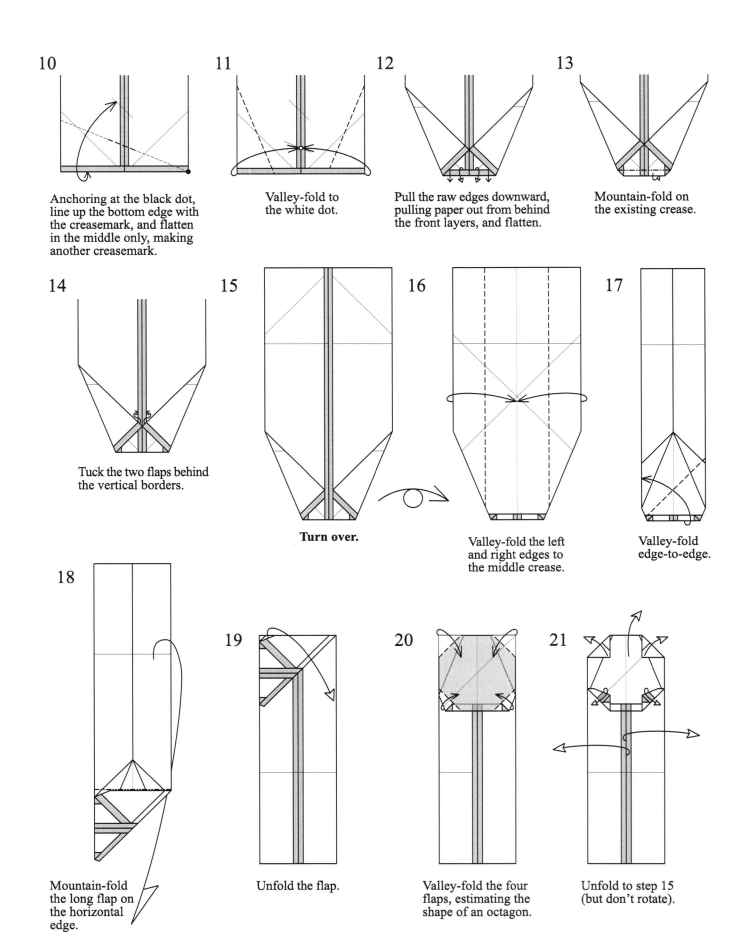

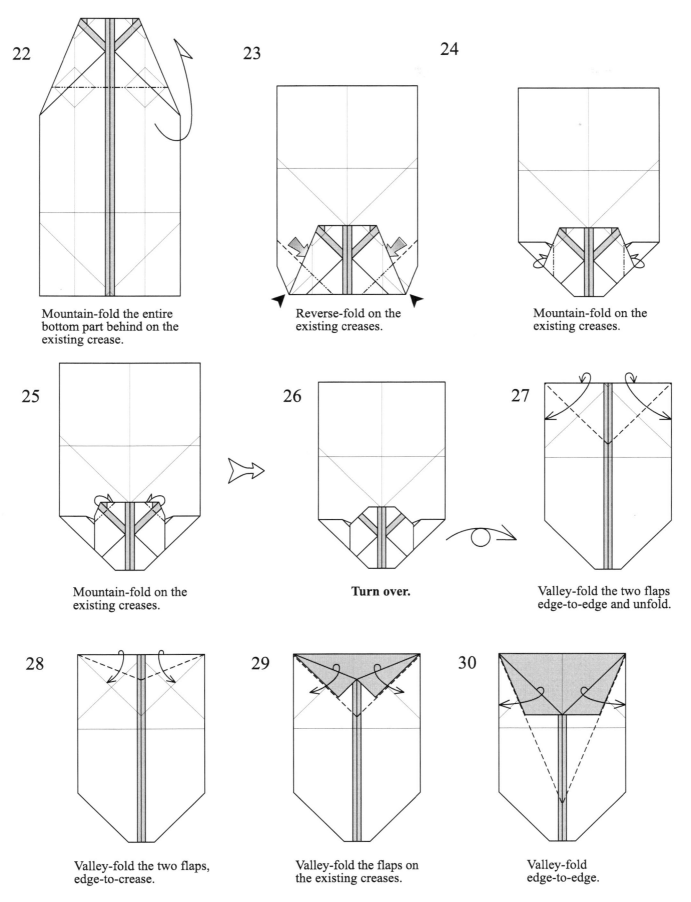

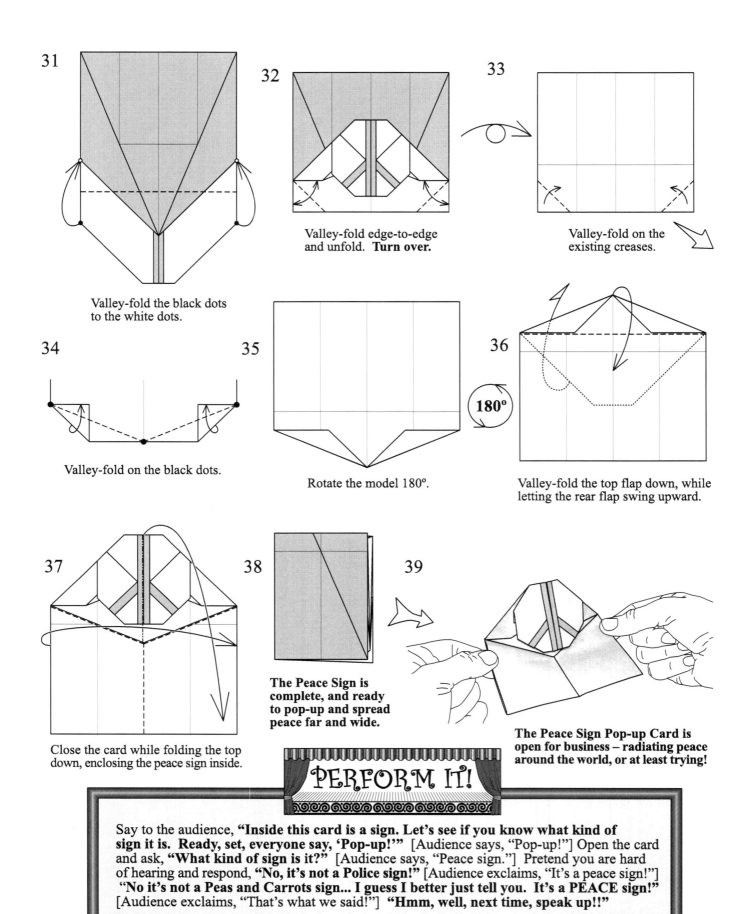

Pop-up Cubicle

By Jeremy Shafer ©2009 (Intermediate)

Perfect for Take your Cubicle to Work Day!

Having trouble getting work done at home? Simply fold this origami Cubicle and your home will instantly transform into an ultra-streamlined work environment for maximum productivity.*

1

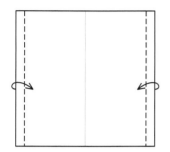

White side up, valley-fold the right and left edges of the paper. These folds need to be exact. Just kidding!

2

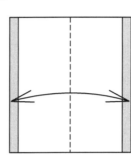

Valley-fold in half and unfold.

3

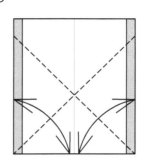

Valley-fold diagonally edge-to-edge. **Turn over.**

4

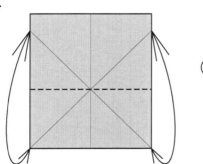

Valley-fold corner-to-crease and unfold. **Turn over top-to-bottom.**

5

Fold a Waterbomb Base on existing creases. What's a Waterbomb Base? See page 14.

6

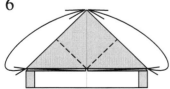

Valley-fold the front flaps corner-to-corner and unfold.

7

Valley-fold corner-to-point and unfold.

8

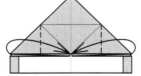

Valley-fold the front flaps to the middle.

---

* This statement has not been evaluated by any government agency, so don't blame me if you still can't get any work done!

9

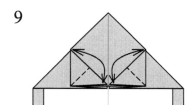

Valley-fold front flaps in half and unfold.

10

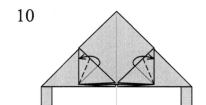

Valley-fold the front flaps crease-to-edge.

11

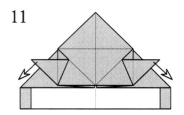

Unfold the two pleats.

12

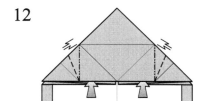

Crimp the front flaps on existing creases.

13

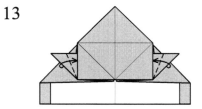

Valley-fold the flaps edge-to-edge.

14

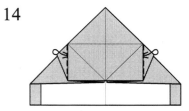

Valley-fold, tucking the flaps into the pockets.

15

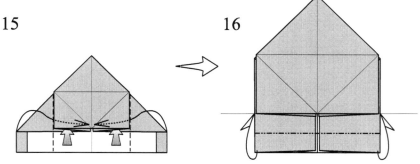

Valley-fold the left and right sides to the middle, inserting them behind the front flaps.

16

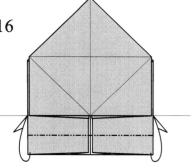

Mountain-fold to the horizonal line.

17

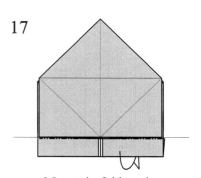

Mountain-fold on the horizontal line.

18

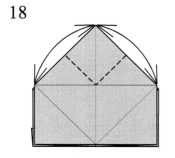

Fold corner-to-corner making two valley creases thru all layers; the two creases should extend to the middle crease.

19

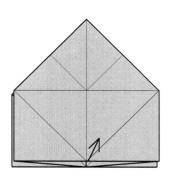

Open the bottom pocket; the model will not lie flat.

20

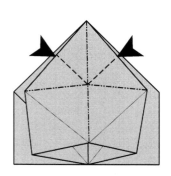

Push where indicated, squeezing together the two edges; the model will still not lie flat, darn it!

218   *Origami Pop-ups*

21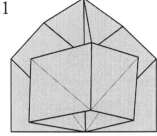

The Cubicle is ready to house a miniature office, or it can be used as the green room for your flea circus.

22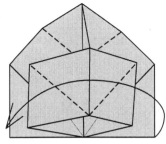

To store, collapse the model on the existing creases as you close the card.

23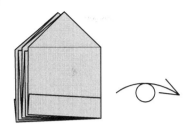

The model is finally lying flat! Yay! Hey, it looks like a house! Perhaps it's time to leave the office and go home! **But first, turn the model over!**

24

The Pop-up Cubicle is done. Open the card...

25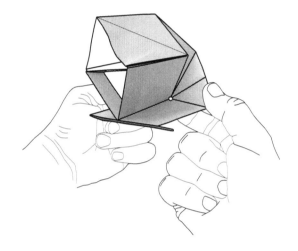

PERFORM IT!

Say to the audience, **"This is a pop-up of a cube with an giant mouth! Ready set, everyone open your mouth wide and yell, 'Pop-up!'"** [Audience yells, "Pop-up!"] Open the card and ask, **"What do you call a cube with a giant mouth?"** [Audience says, "What?"] Answer, **"An open box! Duh!"**

...and it WON'T pop-up as shown above. That's because you haven't pressed the magic button! Holding as shown, press the back of the model at the white dot with your index finger. The cube will not only pop-up into shape, but if you press it repeatedly, it will start to dance – the Rockin' Cubicle!

Warning: Don't get caught folding this model at work or your boss might confiscate not just your origami cubicle – but the real one too!

Note: The original challenge that I set out to try to fold was a Pop-up Cube, but this intermediary model, with only five faces (instead of six), is easier to fold, more efficient, and has a better pop-up action than my final Pop-up Cube (unpublished). So, I thought, why not stop here and call it a Cubicle! The moral of the story is, "When you fall short of any goal, simply reframe the goal, and you can call it a triumph!" I would like to add, though, that although this cube is missing one face, it does have all twelve edges!

Pop-up Cubicle

Cherry Blossom Pop-up Card

My original plan was to design an origami cherry blossom card that I could teach at the San Francisco Cherry Blossom Festival, but this design that I ended up with was too complex to teach to beginners, so I just demonstrated it instead. What I like about this model is how the cherry blossom opens as you open the card, and I also like that it's made from a square even though a cherry blossom has five petals.

(Intermediate)

By Jeremy Shafer ©2011

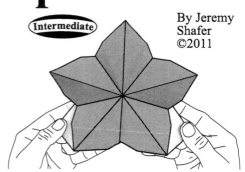

1

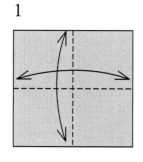

Colored side up, valley-fold in half and unfold in both directions.

2

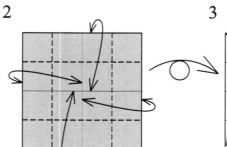

Valley-fold edge-to-crease and unfold on all sides. **Turn over.**

3

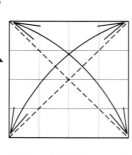

Valley-fold diagonally in half and unfold in both directions.

4

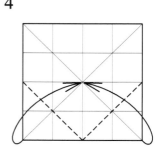

Valley-fold the bottom corners to the center.

5

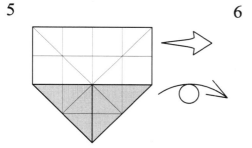

Turn over.

6

Valley-fold edge-to-crease, letting the rear flap swing into view.

7

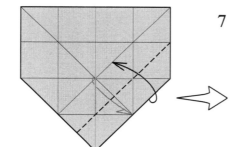

Valley-fold edge-to-crease, letting the rear flap swing into view.

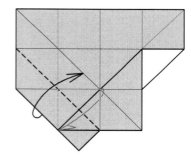

8

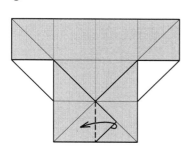

Valley-fold the flap to the left.

9

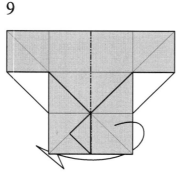

Mountain-fold the model in half.

10

Pull out the flap. Watch the black dot.

11

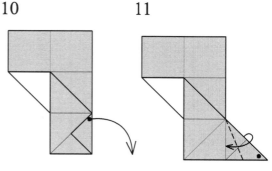

Valley-fold edge-to-crease.

220 *Origami Pop-ups*

12

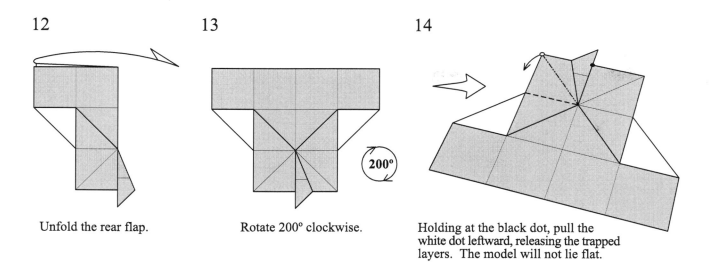

Unfold the rear flap.

13

Rotate 200° clockwise.

14

Holding at the black dot, pull the white dot leftward, releasing the trapped layers. The model will not lie flat.

15

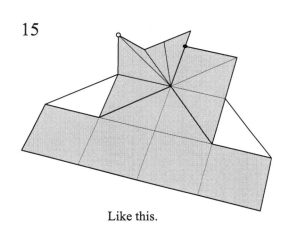

Like this.

16

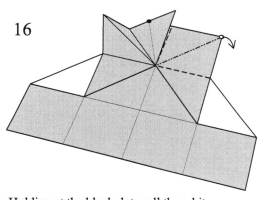

Holding at the black dot, pull the white dot to the right, releasing the layers.

17

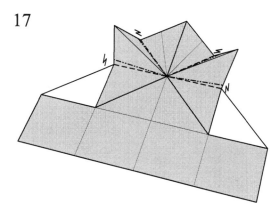

Make four pleats of equal size. The exact size is not important, but the model should still not lie flat.

18

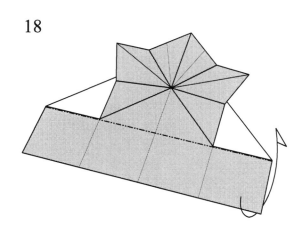

Mountain-fold on the existing crease.

Cherry Blossom Pop-up Card **221**

19

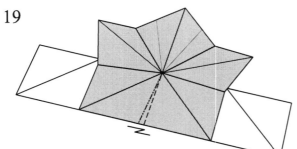

Pleat; the valley fold is on an existing crease and the mountain fold is new. The smaller the pleat, the easier the card will be to fully open but the smaller the crevice between petals will be.

20

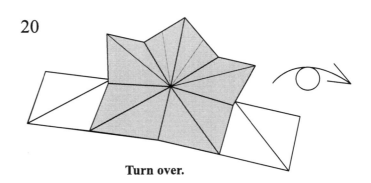

Turn over.

21

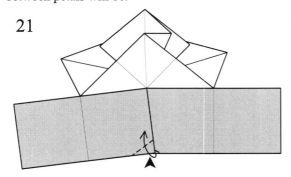

Valley-fold and squash.

22

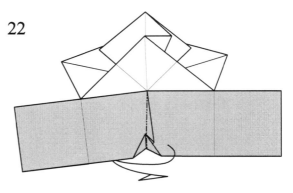

Mountain-fold the card in half and unfold; try not to fold the top part.

23

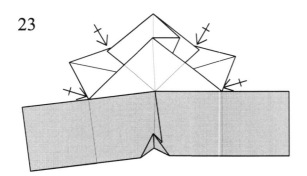

Repeat step 21 on the four remaining pleats.

24

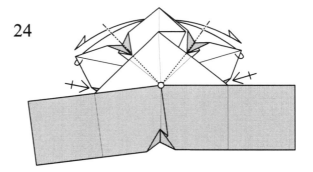

Make two mountain creases that extend behind the front layers to the white dot. **Repeat on the two remaining pleats.**

PERFORM IT!

Say to the audience, **"FORging ahead, FOR our next pop-up we have a metaPHOR FOR bursting FORth into Spring, and it has nothing to do with the number FOUR! Bursting forth into Spring is a... Everyone yell, 'Pop-up!'"** [Audience yells, "Pop-up!"] Open the card and ask, **"What is it?"** If nobody guesses correctly, start slowly saying the answer, **"...is a C-H-E-R-R-Y B-L-O-S-S-O-M"** until someone yells, "Cherry blossom!" and reply, **"YES! And in Japan the cherry blossom is a symbol for the beginning of Spring! Everyone smile like a cherry blossom!"** [Audience smiles.] Exclaim, **"Wow look at those smiles!... You must have really liked this pop-up card!"**

222 *Origami Pop-ups*

25

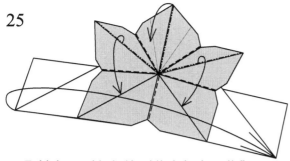

Fold the card in half, while bringing all five petal corners together on existing creases.

26

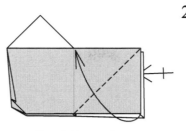

Valley-fold one flap. **Repeat behind.**

27

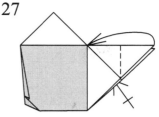

Valley-fold. **Repeat behind.**

28

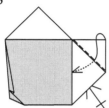

Valley-fold, tucking the flap into the pocket. **Repeat behind.**

29

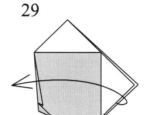

Done! Open the card, being careful that the pleat on the spine of the card does not come undone (hold it together).

Extra Credit:
You've probably noticed that the pleat on the spine tends to come apart when you open the card (if you don't hold it in place). There is a way to rearrange the folds to make it hold together much better but it is rather tricky. It requires unfolding to step 18 and recollapsing on the existing creases made in steps 19, 21 and 22 so that the model looks the same on the front, looks cleaner on the back, and doesn't come apart when the card is opened.
Hint: Step 19 is a crimp instead of a pleat.
Solution: Follow the crease pattern shown to the right.

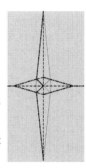

30

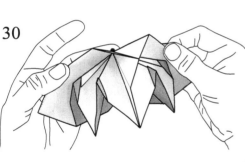

Opening in progress. Make sure that one finger is on the black dot.

31

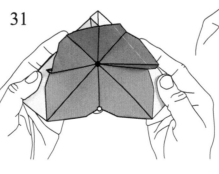

Further in progress. Holding one finger on the white dot (so that the pleat doesn't come undone), push on the black dot from behind, opening the cherry blossom.

32

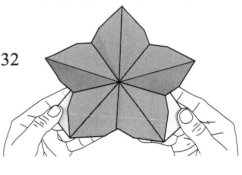

The Finished Cherry Blossom Pop-up Card... greeting yet another Spring.

Video tutorial on youtube.com!
Search: origami cherry blossom

You could try to round the petals with mountain folds to look even more like a cherry blossom (as pictured above), but don't you dare cut it (as I've seen done to the traditional origami Cherry Blossom)!

Cherry Blossom Pop-up Card

Clematis Pop-up Card

By Jeremy Shafer ©2003 (Complex)

Here's a pop-up of a blooming clematis. What's that? Well, it's a flower, and, you see, there's an international organization whose goal it is to see the clematis rival the rose in popularity. In my humble opinion, the first step should be to change the name to something that sounds less like a disease.

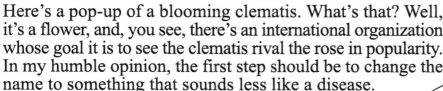

Check out: **http://www.clematisinternational.com**

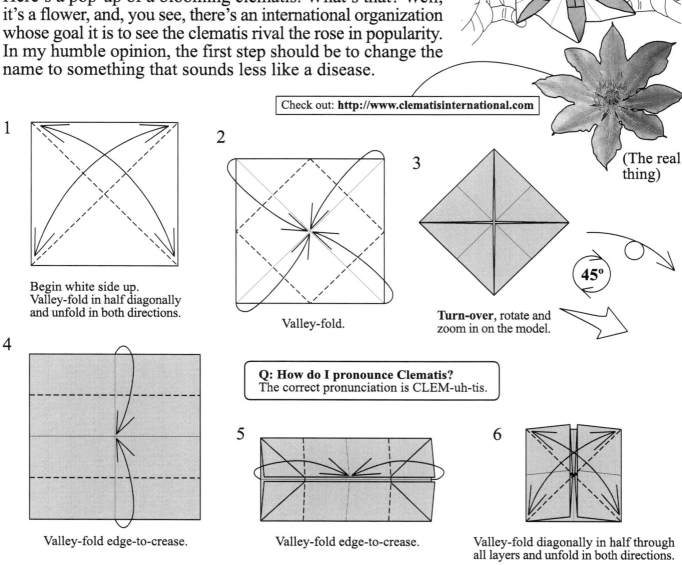

1. Begin white side up. Valley-fold in half diagonally and unfold in both directions.
2. Valley-fold.
3. **Turn-over**, rotate and zoom in on the model.

Q: How do I pronounce Clematis?
The correct pronunciation is CLEM-uh-tis.

4. Valley-fold edge-to-crease.
5. Valley-fold edge-to-crease.
6. Valley-fold diagonally in half through all layers and unfold in both directions.

7. Valley-fold the flaps if you haven't done so already.

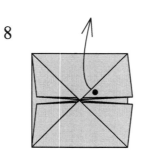

8. Holding the flap at the black dot, slide it upward, freeing the trapped layers. Watch the black dot.

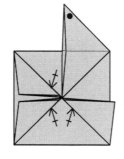

9. Repeat step 8 on the other three flaps.

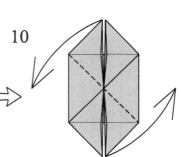

10. Valley-fold the upper left flap and the lower right flap.

224 *Origami Pop-ups*

11

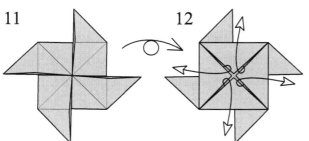

This is called a Blintzed Pinwheel Base. **Turn over.**

12

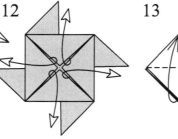

Unfold the four front flaps.

13

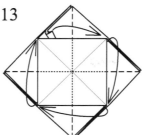

Valley-fold the four interior white flaps in a clockwise direction. The top such flap is shown in progress.

14

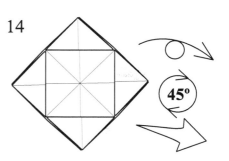

Turn-over, rotate and zoom in on the model.

15

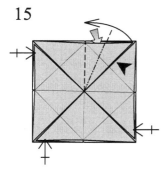

Squash the flap. Repeat on the other three flaps.

16

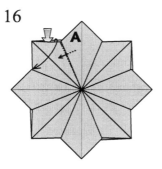

Pull the raw edge downward, pulling paper out from behind flap **A** and flatten. The next step shows this in progress.

17

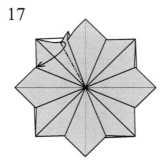

In progress. Continue pulling the raw edge down and flatten. The mountain fold (new) gets formed when you flatten.

18

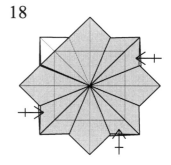

Repeat steps 16-17 on the other such raw edges.

19

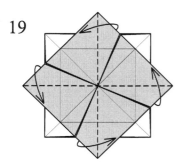

Valley-fold the four flaps.

20

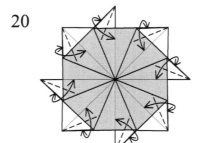

Valley-fold the eight flaps (front layers only) edge-to-crease and unfold.

21

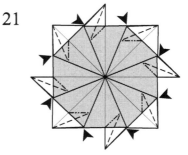

Reverse-fold eight times; the valley folds are on existing creases and the mountain folds (new) extend to the midpoints of the sides of the shaded octagon.

PERFORM IT!

Say to the audience, **"This is a pop-up flower. Everyone yell, 'Pop-up!'"** [Audience yells, "Pop-up!"] Open the card and say, **"Guess how many petals it has."** [Audience says, "Eight."] Pretend you are hard of hearing and respond, **"Eight hundred???"** [Audience says, "No, "EIGHT!"] Respond, **"Eight Thousand??!!"** and so on until you finish the joke by saying, **"No, it only has eight petals! I don't know what you were thinking!"**

Clematis Pop-up Card

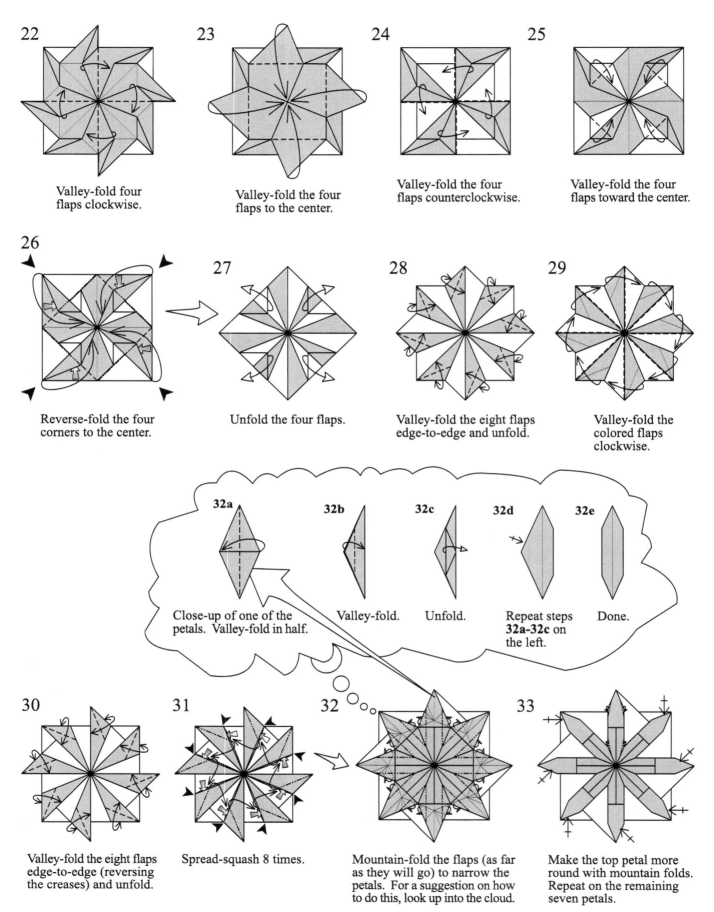

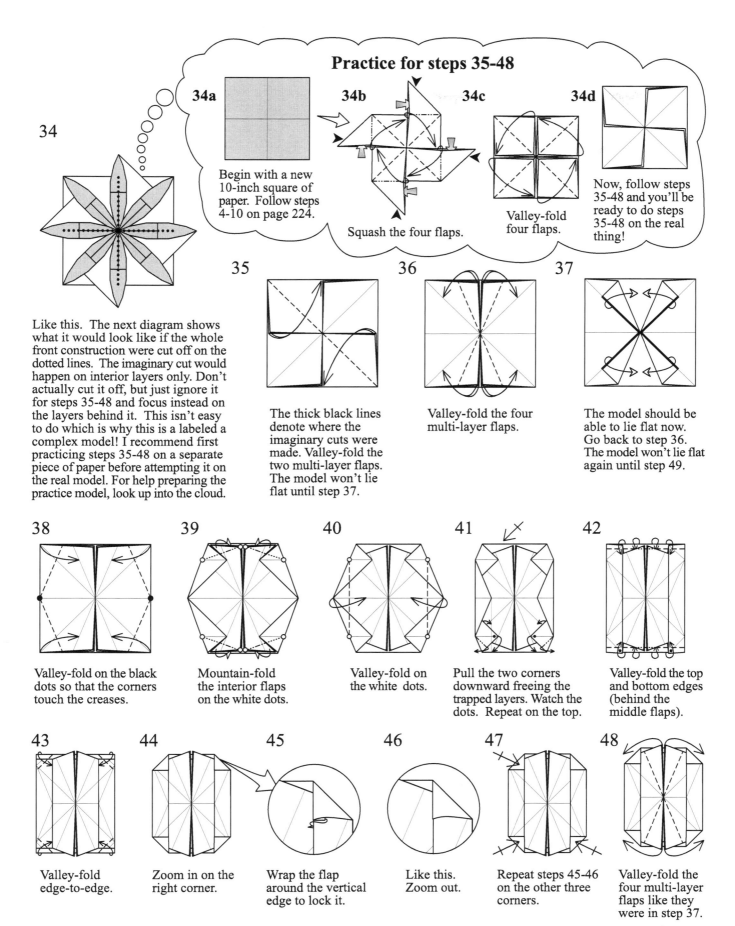

Clematis Pop-up Card 227

49

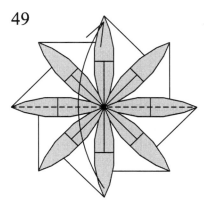

Look, the top construction has magically been restored! Valley-fold the model in half thru all layers...

50

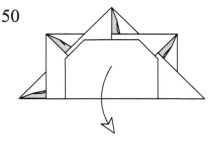

...and unfold.

51

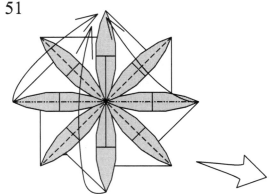

Valley-fold the rear layers in half again, but this time folding the front construction into a Square Base.

52

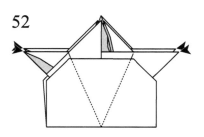

Reverse-fold the four petals that are sticking out.

53

Like this. Now, for the next diagram, imagine that the front petal is torn off.

54

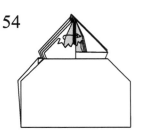

Unfold the colored flap rightward.

55

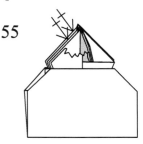

Repeat step 54 on the two remaining left colored flaps.

56   57   58

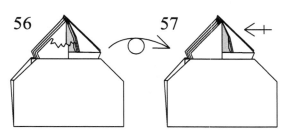

Turn over.   Repeat steps 54-55 on the right side.   **The Pop-up Clematis is ready to open.**

Thoughts Behind the Folds

This model came out of a somewhat mathematical exercise in inside-out origami: Given a square of paper, black on one side and white on the other, what is the maximum length of border between black and white that can be achieved via folding the square. I wasn't able to solve the problem in that there possibly could be an even longer border, but at least my attempt resulted in a black/white border that exceeds the perimeter of the square by roughly 108% (see step 32 and imagine adding microscopic mountain folds on the inner petal edges, to extend the black/white border), and it resulted in a pretty flower too!

59

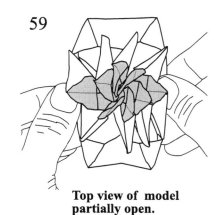

Top view of model partially open. Holding as shown, pull open to a full bloom.

60

Clematis in full bloom. If the flower has trouble returning to its closed position when the card is closed again, you can either accept that it will need assistance or you can try the following: Press the closed model flat between two hard plastic or metal sheets (lids work well) and secure it with clamps or rubber bands. Dunk the whole thing in water and set it out to dry. This should greatly improve the model's ability to close back up.

228 *Origami Pop-ups*

Maple Leaf Pop-up Card

Rather Complex

By Jeremy Shafer
©2012

This model inspired me to learn how to play the Maple Leaf Rag on the piano.

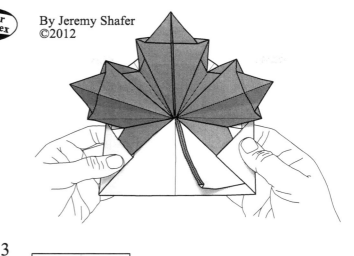

1

White side up, valley-fold and unfold in both directions.

2

Valley-fold the two bottom corners to the center.

3

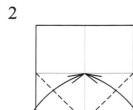

Turn over.

4

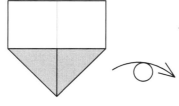

Valley-fold dot-to-dot and unfold, creasing only where indicated. Repeat on the left side.

5

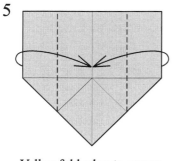

Valley-fold edge-to-crease.

6

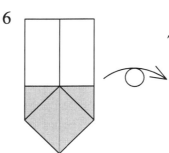

Turn over.

7

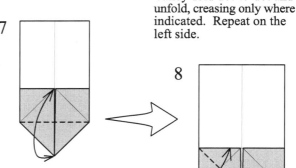

Valley-fold point-to-point and unfold.

8

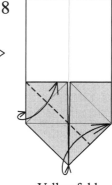

Valley-fold edge-to-edge and unfold.

9

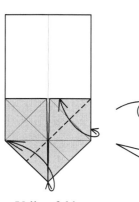

Valley-fold edge-to-edge and unfold. **Turn over.**

10

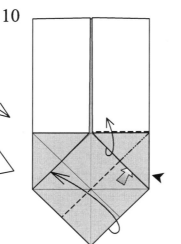

Squash.

11

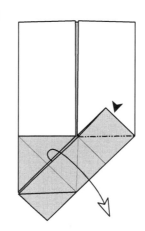

Unsquash! (i.e., return the model to step 10).

Maple Leaf Pop-up Card **229**

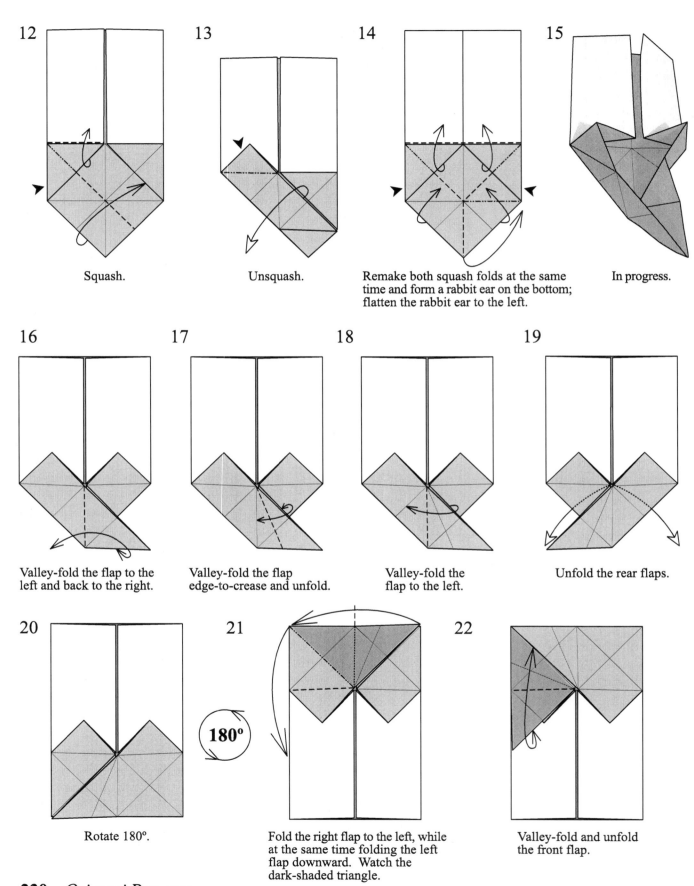

230 *Origami Pop-ups*

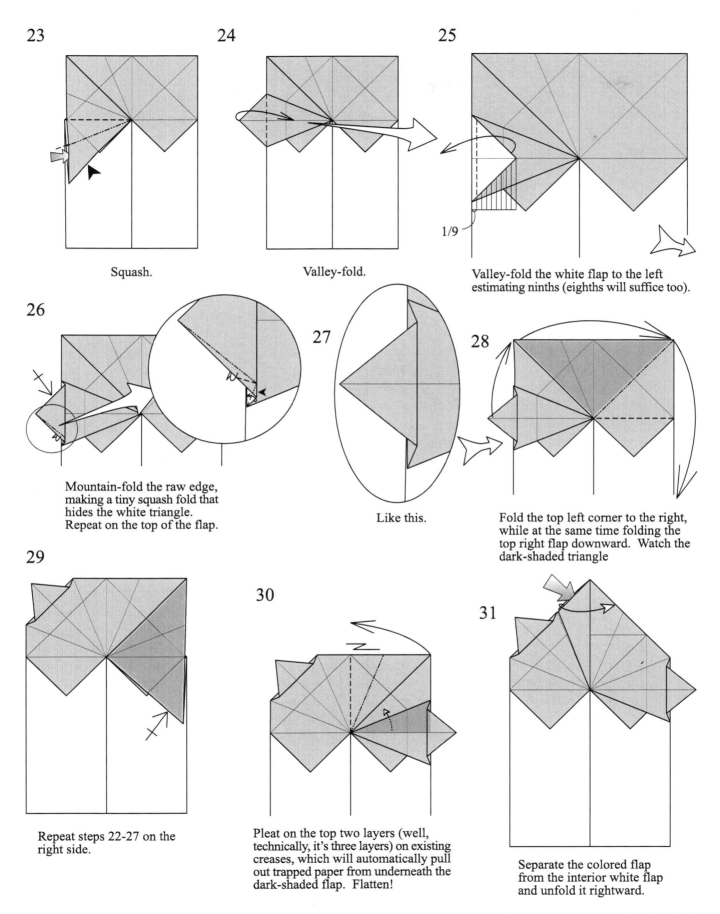

Maple Leaf Pop-up Card 231

32

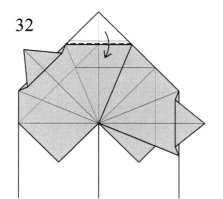

Valley-fold on edge. Don't stress!

33

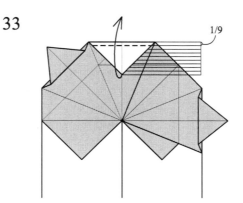

Valley-fold the white flap estimating ninths (eighths will suffice too).

34

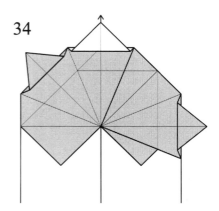

Unfold the white flap.

35

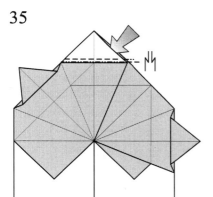

Crimp on existing creases.

36

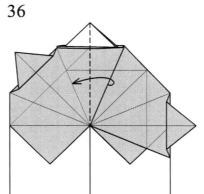

Valley-fold the flap to the left.

37

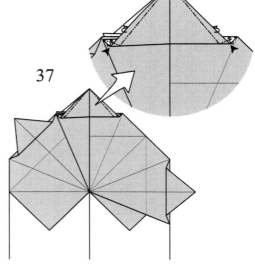

Mountain-fold the two raw edges, making two tiny squash folds that hide the white triangles; the tiny valley folds are edge-to-edge.

38

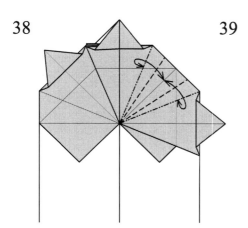

Pleat and unpleat on the top layer only.

39

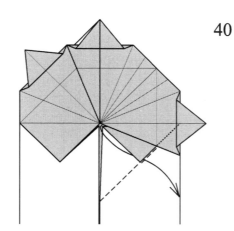

Pull out the interior flap and valley-fold it to the right edge.

40

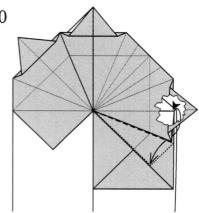

Cut-away view. Pull out the interior flap and valley-fold it to the diagonal folded edge. Flatten.

232 *Origami Pop-ups*

41

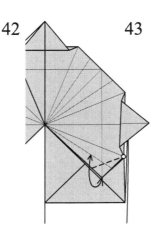

Valley-fold the flap edge-to-crease and unfold.

42

Valley-fold the flap on the white dot so that the corner of the flap hits the existing crease, and unfold.

43

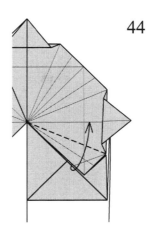

Valley-fold the flap.

44

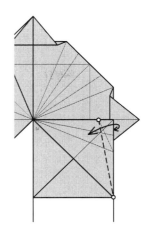

Valley-fold on the white dots (top layer only) and unfold.

45

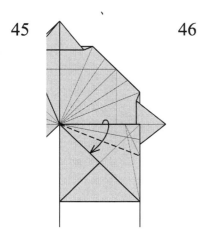

Valley-fold the flap down.

46

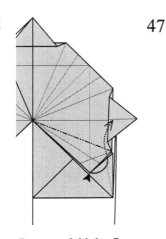

Reverse-fold the flap, returning it to how it was in step 40.

47

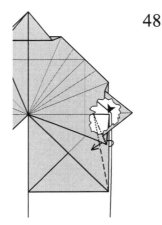

Cut-away view. Reverse-fold the interior flap on existing creases.

48

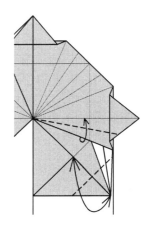

Above: Valley fold the flap edge-to-crease.
Below: Valley-fold the flap point-to-point and unfold.

49

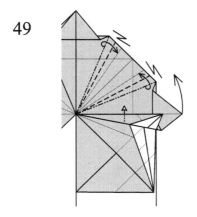

On the top layer only, perform the indicated pleats (crease-to-crease) by pulling out paper from underneath the horizontal edge (the mountains are on existing creases; the valleys are new). Follow the arrows.

50

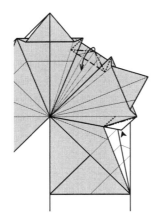

Above: Pull the raw edge downward (as far as it will go) and flatten.
Below: Reverse-fold the small white flap (on edge).

51

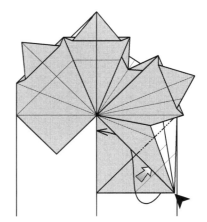

Reverse-fold the flap on the existing creases.

Maple Leaf Pop-up Card 233

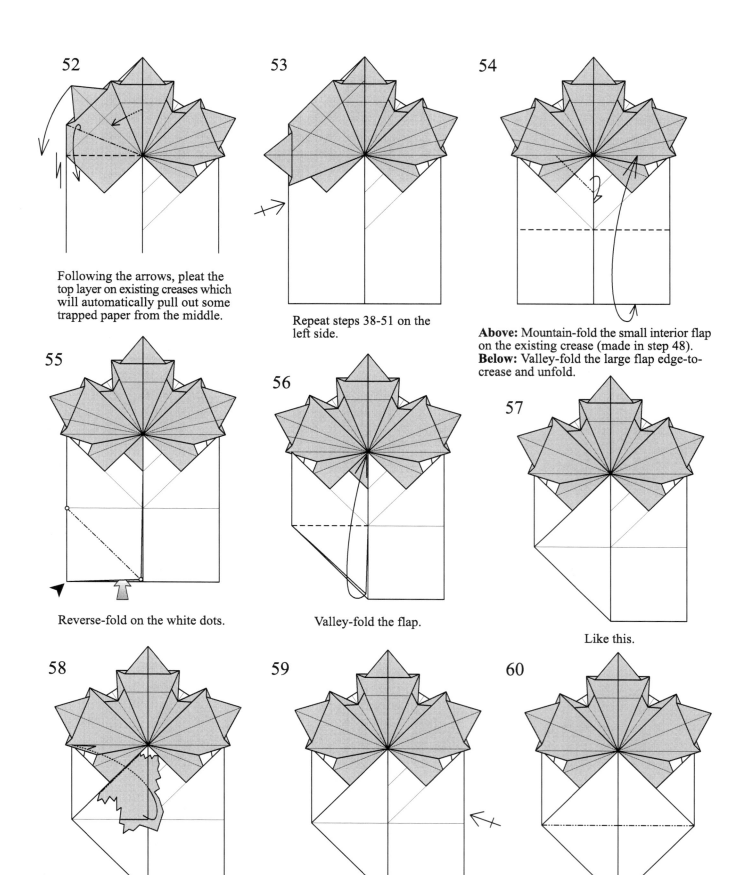

52. Following the arrows, pleat the top layer on existing creases which will automatically pull out some trapped paper from the middle.

53. Repeat steps 38-51 on the left side.

54. **Above:** Mountain-fold the small interior flap on the existing crease (made in step 48). **Below:** Valley-fold the large flap edge-to-crease and unfold.

55. Reverse-fold on the white dots.

56. Valley-fold the flap.

57. Like this.

58. Tear-away view. Mountain-fold the interior flap deep inside the model.

59. Repeat steps 54-58 on the right side.

60. Sink on existing creases.

234 *Origami Pop-ups*

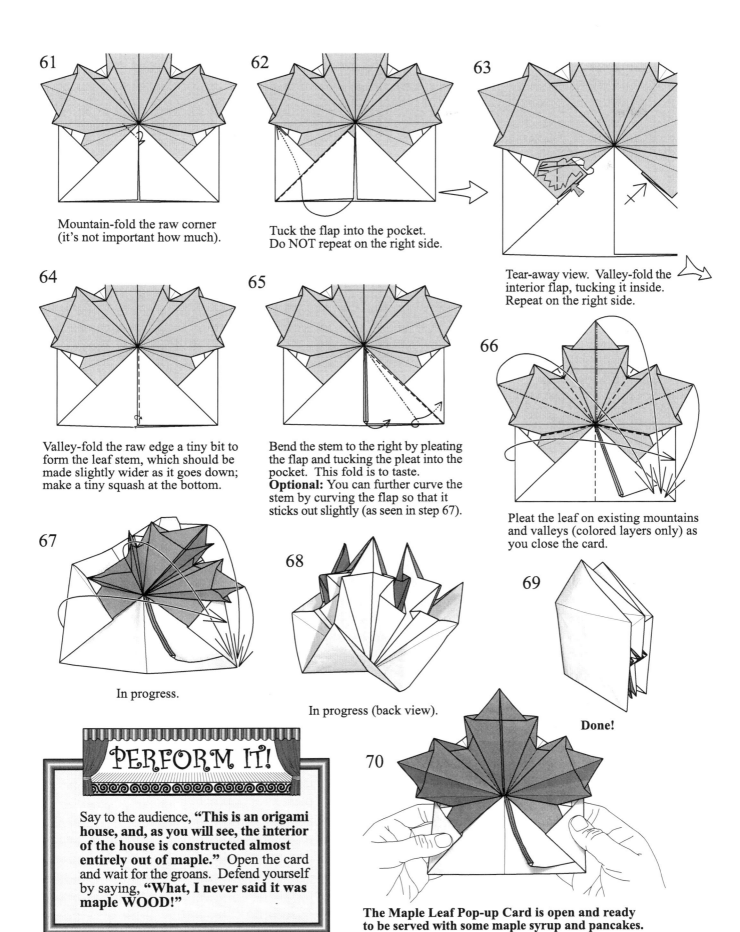

61 Mountain-fold the raw corner (it's not important how much).

62 Tuck the flap into the pocket. Do NOT repeat on the right side.

63 Tear-away view. Valley-fold the interior flap, tucking it inside. Repeat on the right side.

64 Valley-fold the raw edge a tiny bit to form the leaf stem, which should be made slightly wider as it goes down; make a tiny squash at the bottom.

65 Bend the stem to the right by pleating the flap and tucking the pleat into the pocket. This fold is to taste.
Optional: You can further curve the stem by curving the flap so that it sticks out slightly (as seen in step 67).

66 Pleat the leaf on existing mountains and valleys (colored layers only) as you close the card.

67 In progress.

68 In progress (back view).

69 **Done!**

70 The Maple Leaf Pop-up Card is open and ready to be served with some maple syrup and pancakes.

PERFORM IT!

Say to the audience, **"This is an origami house, and, as you will see, the interior of the house is constructed almost entirely out of maple."** Open the card and wait for the groans. Defend yourself by saying, **"What, I never said it was maple WOOD!"**

Maple Leaf Pop-up Card

You've almost reached the end of this book. Just in case some of the models made you feel stressed, well, this final model will hopefully help you get rid of that stress!

Stress Reliever

By Jeremy Shafer ©2011

Full of key pressure points, this model can help manage and relieve mild stress. For extreme stress consult a physician.
Disclaimer: This model is not meant to treat or diagnose any illnesses, but it is darn fun to play with!

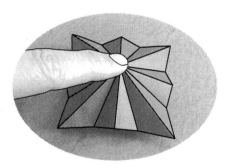

1

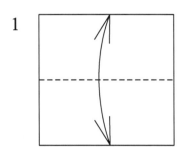

White side up, valley-fold in half and unfold.

2

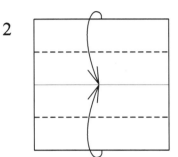

Valley-fold to the crease.

3

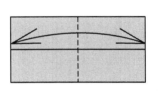

Valley-fold in half and unfold. Rotate 90°.

4

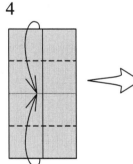

Valley-fold to the crease.

5

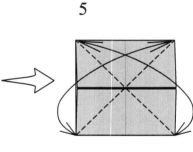

Valley-fold in half diagonally thru all layers and unfold (in both directions).

6

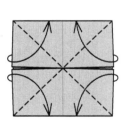

Valley-fold the four flaps (if they are not already folded from the previous step).

7

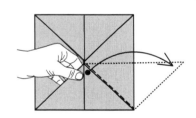

Hold firmly with the left hand as shown. With the right hand, hold at the black dot and pull the flap out to the right, releasing the paper. Watch the black dot.

8   9   10

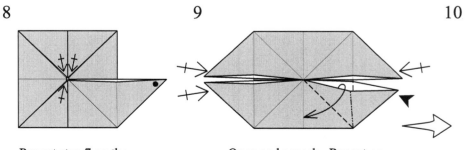

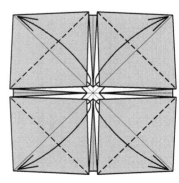

Repeat step 7 on the remaining three flaps.

Open and squash. Repeat on the other three flaps.

Valley-fold the four raw corners.

236 *Origami Pop-ups*

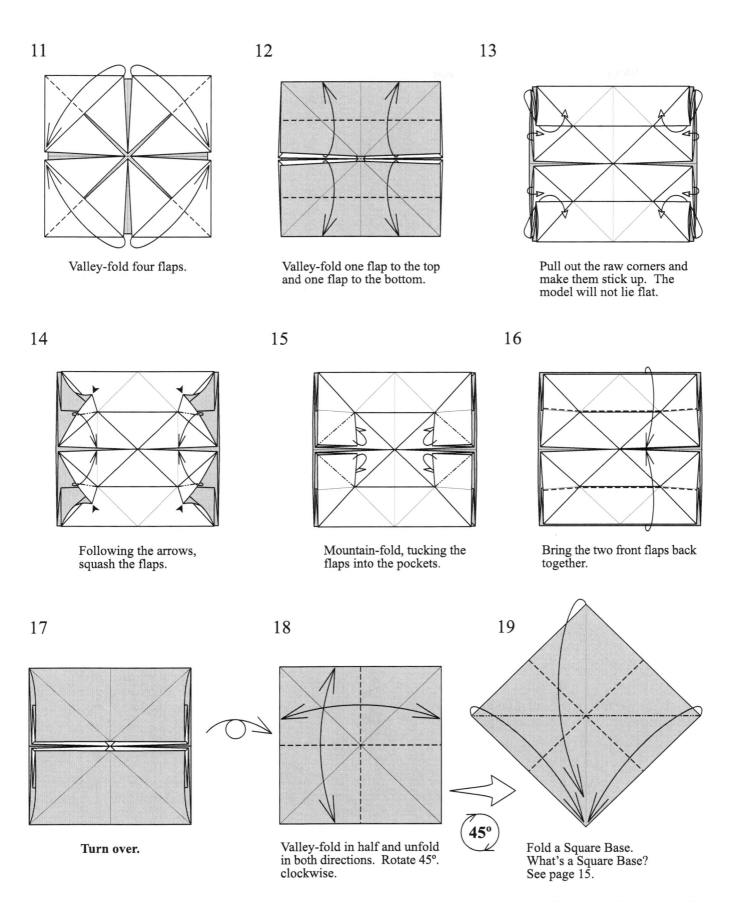

20

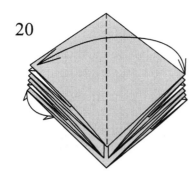

Valley-fold one flap to the left and then back to the right. **Repeat behind.**

21

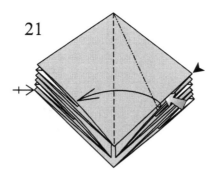

Squash. **Repeat behind.**

22

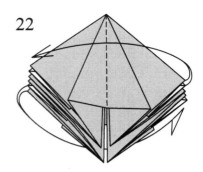

Valley-fold two front flaps to the left. Balance it out by folding two rear flaps to the right.

23

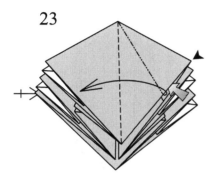

Squash. **Repeat behind.**

24

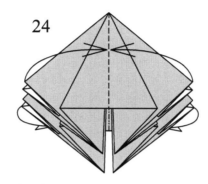

Bring the left and right front flaps together and **repeat behind**, forming an octahedral skeleton. The model will not lie flat.

25

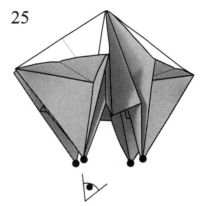

Rotate the model so that the four black dots are pointing toward you.

26

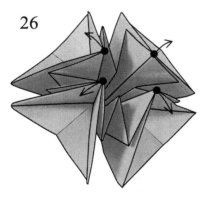

Separate the four black dots so that you can see into the middle.

27

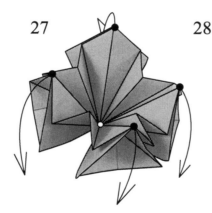

Flip the model inside out so that the white dot pokes up.

28

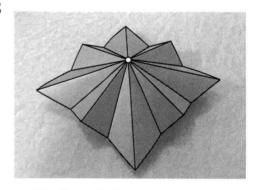

The Stress Reliever is done, and ready to relieve some stress!
Place the model on a smooth surface. See the next page for operating instructions.

PERFORM IT!

Hold the model in the position of step 26 and ask the audience, **"What's this?"** but before they can reply say, **"It's a blooming flower"** (step 26). Then, transforming the model as quickly as you can, say, **"No, it's a Chinese hat"** (step 28). **"No, it's a UFO"** (step 33). **"No it's a Cootie Catcher"** (Step 26). **"No it's a blooming flower"** (step 26)... Continue repeating the routine, but, before it gets old, finish by saying, **"And I hope you caught all of that because there will be an exam after the show!"** [Audience stresses.]

29

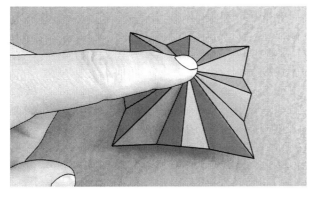

Press the center point down, flipping the model inside out again. The four corners will pop up.

30

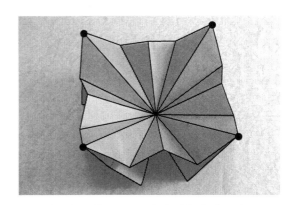

Using four fingers, push the black dots down until the center pops up.

31

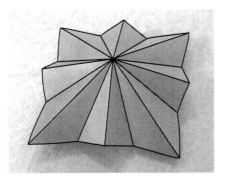

Repeat steps 29 and 30 until your stress is relieved. Stress relief can also be found on the underside of the model. So, **turn over.**

32

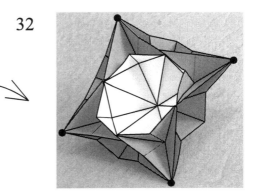

Press the four black dots downward until the middle pops up...

33

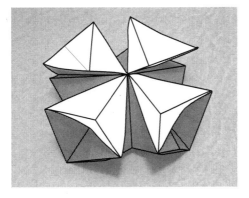

...like this! It's a Maltese Cross! Press the middle and the model will return to step 32.

34

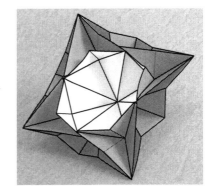

In this position it can also be used as a trophy stand to display your origami stress ball, also known as, a crumpled up ball of paper!

Video tutorial on youtube.com!
Search: shafer youtube stress

Continue flipping the model until you are stress-free. If you still feel stressed, then maybe you should try flipping around other aspects of your life. If you no longer have any stress to relieve (or never had any to begin with), there are other uses for this model:

- In the position shown in step 31 it can be worn as a Chinese Hat. You might want to fold it out of extra large paper (or cardstock) so that it actually fits on your head.
- It spins! In the positions shown in steps 31 and 33 it will spin on top of a pencil or pen if you blow on it just right, and in the step 30 position it will spin on a table if you blow on it from the side (if not, then push it together as pictured in step 27 and try again).
- A candy dish! The position in step 30 makes for one large candy dish while the step 33 position will provide you with 4 small triangular dishes. Sorry, candy not included!

Stress Reliever 239

JeremyShaferOrigami Index

My Origami Tutorials on YouTube
(and how to find them)

www.youtube.com/jeremyshaferorigami

Soon after self-publishing my second origami book "Origami Ooh La La," I decided to start a YouTube origami tutorial channel to help publicize my book. I quickly found out that producing video tutorials is much faster than it was to draw origami diagrams. I also became convinced that, compared to diagrams, video tutorials are easier for the average person to learn from. So, since 2011, I've been publishing my designs exclusively on my YouTube channel instead of drawing diagrams.

In this chapter I've included the thumbnails from almost all of my YouTube origami video tutorials (as of November 2013) along with keywords for how to find them on the Internet. All you have to do is go to **google.com** or **yahoo.com** and type in all of the video's keywords and you should see the video's thumbnail. Click on it and get ready to fold!

240 *Origami Pop-ups*

POP-UPS

Pop-up Pencil Holder

Keywords:
origami
pencil
pop-up
card

Peek-A-Boo Snake Pop-up Snake

Keywords:
origami
pop-up
pyramid
card

Pyramid Pop-up Card

Keywords:
origami
pyramid
pop-up
card

I Love You Peek-A-Boo

Keywords:
origami
love
pop-up
card

Pyramid Pop-up Card

Keywords:
origami
pop-up
pyramid
card

Butterfly Pop-up Card

Keywords:
origami
butterfly
pop-up
card

Magical Transforming Octahedron

Keywords:
origami
transforming
octahedron

Cherry Blossom Pop-up Card

Keywords:
origami
cherry
blossom

Cyclops Jack-o-Lantern Pop-up Card

Keywords:
shafer origami
cyclops

Origami Rocks! Pop-up Card

Keywords:
origami
rocks
pop-up
card

YouTube Tutorials **241**

FLASHERS

Iso-Area Flasher
Keywords:
origami
flasher
iso-area

Easy Flasher Barrister's Wig
Keywords:
origami
barrister
wig

Easy Flasher
Keywords:
origami
easy
flasher

Easy Flasher Baseball Cap
Keywords:
origami
easy
flasher
baseball

Newborn Flasher Hat
Keywords:
origami
newborn
flasher
hat

Flasher Spinner Hat Tent
Keywords:
origami
flasher
spinner
hat
tent

Super Easy Flasher Hat
Keywords:
origami
flasher
hat easy

Hat tent
Keywords:
origami
hat
tent
Palmer

Baby Flasher Hat
Keywords:
origami
baby
flasher
hat

Octopus Flasher
Keywords:
origami
octopus
flasher

Flasher Top Hat
Keywords:
origami
flasher
top
hat

242   *Origami Pop-ups*

STARS

Flasher Deluxe

Keywords:
origami
flasher
deluxe

Levitating Star

Keywords:
origami
levitating star

Flasher Supreme

Keywords:
origami
flasher
supreme

Elf Hat / Star of David Yarmulke

Keywords:
origami
elf
hat

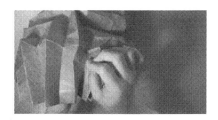

Flasher Sphere

Keywords:
origami
flasher
sphere

One Piece Ninja Star

Keywords:
origami
one piece
shuriken

Flasher Tessellation

Keywords:
origami
easy flasher
tessellation
Jeremy Shafer

8-Pointed Spiral Star

Keywords:
origami
spiral
star
8

Flasher Hat

Keywords:
origami
flasher
hat
part 1

8-Pointed Star Stress Reliever

Keywords:
origami
star
stress
reliever

YouTube Tutorials **243**

HEARTS

Inflatable Heart

Keywords:
origami inflatable heart

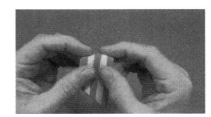

Striped Heart

Keywords:
shafer fold striped heart

Butterfly Heart Card

Keywords:
shafer butterfly heart card

Pyramid Heart

Keywords:
shafer pyramid heart

Heart Ring Diamond Ring

Keywords:
shafer origami diamond ring

Amelia Earhart

Keywords:
youtube origami earhart

Balancing Heart

Keywords:
fold balancing heart

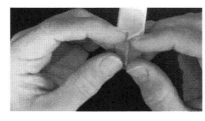

Leaping Heart

Keywords:
shafer leaping heart

Diamond Heart Ring

Keywords:
origami "diamond heart ring"

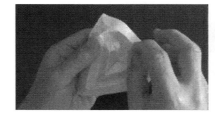

Multiple Rippling Heart

Keywords:
origami multiple rippling heart

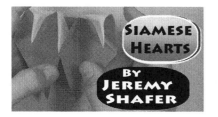

Siamese Hearts

Keywords:
siamese hearts video

Heart Attack

Keywords:
shafer heart attack

244   *Origami Pop-ups*

Heart Box

Keywords: shafer heart box video

FLOWERS

One-Minute Rose

Keywords: origami minute rose

Not Kawasaki Rose

Keywords: not kawasaki rose

8-point Star Box

Keywords: origami shafer 8 starbox

Flower Tower

Keywords: chris palmer flower tower video

Flower Heart Pop-up

Keywords shafer youtube flower heart

EXTREME ACTION

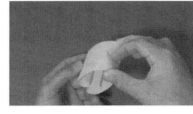

Magical Flying Candy Cane

Keywords: origami flying candy cane

Origami Loud Mouth

Keywords: origami loud mouth

Greeting Card Spinner

Keywords: Youtube origami greeting spinner

Spinning Octahedron

Keywords: shafer spinning octahedron

Cannonball Carrot

Keywords: youtube shafer carrot

Prince Charming

Keywords: youtube shafer prince charming

Super Ninja Dart

Keywords: youtube shafer super dart

Preedo

Keywords: youtube shafer preedo

Moto Spinner

Keywords: youtube shafer moto spinner

Crane Plane

Keywords: youtube shafer crane plane

Octagonal Top

Keywords: youtube shafer octagonal top

Bulldog Butterfly Crane

Keywords: origami shafer bulldog model

Spinning Top

Keywords: origami shafer beyblade

I found the Wakataki!

Keywords: wakataki

Biting Butt Bird

Keywords: youtube shafer biting

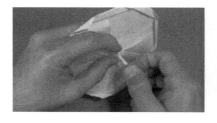

Spinning Top

Keywords: origami Shafer spinning top

246   *Origami Pop-ups*

Flapping Bat

Keywords:
youtube shafer
flapping bat

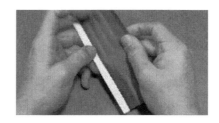

Magic Tap Trap YouTube

Keywords:
Shafer youtube
tap trap

Gulper Eel

Keywords:
youtube shafer
gulper eel

Cootie Catcher Flexahedron

Keywords:
shafer
flexahedron

Spring into Action

Keywords:
beynon spring
shafer

Pyramid Skeleton

Keywords:
shafer youtube
pyramid
skeleton

Spring into Action Tessellation Tower

Keywords:
tessellation
tower

Revolving Flexahedron

Keywords:
shafer youtube
revolving

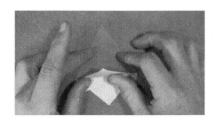

Atom Smasher

Keywords:
shafer atom
smasher

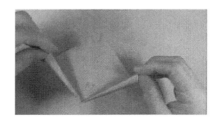

Square to triangle Spinner

Keywords:
Shafer youtube
square triangle

YouTube Tutorials

SCARY ORIGAMI

Monster Envelope
Keywords:
youtube shafer
monster envelope

Blinking Vampire Jack-O-Lantern
Keywords:
youtube shafer
blinking vampire

Ghost & Goblin
Keywords:
origami ghost
goblin

Casket
Keywords:
youtube shafer
casket

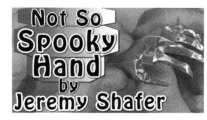

Not So Spooky Hand
Keywords:
not so spooky
hand

Spooky Hand
Keywords:
spooky hand
skeleton
jeremyshaferorigami

Space Monster II
Keywords:
origami video
space monster II

Transforming Piranha
Keywords:
youtube shafer
piranha

Vampire Mouth
Keywords:
youtube shafer
vampire mouth

Vampire Teeth
Keywords:
youtube shafer
vampire teeth

Venus Flytrap
Keywords:
youtube shafer
venus

Space Ball Monster
Keywords:
youtube shafer
spaceball

DOLLAR ORIGAMI

 **$1 HDTV**
Keywords:
shafer youtube
dollar hdtv

 **$1 Spinning Top**
Keywords:
shafer dollar
spinning top

 **$1 Gift Box**
Keywords:
shafer youtube
dollar giftbox

 **$1 Cobra Pop-Up**
Keywords:
shafer youtube
cobra popup

 **$1 Balancing Eagle**
Keywords:
shafer youtube
dollar eagle

 **$1 Minecraft Steve**
Keywords:
shafer youtube
minecraft steve

 **$1 Pyramid**
Keywords:
shafer youtube
dollar pyramid

 **$1 Swiss Army Penguin**
Keywords:
shafer origami
swiss penguin

 **$1 I Love U**
Keywords:
shafer youtube
I love you

 **Fireworks**
Keywords:
shafer youtube
dollar fireworks

YouTube Tutorials

$1 Space Monster

Keywords: dollar space monster

$1 Not Kawasaki Rose

Keywords: origami dollar rose

$1 Piggy Bank

Keywords: $1 piggy bank

$1 Stellated Octahedron

Keywords: origami dollar octahedron

$1 Heart-Shaped Pool

Keywords: origami heart pool

$12 Modular Bouncy Box Dream Cube

Keywords: $12 Bouncy Box

$1 Bow Tie

Keywords: origami $1 bowtie

Ninja Butterfly

Keywords: jeremyshaferorigami ninja butterfly

$1 Giant Cube

Keywords: origami giant cube

POPULAR CULTURE

Facebook Logo

Keywords:
shafer origami
facebook logo

Creeper Body

Keywords:
origami
creeper body
tools

Epic Face

Keywords:
epic face bobble
origami

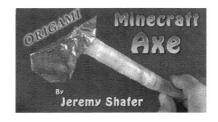

Minecraft Axe

Keywords:
shafer origami
axe

Angry Bird

Keywords:
shafer angry
resentful bird video

Minecraft Sword

Keywords:
shafer origami
diamond sword

X-Wing Fighter

Keywords:
shafer youtube
space ship

Minecraft Sword

Keywords:
shafer origami
gold pickaxe

Creeper Face

Keywords:
shafer origami
minecraft creeper

YouTube Tutorials

ASTONISH AND AMUSE

Bunny Head

Keywords:
youtube shafer
bunny head

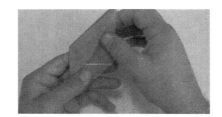

Magic Flap

Keywords:
origami magic flap

Exploding Envelope

Keywords:
youtube shafer
envelope

Two Interlocking rings

Keywords:
shafer origami
interlocking

Blinking Eyes

Keywords:
shafer origami
blinking eyes

Peace Sign

Keywords:
youtube shafer
peace sign

Men's Suit

Keywords:
youtube shafer
mens

Frog's Tongue

Keywords:
origami frog tongue

Dolphin

Keywords:
shafer origami
dolphin

Heart Attack

Keywords:
origami heart attack

Surfer on a Wave
Keywords: origami surfer

Nail Clipper
Keywords: shafer origami nail clipper

Man Swatter
Keywords: origami shafer man swatter

MISCELLANEOUS

4-Fold Surprise
Keywords: origami shafer fold surprise

Blinking Eyes
Keywords: fold dragon shafer

Magic Wand
Keywords: origami magic wand

Squishy Blob
Keywords: fold origami squishy blob

Flapping Bird
Keywords: shafer flapping birds fast

Swiss Army Knife
Keywords: origami shafer army knife

Ninja Butterfly
Keywords: origami flapping ninja butterfly

YouTube Tutorials 253

 **Gotta Go Pee**
Keywords:
shafer origami pee

 **Elf Ears**
Keywords:
origami elf ears tutorial

 **UFO Envelope**
Keywords:
shafer origami ufo

 **Clown Nose**
Keywords:
shafer youtube clown nose

 **Wine Glass**
Keywords:
shafer monolithic wine glass

 **Doodly Bop**
Keywords:
origami doodly bop

 **Angelfish finger puppet**
Keywords:
origami angelfish puppet

 **Origami Transformer**
Keywords:
origami goku sydney

 **Elf Shoes**
Keywords:
shafer youtube elf shoes

 **Cube Dude Wearing Glasses**
Keywords:
origami cube dude

 **Modular Giant Bouncy Box**
Keywords:
shafer origami modular cube video

 **Multiple Rippling Deltoid Design**
Keywords:
multiple rippling deltoid design

Treasure Chest

Keywords:
shafer origami
treasure chest

Ocean Surf Surprise

Keywords:
origami ocean
surf surprise

Pen Holder by Tomoko Fuse

Keywords:
shafer origami
pen holder

Stress Reliever

Keywords:
shafer youtube
stress

HDTV

Keywords:
origami hdtv

Collapsible Cube

Keywords:
jeremy shafer
collapsible cube

Target

Keywords:
youtube origami
target

Magic Hat

Keywords:
shafer origami
magic hat

8 Ball

Keywords:
origami shafer
eight ball

Shark Attack

Keywords:
youtube shafer
shark attack

Flapping Fat Bat Hat

Keywords:
origami flapping
bat hat

Computer Mouse

Keywords:
origami computer
mouse video

Printed in Poland
by Amazon Fulfillment
Poland Sp. z o.o., Wrocław